The Sublime Object
of Ideology

王奕婷

PHRONESIS

*A new series from Verso edited by
Ernesto Laclau and Chantal Mouffe*

There is today wide agreement that the left-wing
project is in crisis. New antagonisms have emerged
– not only in advanced capitalist societies but also in
the Eastern bloc and in the Third World – that
require the reformulation of the socialist ideal in
terms of an extension and deepening of democracy.
However, serious disagreements exist as to the
theoretical strategy needed to carry out such a task.
There are those for whom the current critique of
rationalism and universalism puts into jeopardy the
very basis of the democratic project. Others argue
that the critique of essentialism – a point of
convergence of the most important trends in
contemporary theory: post-structuralism, philosophy of language after the later Wittgenstein, post-
Heideggerian hermeneutics – is the necessary
condition for understanding the widening of the
field of social struggles characteristic of the present
stage of democratic politics. *Phronesis* clearly locates
itself among the latter. Our objective is to establish
a dialogue between these theoretical developments
and left-wing politics. We believe that an anti-
essentialist theoretical stand is the sine qua non of a
new vision for the Left conceived in terms of a
radical and plural democracy.

The Sublime Object
of Ideology

SLAVOJ ŽIŽEK

VERSO

London · New York

First published by Verso 1989
© Slavoj Žižek 1989
All rights reserved

Verso
UK: 6 Meard Street, London W1V 3HR
USA: 29 West 35th Street, New York, NY 10001-2291

Verso is the imprint of New Left Books

British Library Cataloguing in Publication Data
Zizek, Slavoj, *1949-*
    The sublime object of ideology — (Phronesis)
    1. Ideology
    145

    ISBN 0-86091-256-6
    ISBN 0-86091-971-4 pbk

Typeset by Leaper & Gard, Bristol, England
Printed in Great Britain by Bookcraft (Bath) Ltd

For Renata

Contents

Preface

Ernesto Laclau

Like all great intellectual traditions, Lacanian psychoanalytic theory has shed light in a number of directions. Such illuminating effects have tended to present it as a source of diffuse inspiration feeding highly differentiated intellectual currents, rather than a closed and systematic theoretical corpus. The reception given to Lacan has thus varied from country to country; each set of circumstances has emphasized different aspects of a theoretical body of work which had itself undergone considerable transformation over a long period of time. In France, and in Latin countries in general, the influence of Lacan has been mainly clinical and has therefore been closely linked with psychoanalytic practice. The professional training of psychoanalysts has been the most important aspect of this, which has taken place in institutions organized accordingly — first, *L'école freudienne de Paris*, and then *L'école de la cause freudienne*. This does not mean that the cultural impact of Lacanian theory has not extended to broader circles — to literature, philosophy, film theory and so on — but that clinical practice has remained the central point of reference, in spite of these extensions.

In Anglo-Saxon countries this centrality of the clinical aspect has, to a large extent, been absent and the influence of Lacan has revolved almost exclusively around the literature-cinema-feminism triangle. Thus, for example, the work linked to *Screen* magazine during the 1970s (Stephen Heath, Colin MacCabe, Jacqueline Rose) with its theory of 'suture'; or, in the field of feminism, the critical use of certain Lacanian notions, such as the 'phallic signifier', to expose the functioning of the patriarchal order (Juliet Mitchell, Jacqueline Rose and the group surrounding the journal *m/f*). It is also worth mentioning that the tendency in the Anglo-Saxon world has been to emphasize the affinities of Lacanian theory with the general field of 'post-structuralism' — deconstruction, for instance —

while in France greater degrees of demarcation and confrontation have been maintained between intellectual currents.

To these national variants we must also add a differentiation in terms of the diverse *interpretations* of the Lacanian corpus, as well as the various attempts to articulate this with *other* theoretical approaches. As regards interpretation, we should point to the opposition that exists in France between the different Lacanian 'generations'. On the one hand, we find the approach of the 'old school' or first generation of Lacanians (Octave and Maud Mannoni, Serge Leclaire, Moustafa Safouan etc.), who emphasize clinical problems and the crucial role of the *Symbolic* in the psychoanalytical process. This approach is largely based on Lacan's writing in the 1950s, the era of high structuralism, in which the Imaginary register is presented as a series of variants that must be referred to a stable symbolic matrix. On the other hand, the younger generation (Michel Silvestre, Alain Grosrichard etc., led by Jacques-Alain Miller) has attempted to formalize Lacanian theory, pointing out the distinctions between the different stages of his teaching, and placing an accent on the theoretical importance of the last stage, in which a central role is granted to the notion of the *Real* as that which resists symbolization. As regards the attempts to articulate Lacanian theory with other theoretical approaches, it is worth mentioning in the first instance the hermeneutical appropriation of Lacan that has taken place, principally in German (Hermann Lang, Manfred Frank etc.). This consists mainly in an attempt to show that the hermeneutical 'horizon of prejudices' can offer the proper philosophical foundation to psychoanalysis. To this one should add the Marxist–structuralist interpretation of Lacan carried out by Althusser and his followers (especially Michel Pêcheux). In this reading, Lacanian psychoanalysis is presented as the only psychological theory which contains a notion of the subject that is compatible with historical materialism.

Within this general framework, the Slovenian Lacanian school, to which this book by Žižek belongs, possesses highly original features. In contrast with the Latin and Anglo-Saxon world, Lacanian categories have been used in a reflection which is essentially *philosophical* and *political*. And while the Slovenian theoreticians make some effort to extend their analysis to the domain of literature and film, the clinical dimension is totally absent. Two main features characterize this school. The first is its insistent reference to the ideological–political field: its description and theorization of the fundamental mechanisms of ideology (identification, the role of the master signifier, ideological fantasy); its attempts to define the specificity of 'totalitarianism' and its different variants (Stalinism, fascism), and to outline the main characteristics of radical democratic struggles in Eastern European societies. The Lacanian notion of the *point de capiton* is conceived as the fundamental ideological operation; 'fantasy' becomes an imaginary scenario concealing the fundamental split or 'antagonism' around which the social field is structured; 'identification' is seen as the process through which the ideological field is constituted; enjoyment, or *jouissance* enables us to understand the logic of exclusion operating in discourses such as racism. The second distinctive feature of the Slovenian school is the use of Lacanian categories in the analysis of classical philosophical texts: Plato, Descartes, Leibniz, Kant, Marx, Heidegger, the Anglo-Saxon analytical tradition and, above all, Hegel. The specific 'flavour' of the Slovenian theorists is given by their Hegelian orientation: they attempt to articulate a new reading of Hegel's philosophy which leaves behind such long-established assumptions as Hegel's presumed pan-logicism or the notion that the systematic character of his reflection leads to the abolition of all differences in the final mediation by Reason.

The production of the Slovenian school is already considerable.* Today, Lacanian theory is the main philosophical orientation in Slovenia. It has also been one of the principal reference points of the so-called 'Slovenia Spring' — that is to say the democratization campaigns that have taken place in recent years. The weekly *Mladina*, on which Žižek is the main political columnist, is the most important mouthpiece of this movement.

The interest of the Slovenian theoreticians in the problems of a radical democracy and their efforts to link the Lacanian Real to what in *Hegemony*

Everything You Want to Know about Lacan (But were Afraid to Ask Hitchcock) London: Routledge, 1992.

*Two of their books have recently been translated into French: the co-lective volume *Tout ce que vous avez toujours voulu savoir sur Lacan, sans jamais oser le demander à Hitchcock* (Navarin, Paris 1988); and Slavoj Žižek's *Le plus sublime des hystériques — Hegel passe* (Point Hors Ligne, Paris 1988). But in Slovenian there are already more than twenty volumes published. Among them we should mention *Hegel and the Signifier* (Slavoj Žižek, Ljubljana 1980); *History and the Unconscious* (Slavoj Žižek, Ljubljana 1982); *Hegel and the Object*, (Mladen Dolar and Slavoj Žižek, Ljubljana 1985); *Problems and the Theory of Fetishism* (Rado Riha and Slavoj Žižek, Ljubljana 1985); *The Structure of Fascist Domination* (Mladen Dolar, Ljubljana 1982); *Philosophy in the Science* (Raho Riha, Ljubljana 1982). Apart from Žižek, we should mention the important theoretical contributions of Miran Božovič (readings of Descartes, Leibniz and Spinoza); Zravko Kobe (studies in Hegel's logic); Zdenko Vrdlovec, Stojan Pelko and Marcel Stefančič (film theory); Eva D. Bahovec (epistemology); Jelica Sumič-Riha (analytical philosophy); and Renata Salecl (law).

and Socialist Strategy Chantal Mouffe and I have called the 'constitutive character of antagonisms', have created the possibility for fruitful intellectual exchange. Žižek has visited our research programme on Ideology and Discourse Analysis at the Department of Government at the University of Essex on many occasions; a number of joint research projects have stemmed from these contacts. This does not mean, of course, that there has been complete agreement: in our view, the Slovenian school initially drew too drastic a line of separation between Lacanian theory and post-structuralism; we also have a number of reservations about their reading of Hegel. If, in the first case, our differences have tended to diminish in the course of debate, in the second, discussions are still taking place. Nevertheless, in spite of these differences, there can be no doubt as to the richness and depth offered by the Slovenian school's interpretation of Hegel. Its special combination of Hegelianism and Lacanian theory currently represents one of the most innovative and promising theoretical projects on the European intellectual scene.

At this point I would like to offer a series of suggestions for the reading of this book. The reader could quite easily end up disorientated as to its literary genre. It is certainly not a book in the classical sense; that is to say, a systematic structure in which an argument is developed according to a pre-determined plan. Nor is it a collection of essays, each of which constitutes a finished product and whose 'unity' with the rest is merely the result of its thematic discussion of a common problem. It is rather a series of theoretical interventions which shed mutual light on each other, not in terms of the *progression* of an argument, but in terms of what we could call the *reiteration* of the latter in different discursive contexts. The basic thesis of the book — that the category of 'subject' cannot be reduced to the 'positions of subject', since before subjectivation the subject is the subject of a lack — is formulated in the first chapter: each of the subsequent chapters which reiterate this thesis does so in a new discursive context which sheds light on it from a different angle. But as this process of refinement is not the result of a necessary progression, the text reaches a point of interruption rather than conclusion, thus inviting the reader to continue for him- or herself the discursive proliferation in which the author has been engaged. Thus, where Žižek has spoken of Lacan, Hegel, Kripke, Kafka or Hitchcock, the reader could continue, referring to Plato, Wittgenstein, Leibniz, Gramsci or Sorel. And each of these reiterations partially *constructs* the argument instead of simply repeating it. Žižek's text is an eminent example of what Barthes has called a 'writerly text'.

This book also contains an implicit invitation to break the barrier separating theoretical languages from those of everyday life. Contemporary criticism of the notion of meta-language has paved the way for a generalized transgression of boundaries, but Žižek's text — with its movement from film to philosophy, from literature to politics — is especially rich in this respect. No one who attaches a 'super-hard transcendentiality' to their own theoretical perspective or who continues to live in the mythological world of 'case studies' will feel comfortable reading this book. The limits which the presence of the Real imposes on all symbolization also affect theoretical discourses; the radical contingency that this introduces is based on an almost pragmatist 'constitutive incompletion'. From this point of view, the emphasis on the Real necessarily leads to a deeper exploration of the *conditions of possibility* of any objectivity.

It would be a betrayal of Žižek's text if I were to attempt to draw up a systematic picture of its categories, when the author has preferred to establish a much subtler process of open reference between them. Nevertheless, I would like to draw attention to two key points in the text, given their productiveness in terms of political analysis. The first refers to the use which is made of Saul Kripke's anti-descriptivism in political analysis. The dispute between descriptivists and anti-descriptivists revolves around the question of the way in which names refer to objects. According to the descriptivists, the link is the result of the *meaning* of a name — that is to say, each name involves a cluster of descriptive features and refers to those objects in the real world displaying those features. For the anti-descriptivists, on the other hand, the name refers to the object by means of what they call a 'primal baptism' in which the name continues to refer to that *object* even if all the descriptive features of the object at the time of its baptism have disappeared. Like myself, Žižek sides with the anti-descriptivists. But he also introduces a variant into the argument which is of crucial importance. The central problem for any anti-descriptivist approach is to determine what it is in the object, beyond its descriptive features, that constitutes its identity — that is to say, what it is that constitutes the objective correlative of the 'rigid designator'. On this point, Žižek presents the following argument: 'What is overlooked, at least in the standard version of anti-descriptivism, is that this guaranteeing the identity of an object in all counterfactual situations, that is, through a change of all its descriptive features, is the *retroactive effect of naming itself*: it is the name itself, the signifier, which supports the identity of the object. That "surplus" in the object which stays the same in all possible worlds is "something in it more than itself", that is to say the Lacanian *objet petit a*: we search in vain for it in positive reality because it has no positive consistency, that is, because it is just a positivation of a void — of a discontinuity opened in reality by the emergence of the signifier.' Now this argument is crucial. For if the unity of the object is the retroactive effect of naming itself, then naming is not just the pure nominalistic game of attributing an empty name to a preconstituted subject. It is the discursive construction of the object itself. The consequences of this argument for a theory of hegemony or politics are easy to see. If the descriptivist approach were correct, then the meaning of the name and the descriptive features of the objects would be given beforehand, thus discounting the possibility of any discursive hegemonic variation that could open the space for a political construction of social identities. But if the process of naming of objects amounts to the very act of their constitution, then their descriptive features will be fundamentally unstable and open to all kinds of hegemonic rearticulations. The essentially performative character of naming is the precondition for all hegemony and politics.

The second point refers to the substance–subject relationship which is discussed in the final chapter of the book. The reduction of the subject to substance is the central proposition of Spinoza's philosophy and this has been adopted as a banner by such Marxist currents as Althusserianism ('history is a process without subject'). All radical objectivism can only be affirmed by means of this reduction. It is important to point out that this essentialism of the substance has usually been presented as the only alternative to the essentialism of the subject, which would affirm the fullness and positivity of the latter (remember how the Cartesian *cogito* grants the unmodified category of substance to the subject itself). But Žižek's reintroduction of the category of subject deprives it of all substantiality: 'If the essence is not in itself split, if — in the movement of extreme alienation — it does not perceive itself as an alien Entity, then the very difference essence/appearance cannot establish itself. *This self-fissure of the essence means that the essence is "subject" and not only "substance"*: to put things in a simplified way, "substance" is the essence insofar as it reflects itself in the world of appearance, in phenomenal objectivity, and "subject" is the substance insofar as it is itself split and experiences itself as some alien, positively given Entity. In a paradoxical way, we could say that subject is precisely the *substance insofar as it experiences itself as substance* (i.e. as some alien, given, external, positive Entity, existing in itself); "subject" is nothing but the name for this inner distance of the "substance" towards itself, the name for this empty place from which the substance can perceive itself as something alien.'

These are affirmations to which I can only strongly subscribe, since they tend to break with the structure-subject dualism, positing the question of 'social agency' in terms which clearly go beyond all objectivism. There is subject because the substance — objectivity — does not manage to constitute itself fully; the location of the subject is that of a fissure at the very centre of the structure. The traditional debate as to the relationship between agent and structure thus appears fundamentally displaced: the issue is no longer a problem of *autonomy*, of determinism versus free will, in which two entities fully constituted as 'objectivities' mutually limit each other. On the contrary, the subject emerges as a result of the failure of substance in the process of its self-constitution. In my view, this is where the theory of deconstruction can make a contribution to a theory of the *space of the subject*. Indeed, deconstruction reveals that it is the 'undecidables' which form the ground on which any structure is based. I have elsewhere sustained that in this sense, the subject is merely the distance between the undecidable structure and the decision. And analysis of the exact dimensions of any decision reached on an undecidable terrain is the central task of a theory of politics, a theory which has to show the contingent 'origins' of all objectivity. The theory which Žižek has begun to elaborate in this book represents a contribution of the highest order in this challenge.

These are just some of the principal themes dealt with by this book. For all those interested in the elaboration of a theoretical perspective that seeks to address the problems of constructing a democratic socialist political project in a post-Marxist age, it is essential reading.

Translated by Jon Barnes

Acknowledgements

The author wishes to acknowledge his indebtedness and gratitude to Jacques-Alain Miller, whose Seminar at the University of Paris VIII paved the way to Lacan for him, and to Ernesto Laclau and Chantal Mouffe, whose work — above all their book *Hegemony and Socialist Strategy* — orientated him in his attempt to use Lacanian conceptual apparatus as a tool in the analysis of ideology.

Preliminary versions of some of the material contained in this book were presented as the following publications: 'The Object as a Limit to Discourse' (intervention at the *Lacan: Television* conference, New York, 10 April 1987, published in *Lacan and Discourse*, a special issue of *Prose Studies*, Kent State University 1989); 'The Real in Ideology' (intervention at the conference *Gramsci: Wars of Persuasion and Mass Culture*, organized by the Center for Studies in Contemporary Culture, University of Massachusetts, 24–26 April 1987, published in *PsychCritique* 2:3 (1987), New York; 'Why Lacan Is Not a Post-Structuralist' (published in *Newsletter of the Freudian Field* 2, 1988, Florida State University); 'The Truth Arises from Misrecognition' (intervention at the conference *Lacan, Language and Literature*, Kent State University, 27–30 May 1988, to be published by Illinois University Press in a volume containing papers from the conference).

Introduction

The Philosophical Discourse of Modernity

In that book of Habermas's which specifically addresses the issue of so-called 'post-structuralism', *Der philosophische Diskurs der Moderne* (Habermas, 1985), there is a curious detail concerning Lacan's name: it is mentioned only five times and each time in conjunction with other names. (Let us cite all five instances: p. 70 — 'von Hegel und Marx bis Nietzsche und Heidegger, von Bataille und Lacan bis Foucault und Derrida'; p. 120 — 'Bataille, Lacan und Foucault'; p. 311 — 'mit Lévi-Strauss und Lacan'; p. 313 — 'den zeitgenössischen Strukturalismus, die Ethnologie von Lévi-Strauss und die Lacanische Psychoanalyse'; p. 359 — 'von Freud oder C. G. Jung, von Lacan oder Lévi-Strauss'.) Lacanian theory is not, then, perceived as a specific entity; it is — to use Laclau and Mouffe's term — always articulated in a series of equivalences. Why this refusal to confront Lacan directly, in a book which includes lengthy discussions of Bataille, Derrida and, above all, Foucault, the real partner of Habermas?

The answer to this enigma is to be found in another curiosity of the Habermas book, in a curious accident concerning Althusser. Of course, we are using the term 'curious accident' in a Sherlock Holmesian sense: Althusser's name is not even mentioned in Habermas's book, and that is the curious accident. So our first thesis would be that the great debate occupying the foreground of today's intellectual scene, the Habermas–Foucault debate, is masking another opposition, another debate which is theoretically more far-reaching: the Althusser–Lacan debate. There is something enigmatic in the sudden eclipse of the Althusserian school: it cannot be explained away in terms of a theoretical defeat. — It is more as if there were, in Althusser's theory, a traumatic kernel which had to be quickly forgotten, 'repressed'; it is an effective case of theoretical amnesia. Why, then, was the opposition Althusser–Lacan replaced, in a kind of metaphorical substitution, by the opposition Habermas–Foucault? At stake here are four different ethical positions, and at the same time four different notions of the subject.

With Habermas, we have the ethics of the unbroken communication, the Ideal of the universal, transparent intersubjective community; the notion of the subject behind this is, of course, the philosophy-of-language version of the old subject of transcendental reflection. With Foucault, we have a turn against that universalist ethics which results in a kind of aestheticization of ethics: each subject must, without any support from universal rules, build his own mode of self-mastery; he must harmonize the antagonism of the powers within himself – invent himself, so to speak, produce himself as subject, find his own particular art of living. This is why Foucault was so fascinated by marginal lifestyles constructing their particular mode of subjectivity (the sadomasochistic homosexual universe, for example: see Foucault, 1984).

It is not very difficult to detect how this Foucauldian notion of subject enters the humanist–elitist tradition: its closest realization would be the Renaissance ideal of the 'all-round personality' mastering the passions within himself and making out of his own life a work of art. Foucault's notion of the subject is, rather, a classical one: subject as the power of self-mediation and harmonizing the antagonistic forces, as a way of mastering the 'use of pleasures' through a restoration of the image of self. Here Habermas and Foucault are the two sides of the same coin – the real break is represented by Althusser, by his insistence on the fact that a certain cleft, a certain fissure, misrecognition, characterizes the human condition as such: by the thesis that the idea of the possible end of ideology is an ideological idea *par excellence* (Althusser, 1965).

Although Althusser has not written extensively about ethical problems, it is clear that the whole of his work embodies a certain radical ethical attitude which we might call the heroism of alienation or of subjective destitution (although, or rather precisely, *because* Althusser refuses the very notion of 'alienation' as ideological). The point is not just that we must unmask the structural mechanism which is producing the effect of subject as ideological misrecognition, but that we must at the same time fully acknowledge this misrecognition as unavoidable – that is, we must accept a certain delusion as a condition of our historical activity, of assuming a role as agent of the historical process.

In this perspective, the subject as such is constituted through a certain misrecognition: the process of ideological interpellation through which the subject 'recognizes' itself as the addressee in the calling up of the ideological cause implies necessarily a certain short circuit, an illusion of the type 'I was already there' which, as Michel Pêcheux — who has given us the most elaborated version of the theory of interpellation — pointed out (Pêcheux, 1975), is not without its comical effects: the short circuit of 'no wonder you were interpellated as proletarian, when you are a proletarian'. Here, Pêcheux is supplementing Marxism with the Marx Brothers, whose well-known joke goes: 'You remind me of Emanuel Ravelli.' 'But I am Emanuel Ravelli.' 'Then no wonder you look like him!'

In contrast to this Althusserian ethics of *alienation* in the symbolic 'process without subject', we may denote the ethics implied by Lacanian psychoanalysis as that of *separation*. The famous Lacanian motto not to give way on one's desire [*ne pas céder sur son desir*] — is aimed at the fact that we must not obliterate the distance separating the Real from its symbolization: it is this surplus of the Real over every symbolization that functions as the object-cause of desire. To come to terms with this surplus (or, more precisely, leftover) means to acknowledge a fundamental deadlock ('antagonism'), a kernel resisting symbolic integration-dissolution. The best way to locate such an ethical position is via its opposition to the traditional Marxist notion of social antagonism. This traditional notion implies two interconnected features: (1) there exists a certain fundamental antagonism possessing an ontological priority to 'mediate' all other antagonisms, determining their place and their specific weight (class antagonism, economic exploitation); (2) historical development brings about, if not a necessity, at least an 'objective possibility' of solving this fundamental antagonism and, in this way, mediating all other antagonisms — to recall the well-known Marxist formulation, the same logic which drove mankind into alienation and class division also creates the condition for its abolition — '*die Wunde schliesst der Speer nur, der sie schlug*' (the wound can be healed only by the spear which made it) — as Wagner, Marx's contemporary, said through the mouth of Parsifal.

It is upon the unity of these two features that the Marxist notion of the revolution, of the revolutionary situation, is founded: a situation of metaphorical condensation in which it finally becomes clear to the everyday consciousness that it is not possible to solve any particular question without solving them all — that is, without solving the fundamental question which embodies the antagonistic character of the social totality. In a 'normal', pre-revolutionary state of things, everybody is fighting his own particular battles (workers are striking for better wages, feminists are fighting for the rights of women, democrats for political and social freedoms, ecologists against the exploitation of nature, participants in the peace movements against the danger of war, and so on). Marxists are using all their skill and adroitness of argument to convince the participants in these particular struggles that the only real solution to their problem is to be found in the global revolution: as long as social relations are dominated by Capital, there will always be sexism in relations between the sexes, there will always be a threat of global war, there will always be a danger that political and social freedoms will be suspended, nature itself will always remain an object of ruthless exploitation. . . . The global revolution will then abolish the basic social antagonism, enabling the formation of a transparent, rationally governed society.

The basic feature of so-called 'post-Marxism' is, of course, the break with this logic — which, incidentally, does not necessarily have a Marxist connotation: almost any of the antagonisms which, in the light of Marxism, appear to be secondary can take over this essential role of mediator for all the others. We have, for example, feminist fundamentalism (no global liberation without the emancipation of women, without the abolition of sexism); democratic fundamentalism (democracy as the fundamental value of Western civilization; all other struggles — economic, feminist, of minorities, and so on — are simply further applications of the basic democratic, egalitarian principle); ecological fundamentalism (ecological deadlock as the fundamental problem of mankind); and — why not? — also psychoanalytic fundamentalism as articulated in Marcuse's *Eros and Civilization* (the key to liberation lies in changing the repressive libidinal structure: see Marcuse, 1955).

Psychoanalytic 'essentialism' is paradoxical in so far as it is precisely psychoanalysis — at least in its Lacanian reading — which presents the real break with essentialist logic. That is to say, Lacanian psychoanalysis goes a decisive step further than the usual 'post-Marxist' anti-essentialism affirming the irreducible plurality of particular struggles — in other words, demonstrating how their articulation into a series of equivalences depends always on the radical contingency of the social–historical process: it enables us to grasp this plurality itself as a multitude of responses to the same impossible–real kernel.

Let us take the Freudian notion of the 'death drive'. Of course, we have to abstract Freud's biologism: 'death drive' is not a biological fact but a notion indicating that the human psychic apparatus is subordinated to a blind automatism of repetition beyond pleasure-seeking, self-preservation, accordance between man and his milieu. Man is — Hegel *dixit* — 'an animal sick unto death', an animal extorted by an insatiable parasite (reason, *logos*, language). In this perspective, the 'death drive', this dimension of radical negativity, cannot be reduced to an expression of alienated social conditions, it defines *la condition humaine* as such: there is no solution, no escape from it; the thing to do is not to 'overcome', to 'abolish' it, but to come to terms with it, to learn to recognize it in its terrifying dimension and then, on the basis of this fundamental recognition, to try to articulate a *modus vivendi* with it.

All 'culture' is in a way a reaction-formation, an attempt to limit, canalize — to *cultivate* this imbalance, this traumatic kernel, this radical antagonism through which man cuts his umbilical cord with nature, with animal homeostasis. It is not only that the aim is no longer to abolish this drive antagonism, but the aspiration to abolish it is precisely the source of totalitarian temptation: the greatest mass murders and holocausts have always been perpetrated in the name of man as harmonious being, of a New Man without antagonistic tension.

We have the same logic with ecology: man as such is 'the wound of nature', there is no return to the natural balance; to accord with his milieu, the only thing man can do is accept fully this cleft, this fissure, this structural rooting-out, and to try as far as possible to patch things up afterwards; all other solutions — the illusion of a possible return to nature, the idea of a total socialization of nature — are a direct path to totalitarianism. We have the same logic with feminism: 'there is no sexual relationship': that is, the relation between sexes is by definition 'impossible', antagonistic; there is no final solution, and the only basis for a somewhat bearable relation between the sexes is an acknowledgement of this basic antagonism, this basic impossibility.

We have the same logic with democracy: it is — to use the worn-out phrase attributed to Churchill — the worst of all possible systems; the only problem is that there is no other which would be better. That is to say, democracy always entails the possibility of corruption, of the rule of dull mediocrity; the only problem is that every attempt to elude this inherent risk and to restore 'real' democracy necessarily brings about its opposite — it ends in the abolition of democracy itself. Here it would be possible to defend a thesis that the first post-Marxist was none other than Hegel himself: according to Hegel, the antagonism of civil society cannot be suppressed without a fall into totalitarian terrorism — only afterwards can the state limit its disastrous effects.

It is the merit of Ernest Laclau and Chantal Mouffe that they have, in *Hegemony and Socialist Strategy* (Laclau–Mouffe 1985), developed a theory of the social field founded on such a notion of antagonism — on an acknowledgement of an original 'trauma', an impossible kernel which resists symbolization, totalization, symbolic integration. Every attempt at symbolization–totalization comes afterwards: it is an attempt to suture an original cleft — an attempt which is, in the last resort, by definition doomed to failure. They emphasize that we must not be 'radical' in the sense of aiming at a radical solution: we always live in an interspace and in borrowed time; every solution is provisional and temporary, a kind of postponing of a fundamental impossibility. Their term 'radical democracy' is thus to be taken somehow paradoxically: it is precisely *not* 'radical' in the sense of pure, true democracy; its radical character implies, on the contrary, that we can save democracy only by *taking into account its own radical impossibility*. Here we can see how we have reached the opposite extreme of the traditional Marxist standpoint: in traditional Marxism, the global solution-revolution is the condition of the effective solution of all particular problems, while here every provisional, temporarily successful solution of a particular problem entails an acknowledgement of the global radical deadlock, impossibility, the acknowledgement of a fundamental antagonism.

My thesis (developed in *Le plus sublime des hystériques: Hegel passe*, Paris 1988), is that the most consistent model of such an acknowledgement of antagonism is offered by Hegelian dialectics: far from being a story of its progressive overcoming, dialectics is for Hegel a systematic notation of the failure of all such attempts — 'absolute knowledge' denotes a subjective position which finally accepts 'contradiction' as an internal condition of every identity. In other words, Hegelian 'reconciliation' is not a 'panlogicist' sublation of all reality in the Concept but a final consent to the fact that the Concept itself is 'not-all' (to use this Lacanian term). In this sense we can repeat the thesis of Hegel as the first post-Marxist: he opened up the field of a certain fissure subsequently 'sutured' by Marxism.

Such an understanding of Hegel inevitably runs counter to the accepted notion of 'absolute knowledge' as a monster of conceptual totality devouring every contingency; this commonplace of Hegel simply *shoots too fast*, like the patrolling soldier of the well-known joke from Jaruzelski's Poland immediately after the military coup. At that time, military patrols had the right to shoot without warning at people walking on the streets after curfew (ten o'clock); one of the two soldiers on patrol sees somebody in a hurry at ten minutes to ten and shoots him immediately. When his colleague asks him why he shot when it was only ten to ten, he answers: 'I knew the fellow — he lived far from here and in any case would not be able to reach his home in ten minutes, so to simplify matters, I shot him now. . . .' This is exactly how the critics of Hegel's presumed 'panlogicism' proceed: they condemn absolute knowledge 'before it is ten o'clock', without reaching it — that is, they refute nothing with their criticism but their own prejudices about it.

The aim of this book is thus threefold:

- to serve as an introduction to some of the fundamental concepts of Lacanian psychoanalysis: against the distorted picture of Lacan as belonging to the field of 'post-structuralism', the book articulates his radical break with 'post-structuralism'; against the distorted picture of Lacan's obscurantism, it locates him in the lineage of rationalism. Lacanian theory is perhaps the most radical contemporary version of the Enlightenment.

- to accomplish a kind of 'return to Hegel' — to reactualize Hegelian dialectics by giving it a new reading on the basis of Lacanian psychoanalysis. The current image of Hegel as an 'idealist-monist' is totally misleading: what we find in Hegel is the strongest affirmation yet of difference and contingency — 'absolute knowledge' itself is nothing but a name for the acknowledgement of a certain radical loss.

- to contribute to the theory of ideology via a new reading of some well-known classical motifs (commodity fetishism, and so on) and of some crucial Lacanian concepts which, on a first approach, have nothing to offer to the theory of ideology: the 'quilting point' (*le point de capiton*: 'upholstery button'), sublime object, surplus-enjoyment, and so on.

It is my belief that these three aims are deeply connected: the only way to 'save Hegel' is through Lacan, and this Lacanian reading of Hegel and the Hegelian heritage opens up a new approach to ideology, allowing us to grasp contemporary ideological phenomena (cynicism, 'totalitarianism', the fragile status of democracy) without falling prey to any kind of 'postmodernist' traps (such as the illusion that we live in a 'post-ideological' condition).

PART I

The Symptom

1

How Did Marx Invent the Symptom?

Marx, Freud: the Analysis of Form

According to Lacan, it was none other than Karl Marx who invented the
notion of symptom. Is this Lacanian thesis just a sally of wit, a vague
analogy, or does it possess a pertinent theoretical foundation? If Marx
really articulated the notion of the symptom as it is also at work in the
Freudian field, then we must ask ourselves the Kantian question
concerning the epistemological 'conditions of possibility' of such an
encounter: how was it possible for Marx, in his analysis of the world of
commodities, to produce a notion which applies also to the analysis of
dreams, hysterical phenomena, and so on?

The answer is that there is a fundamental homology between the
interpretative procedure of Marx and Freud — more precisely, between
their analysis of commodity and of dreams. In both cases the point is to
avoid the properly fetishistic fascination of the 'content' supposedly
hidden behind the form: the 'secret' to be unveiled through analysis is
not the content hidden by the form (the form of commodities, the form
of dreams) but, on the contrary, *the 'secret' of this form itself*. The theoretical
intelligence of the form of dreams does not consist in penetrating from
the manifest content to its 'hidden kernel', to the latent dream-thoughts;
it consists in the answer to the question: why have the latent dream-
thoughts assumed such a form, why were they transposed into the form
of a dream? It is the same with commodities: the real problem is not to
penetrate to the 'hidden kernel' of the commodity — the determination
of its value by the quantity of the work consumed in its production —
but to explain why work assumed the form of the value of a commodity,
why it can affirm its social character only in the commodity-form of its
product.

The notorious reproach of 'pansexualism' addressed at the Freudian interpretation of dreams is already a commmonplace. Hans-Jürgen Eysenck, a severe critic of psychoanalysis, long ago observed a crucial paradox in the Freudian approach to dreams: according to Freud, the desire articulated in a dream is supposed to be — as a rule, at least — unconscious and at the same time of a sexual nature, which contradicts the majority of examples analysed by Freud himself, starting with the dream he chose as an introductory case to exemplify the logic of dreams, the famous dream of Irma's injection. The latent thought articulated in this dream is Freud's attempt to get rid of the responsibility for the failure of his treatment of Irma, a patient of his, by means of arguments of the type 'it was not my fault, it was caused by a series of circumstances . . .'; but this 'desire', the meaning of the dream, is obviously neither of a sexual nature (it rather concerns professional ethics) nor unconscious (the failure of Irma's treatment was troubling Freud day and night) (Eysenck, 1966).

This kind of reproach is based on a fundamental theoretical error: the identification of the unconscious desire at work in the dream with the 'latent thought' — that is, the signification of the dream. But as Freud continually emphasizes, *there is nothing 'unconscious' in the 'latent dream-thought'*: this thought is an entirely 'normal' thought which can be articulated in the syntax of everyday, common language; topologically, it belongs to the system of 'consciousness/preconsciousness'; the subject is usually aware of it, even excessively so; it harasses him all the time. . . . Under certain conditions this thought is pushed away, forced out of the consciousness, drawn into the unconscious — that is, submitted to the laws of the 'primary process', translated into the 'language of the unconscious'. The relationship between the 'latent thought' and what is called the 'manifest content' of a dream — the text of the dream, the dream in its literal phenomenality — is therefore that between some entirely 'normal', (pre)conscious thought and its translation into the 'rebus' of the dream. The essential constitution of dream is thus not its 'latent thought' but this work (the mechanisms of displacement and condensation, the figuration of the contents of words or syllables) which confers on it the form of a dream.

Herein, then, lies the basic misunderstanding: if we seek the 'secret of the dream' in the latent content hidden by the manifest text, we are doomed to disappointment: all we find is some entirely 'normal' — albeit usually unpleasant — thought, the nature of which is mostly non-sexual and definitely not 'unconscious'. This 'normal', conscious/preconscious thought is not drawn towards the unconscious, repressed simply because of its 'disagreeable' character for the conscious, but because it achieves a kind of 'short circuit' between it and another desire which is already repressed, located in the unconscious, *a desire which has nothing whatsoever to do with the 'latent dream-thought'*. 'A normal train of thought' — normal and therefore one which can be articulated in common, every-day language: that is, in the syntax of the 'secondary process' — 'is only submitted to the abnormal psychical treatment of the sort we have been describing' — to the dream-work, to the mechanisms of the 'primary process' — 'if an unconscious wish, derived from infancy and in a state of repression, has been transferred on to it' (Freud, 1977, p. 757).

It is this unconscious/sexual desire which cannot be reduced to a 'normal train of thought' because it is, from the very beginning, con-stitutively repressed (Freud's *Urverdrängung*) — because it has no 'original' in the 'normal' language of everyday communication, in the syntax of the conscious/preconscious; its only place is in the mechanisms of the 'primary process'. This is why we should not reduce the interpretation of dreams, or symptoms in general, to the retranslation of the 'latent dream-thought' into the 'normal', everyday common language of inter-subjective communication (Habermas's formula). The structure is always triple; there are always *three* elements at work: the *manifest dream-text*, the *latent dream-content* or thought and the *unconscious desire* articulated in a dream. This desire attaches itself to the dream, it intercalates itself in the interspace between the latent thought and the manifest text; it is there-fore not 'more concealed, deeper' in relation to the latent thought, it is decidedly more 'on the surface', consisting entirely of the signifier's mechanisms, of the treatment to which the latent thought is submitted. In other words, its only place is in the *form* of the 'dream': the real subject matter of the dream (the unconscious desire) articulates itself in the dream-work, in the elaboration of its 'latent content'.

As is often the case with Freud, what he formulates as an empirical observation (although of 'quite surprising frequency') announces a fun-damental, universal principle: 'The form of a dream or the form in which it is dreamt is used with quite surprising frequency for represent-ing its concealed subject matter' (Freud, 1977, p. 446). This, then, is the basic paradox of the dream: the unconscious desire, that which is sup-posedly its most hidden kernel, articulates itself precisely through the dissimulation work of the 'kernel' of a dream, its latent thought, through the work of disguising this content-kernel by means of its translation into the dream-rebus. Again, as characteristically, Freud gave this paradox its final formulation in a footnote added in a later edition:

> I used at one time to find it extraordinarily difficult to accustom readers to
> the distinction between the manifest content of dreams and the latent
> dream-thoughts. Again and again arguments and objections would be
> brought up based upon some uninterpreted dream in the form in which it
> had been retained in the memory, and the need to interpret it would be
> ignored. But now that analysts at least have become reconciled to replacing
> the manifest dream by the meaning revealed by its interpretation, many of
> them have become guilty of falling into another confusion which they cling
> to with an equal obstinacy. They seek to find the essence of dreams in their
> latent content and in so doing they overlook the distinction between the
> latent dream-thoughts and the dream-work.
>
> At bottom, dreams are nothing other than a particular form of thinking,
> made possible by the conditions of the state of sleep. It is the dream-work
> which creates that form, and it alone is the essence of dreaming — the
> explanation of its peculiar nature. (Freud, 1977, p.650)

Freud proceeds here in two stages:

- First, we must break the appearance according to which a dream is
  nothing but a simple and meaningless confusion, a disorder caused by
  physiological processes and as such having nothing whatsoever to do
  with signification. In other words, we must accomplish a crucial step
  towards a *hermeneutical* approach and conceive the dream as a meaningful phenomenon, as something transmitting a repressed message
  which has to be discovered by an interpretative procedure;

- Then we must get rid of the fascination in this kernel of signification,
  in the 'hidden meaning' of the dream — that is to say, in the content
  concealed behind the form of a dream — and centre our attention on
  this form itself, on the dream-work to which the 'latent dream-
  thoughts' were submitted.

The crucial thing to note here is that we find exactly the same articulation in two stages with Marx, in his analysis of the 'secret of the
commodity-form':

- First, we must break the appearance according to which the value of a
  commodity depends on pure hazard — on an accidental interplay

between supply and demand, for example. We must accomplish the crucial step of conceiving the hidden 'meaning' behind the commodity-form, the signification 'expressed' by this form; we must penetrate the 'secret' of the value of commodities:

The determination of the magnitude of value by labour-time is therefore a secret, hidden under the apparent fluctuations in the relative values of commodities. Its discovery, while removing all appearance of mere accidentality from the determination of the magnitude of the values of products, yet in no way alters the mode in which that determination takes place. (Marx, 1974, p.80)

– But as Marx points out, there is a certain 'yet': the unmasking of the secret *is not sufficient.* Classical bourgeois political economy has already discovered the 'secret' of the commodity-form; its limit is that it is not able to disengage itself from this fascination in the secret hidden behind the commodity-form — that its attention is captivated by labour as the true source of wealth. In other words, classical political economy is interested only in contents concealed behind the commodity-form, which is why it cannot explain the true secret, not the secret *behind* the form but *the secret of this form itself.* In spite of its quite correct explanation of the 'secret of the magnitude of value', the commodity remains for classical political economy a mysterious, enigmatic thing — it is the same as with the dream: even after we have explained its hidden meaning, its latent thought, the dream remains an enigmatic phenomenon; what is not yet explained is simply its form, the process by means of which the hidden meaning disguised itself in such a form.

We must, then, accomplish another crucial step and analyse the genesis of the commodity-form itself. It is not sufficient to reduce the form to the essence, to the hidden kernel, we must also examine the process — homologous to the 'dream-work' — by means of which the concealed content assumes such a form, because, as Marx points out: 'Whence, then, arises the enigmatical character of the product of labour, as soon as it assumes the form of commodities? Clearly from this form itself' (Marx, 1974, p. 76). It is this step towards the genesis of the form that classical political economy cannot accomplish, and this is its crucial weakness:

Political economy has indeed analysed value and its magnitude, however

incompletely, and has uncovered the content concealed within these forms.
But it has never once asked the question why this content has assumed that
particular form, that is to say, why labour is expressed in value, and why the
measurement of labour by its duration is expressed in the magnitude of the
value of the product. (Sohn-Rethel, 1978, p.31)

The Unconscious of the Commodity-form

Why did the Marxian analysis of the commodity-form — which, *prima
facie*, concerns a purely economic question — exert such an influence in
the general field of social sciences; why has it fascinated generations of
philosophers, sociologists, art historians, and others? Because it offers a
kind of matrix enabling us to generate all other forms of the 'fetishistic
inversion': it is as if the dialectics of the commodity-form presents us
with a pure — distilled, so to speak — version of a mechanism offering us
a key to the theoretical understanding of phenomena which, at first
sight, have nothing whatsoever to do with the field of political economy
(law, religion, and so on). In the commodity-form there is definitely
more at stake than the commodity-form itself, and it was precisely this
'more' which exerted such a fascinating power of attraction. The theo-
retician who has gone furthest in unfolding the universal reach of the
commodity-form is indubitably Alfred Sohn-Rethel, one of the 'fellow-
travellers' of the Frankfurt School. His fundamental thesis was that

> the formal analysis of the commodity holds the key not only to the critique
> of political economy, but also to the historical explanation of the abstract
> conceptual mode of thinking and of the division of intellectual and manual
> labour which came into existence with it. (Sohn-Rethel, 1978, p. 33)

In other words, in the structure of the commodity-form it is possible to
find the transcendental subject: the commodity-form articulates in
advance the anatomy, the skeleton of the Kantian transcendental subject
— that is, the network of transcendental categories which constitute the a
priori frame of 'objective' scientific knowledge. Herein lies the paradox
of the commodity-form: it — this inner-worldly, 'pathological' (in the
Kantian meaning of the word) phenomenon — offers us a key to solving
the fundamental question of the theory of knowledge: objective knowledge with universal validity — how is this possible?
After a series of detailed analyses, Sohn-Rethel came to the following

conclusion: the apparatus of categories presupposed, implied by the scientific procedure (that, of course of the Newtonian science of nature), the network of notions by means of which it seizes nature, is already present in the social effectivity, already at work in the act of commodity exchange. Before thought could arrive at pure *abstraction*, the abstraction was already at work in the social effectivity of the market. The exchange of commodities implies a double abstraction: the abstraction from the changeable character of the commodity during the act of exchange and the abstraction from the concrete, empirical, sensual, particular character of the commodity (in the act of exchange, the distinct, particular quali- tative determination of a commodity is not taken into account; a commodity is reduced to an abstract entity which — irrespective of its particular nature, of its 'use-value' — possesses 'the same value' as another commodity for which it is being exchanged).

Before thought could arrive at the idea of a purely *quantitative* deter- mination, a *sine qua non* of the modern science of nature, pure quantity was already at work in money, that commodity which renders possible the commensurability of the value of all other commodities notwith- standing their particular qualitative determination. Before physics could articulate the notion of a purely abstract *movement* going on in a geo- metric space, independently of all qualitative determinations of the moving objects, the social act of exchange had already realized such a 'pure', abstract movement which leaves totally intact the concrete- sensual properties of the object caught in movement: the transference of property. And Sohn-Rethel demonstrated the same about the relationship of substance and its accidents, about the notion of causality operative in Newtonian science — in short, about the whole network of categories of pure reason.

In this way, the transcendental subject, the support of the net of a priori categories, is confronted with the disquieting fact that it depends, in its very formal genesis, on some inner-worldly, 'pathological' process — a scandal, a nonsensical impossibility from the transcendental point of view, in so far as the formal–transcendental a priori is by definition independent of all positive contents: a scandal corresponding perfectly to the 'scandalous' character of the Freudian unconscious, which is also unbearable from the transcendental–philosophical perspective. That is to say, if we look closely at the ontological status of what Sohn-Rethel calls the 'real abstraction' [*das reale Abstraktion*] (that is, the act of abstraction at work in the very *effective* process of the exchange of commodities), the homology between its status and that of the unconscious, this signifying chain which persists on 'another Scene', is striking: *the 'real abstraction' is the unconscious of the transcendental subject,* the support of objective-universal scientific knowledge.

On the one hand, the 'real abstraction' is of course not 'real' in the sense of the real, effective properties of commodities as material objects: the object-commodity does not contain 'value' in the same way as it possesses a set of particular properties determining its 'use-value' (its form, colour, taste, and so on). As Sohn-Rethel pointed out, its nature is that of a *postulate* implied by the effective act of exchange — in other words, that of a certain 'as if' [*als ob*]: during the act of exchange, individuals proceed *as if* the commodity is not submitted to physical, material exchanges; *as if* it is excluded from the natural cycle of generation and corruption; although on the level of their 'consciousness' they 'know very well' that this is not the case.

The easiest way to detect the effectivity of this postulate is to think of the way we behave towards the materiality of money: we know very well that money, like all other material objects, suffers the effects of use, that its material body changes through time, but in the social *effectivity* of the market we none the less *treat* coins as if they consist 'of an immutable substance, a substance over which time has no power, and which stands in antithetic contrast to any matter found in nature' (Sohn-Rethel, 1978, p. 59). How tempting to recall here the formula of fetishistic disavowal: 'I know very well, but still . . .'. To the current exemplifications of this formula ('I know that Mother has not got a phallus, but still . . . [I believe she has got one]'; 'I know that Jews are people like us, but still . . . [there is something in them]') we must undoubtedly add also the variant of money: 'I know that money is a material object like others, but still . . . [it is as if it were made of a special substance over which time has no power]'.

Here we have touched a problem unsolved by Marx, that of the *material* character of money: not of the empirical, material stuff money is made of, but of the *sublime* material, of that other 'indestructible and immutable' body which persists 'beyond the corruption of the body physical — this other body of money is like the corpse of the Sadeian victim which endures all torments and survives with its beauty immaculate. This immaterial corporality of the 'body within the body' gives us a precise definition of the sublime object, and it is in this sense only that the psychoanalytic notion of money as a 'pre-phallic', 'anal' object is acceptable — provided that we do not forget how this postulated existence of the sublime body depends on the symbolic order: the indestructible 'body-within-the-body' exempted from the effects of wear and tear is always sustained by the guarantee of some symbolic authority:

> A coin has it stamped upon its body that it is to serve as a means of exchange and not as an object of use. Its weight and metallic purity are guaranteed by the issuing authority so that, if by the wear and tear of circulation it has lost in weight, full replacement is provided. Its physical matter has visibly become a mere carrier of its social function. (Sohn-Rethel, 1978, p. 59)

If, then, the 'real abstraction' has nothing to do with the level of 'reality', of the effective properties, of an object, it would be wrong for that reason to conceive of it as a 'thought-abstraction', as a process taking place in the 'interior' of the thinking subject: in relation to this 'interior', the abstraction appertaining to the act of exchange is in an irreducible way external, decentred — or, to quote Sohn-Rethel's concise formulation: 'The exchange abstraction *is not* thought, but it has the *form* of thought.'

Here we have one of the possible definitions of the unconscious: *the form of thought whose ontological status is not that of thought,* that is to say, the form of thought external to the thought itself — in short, some Other Scene external to the thought whereby the form of the thought is already articulated in advance. The symbolic order is precisely such a formal order which supplements and/or disrupts the dual relationship of 'external' factual reality and 'internal' subjective experience; Sohn-Rethel is thus quite justified in his criticism of Althusser, who conceives abstraction as a process taking place entirely in the domain of knowledge and refuses for that reason the category of 'real abstraction' as the expression of an 'epistemological confusion'. The 'real abstraction' is unthinkable in the frame of the fundamental Althusserian epistemological distinction between the 'real object' and the 'object of knowledge' in so far as it introduces a third element which subverts the very field of this distinction: the form of the thought previous and external to the thought — in short the symbolic order.

We are now able to formulate precisely the 'scandalous' nature of Sohn-Rethel's undertaking for philosophical reflection: he has confronted the closed circle of philosophical reflection with an external place where its form is already 'staged'. Philosophical reflection is thus subjected to an uncanny experience similar to the one summarized by the old oriental formula 'thou art that': there, in the external effectivity of the exchange process, is your proper place; there is the theatre in which your truth was performed before you took cognizance of it. The confrontation with this place is unbearable because philosophy as such *is defined by* its blindness to this place: it cannot take it into consideration without dissolving itself, without losing its consistency.

This does not mean, on the other hand, that everyday 'practical' consciousness, as opposed to the philosophical-theoretical one – the consciousness of the individuals partaking in the act of exchange – is not also subjected to a complementary blindness. During the act of exchange, individuals proceed as 'practical solipsists', they misrecognize the socio-synthetic function of exchange: that is the level of the 'real abstraction' as the form of socialization of private production through the medium of the market. 'What the commodity owners do in an exchange relation is practical solipsism – irrespective of what they think and say about it' (Sohn-Rethel, 1978, p. 42). Such a misrecognition is the *sine qua non* of the effectuation of an act of exchange – if the participants were to take note of the dimension of 'real abstraction', the 'effective' act of exchange itself would no longer be possible:

> Thus, in speaking of the abstractness of exchange we must be careful not to apply the term to the consciousness of the exchange agents. They are supposed to be occupied with the use of the commodities they see, but occupied in their imagination only. It is the action of exchange, and the action alone, that is abstract ... the abstractness of that action cannot be noted when it happens because the consciousness of its agents is taken up with their business and with the empirical appearance of things which pertain to their use. One could say that the abstractness of their action is beyond realization by the actors because their very consciousness stands in the way. Were the abstractness to catch their minds their action would cease to be exchange and the abstraction would not arise. (Sohn-Rethel, 1978, pp. 26–7)

This misrecognition brings about the fissure of the consciousness into 'practical' and 'theoretical': the proprietor partaking in the act of exchange proceeds as a 'practical solipsist': he overlooks the universal, socio-synthetic dimension of his act, reducing it to a casual encounter of atomized individuals in the market. This 'repressed' *social* dimension of his act emerges thereupon in the form of its contrary – as universal Reason turned towards the observation of nature (the network of categories of 'pure reason' as the conceptual frame of natural sciences).

The crucial paradox of this relationship between the social effectivity of the commodity exchange and the 'consciousness' of it is that – to use again a concise formulation by Sohn-Rethel – 'this non-knowledge of the reality is part of its very essence': the social effectivity of the exchange process is a kind of reality which is possible only on condition that the individuals partaking in it are *not* aware of its proper logic; that is, a kind of reality *whose very ontological consistency implies a certain non-knowledge of its participants* — if we come to 'know too much', to pierce the true functioning of social reality, this reality would dissolve itself.

This is probably the fundamental dimension of 'ideology': ideology is not simply a 'false consciousness', an illusory representation of reality, it is rather this reality itself which is already to be conceived as 'ideological' — *'ideological' is a social reality whose very existence implies the non-knowledge of its participants as to its essence* — that is, the social effectivity, the very reproduction of which implies that the individuals 'do not know what they are doing'. *'Ideological' is not the 'false consciousness' of a (social) being but this being itself in so far as it is supported by 'false consciousness'*. Thus we have finally reached the dimension of the symptom, because one of its possible definitions would also be 'a formation whose very consistency implies a certain non-knowledge on the part of the subject': the subject can 'enjoy his symptom' only in so far as its logic escapes him — the measure of the success of its interpretation is precisely its dissolution.

The Social Symptom

How, then, can we define the Marxian symptom? Marx 'invented the symptom' (Lacan) by means of detecting a certain fissure, an asymmetry, a certain 'pathological' imbalance which belies the universalism of the bourgeois 'rights and duties'. This imbalance, far from announcing the 'imperfect realization' of these universal principles — that is, an insufficiency to be abolished by further development — functions as their constitutive moment: the 'symptom' is, strictly speaking, a particular element which subverts its own universal foundation, a species subverting its own genus. In this sense, we can say that the elementary Marxian procedure of 'criticism of ideology' is already 'symptomatic': it consists in detecting a point of breakdown *heterogenous* to a given ideological field and at the same time *necessary* for that field to achieve its closure, its accomplished form.

This procedure thus implies a certain logic of exception: every ideological Universal — for example freedom, equality — is 'false' in so far as it necessarily includes a specific case which breaks its unity, lays open its falsity. Freedom, for example: a universal notion comprising a number of species (freedom of speech and press, freedom of consciousness, freedom of commerce, political freedom, and so on) but also, by means of a structural necessity, a specific freedom (that of the worker to sell freely his own labour on the market) which subverts this universal notion. That is to say, this freedom is the very opposite of effective freedom: by selling his labour 'freely', the worker *loses* his freedom — the real content of this free act of sale is the worker's enslavement to capital. The crucial point is, of course, that it is precisely this paradoxical freedom, the form of its opposite, which closes the circle of 'bourgeois freedoms'.

The same can also be shown for fair, equivalent exchange, this ideal of the market. When, in pre-capitalist society, the production of commodities has not yet attained universal character — that is, when it is still so-called 'natural production' which predominates — the proprietors of the means of production are still themselves producers (as a rule, at least): it is artisan production; the proprietors themselves work and sell their products on the market. At this stage of development there is no exploitation (in principle, at least — that is, if we do not consider the exploitation of apprentices, and so on); the exchange on the market is equivalent, every commodity is paid its full value. But as soon as production for the market prevails in the economic edifice of a given society, this *generalization* is necessarily accompanied by the appearance of a new, paradoxical type of commodity: the labour force, the workers who are not themselves proprietors of the means of production and who are consequently obliged to sell on the market their own labour instead of the products of their labour.

With this new commodity, the equivalent exchange becomes its own negation — the very form of exploitation, of appropriation of the surplus-value. The crucial point not to be missed here is that this negation is strictly *internal* to equivalent exchange, not its simple violation: the labour force is not 'exploited' in the sense that its full value is not remunerated; in principle at least, the exchange between labour and capital is wholly equivalent and equitable. The catch is that the labour force is a peculiar commodity, the use of which — labour itself — produces a certain surplus-value, and it is this surplus over the value of the labour force itself which is appropriated by the capitalist.

We have here again a certain ideological Universal, that of equivalent and equitable exchange, and a particular paradoxical exchange — that of the labour force for its wages — which, precisely as an equivalent, functions as the very form of exploitation. The 'quantitative' development itself, the universalization of the production of commodities, brings about a new 'quality', the emergence of a new commodity representing the internal negation of the universal principle of equivalent exchange of commodities; in other words, *it brings about a symptom*. And in the Marxian perspective, *utopian* socialism consists in the very belief that a society is possible in which the relations of exchange are universalized and production for the market predominates, but workers themselves none the less remain proprietors of their means of production and are therefore not exploited — in short, 'utopian' conveys a belief in the possibility of *a universality without its symptom*, without the point of exception functioning as its internal negation.

This is also the logic of the Marxian critique of Hegel, of the Hegelian notion of society as a rational totality: as soon as we try to conceive the existing social order as a rational totality, we must include in it a para-doxical element which, without ceasing to be its internal constituent, functions as its symptom — subverts the very universal rational principle of this totality. For Marx, this 'irrational' element of the existing society was, of course, the proletariat, 'the unreason of reason itself' (Marx), the point at which the Reason embodied in the existing social order encounters its own unreason.

Commodity Fetishism

In his attribution of the discovery of symptom to Marx, Lacan is, however, more distinct: he locates this discovery in the way Marx conceived the *passage* from feudalism to capitalism: 'One has to look for the origins of the notion of symptom not in Hippocrates but in Marx, in the connection he was first to establish between capitalism and what? — the good old times, what we call the feudal times' (Lacan, 1975a, p. 106). To grasp the logic of this passage from feudalism to capitalism we have first to elucidate its theoretical background, the Marxian notion of commodity fetishism.

In a first approach, commodity fetishism is 'a definite social relation between men, that assumes, in their eyes, the fantastic form of a relation between things' (Marx, 1974, p. 77). The *value* of a certain commodity, which is effectively an insignia of a network of social relations between producers of diverse commodities, assumes the form of a quasi-'natural' property of another thing-commodity, money: we say that the value of a certain commodity is such-and-such amount of money. Consequently, the essential feature of commodity fetishism does not consist of the famous replacement of men with things ('a relation between men

assumes the form of a relation between things'); rather, it consists of a
certain misrecognition which concerns the relation between a structured
network and one of its elements: what is really a structural effect, an
effect of the network of relations between elements, appears as an immediate property of one of the elements, as if this property also belongs to it
outside its relation with other elements.

Such a misrecognition can take place in a 'relation between things' as
well as in a 'relation between men' — Marx states this explicitly apropos
of the simple form of the value-expression. The commodity A can
express its value only by referring itself to another commodity, B, which
thus becomes its equivalent: in the value relationship, the natural form of
the commodity B (its use-value, its positive, empirical properties)
functions as a form of value of the commodity A; in other words, the
body of B becomes for A the mirror of its value. To these reflections,
Marx added the following note:

> In a sort of way, it is with man as with commodities. Since he comes into the
> world neither with a looking-glass in his hand, nor as a Fichtian philos-
> opher, to whom 'I am I' is sufficient, man first sees and recognizes himself in
> other men. Peter only establishes his own identity as a man by first com-
> paring himself with Paul as being of like kind. And thereby Paul, just as he
> stands in his Pauline personality, becomes to Peter the type of the genus
> homo. (Marx, 1974, p. 59)

This short note anticipates in a way the Lacanian theory of the mirror
stage: only by being reflected in another man — that is, in so far as this
other man offers it an image of its unity — can the ego arrive at its self-
identity; identity and alienation are thus strictly correlative. Marx
pursues this homology: the other commodity (B) is an equivalent only in
so far as A relates to it as to the form-of-appearance of its own value,
only within this relationship. But the appearance — and herein lies the
effect of inversion proper to fetishism — the appearance is exactly opposite: A seems to relate to B as if, for B, to be an equivalent of A would not
be a 'reflexive determination' (Marx) of A — that is as if B would *already
in itself* be the equivalent of A; the property of 'being-an-equivalent'
appears to belong to it even outside its relation to A, on the same level as
its other 'natural' effective properties constituting its use-value. To these
reflections, Marx again added a very interesting note:

> Such expressions of relations in general, called by Hegel reflex-categories,

form a very curious class. For instance, one man is king only because other men stand in the relation of subjects to him. They, on the contrary, imagine that they are subjects because he is king. (Marx, 1974, p. 63)

'Being-a-king' is an effect of the network of social relations between a 'king' and his 'subjects'; but — and here is the fetishistic misrecognition — to the participants of this social bond, the relationship appears necessarily in an inverse form: they think that they are subjects giving the king royal treatment because the king is already in himself, outside the relationship to his subjects, a king; as if the determination of 'being-a-king' were a 'natural' property of the person of a king. How can one not remind oneself here of the famous Lacanian affirmation that a madman who believes himself to be a king is no more mad than a king who believes himself to be a king — who, that is, identifies immediately with the mandate 'king'?

What we have here is thus a parallel between two modes of fetishism, and the crucial question concerns the exact relationship between these two levels. That is to say, this relationship is by no means a simple homology: we cannot say that in societies in which production for the market predominates — ultimately, that is, in capitalist societies — 'it is with man as with commodities'. Precisely the opposite is true: commodity fetishism occurs in capitalist societies, but in capitalism relations between men are definitely *not* 'fetishized'; what we have here are relations between 'free' people, each following his or her proper egoistic interest. The predominant and determining form of their interrelations is not domination and servitude but a contract between free people who are equal in the eyes of the law. Its model is the market exchange: here, two subjects meet, their relation is free of all the lumber of veneration of the Master, of the Master's patronage and care for his subjects; they meet as two persons whose activity is thoroughly determined by their egoistic interest; every one of them proceeds as a good utilitarian; the other person is for him wholly delivered of all mystical aura; all he sees in his partner is another subject who follows his interest and interests him only in so far as he possesses something — a commodity — that could satisfy some of his needs.

The two forms of fetishism are thus *incompatible*: in societies in which commodity fetishism reigns, the 'relations between men' are totally de-fetishized, while in societies in which there is fetishism in 'relations between men' — in pre-capitalist societies — commodity fetishism is not yet developed, because it is 'natural' production, not production for the market which predominates. This fetishism in relations between men has to be called by its proper name: what we have here are, as Marx points out, 'relations of domination and servitude' — that is to say, precisely the relation of Lordship and Bondage in a Hegelian sense;* and it is as if the retreat of the Master in capitalism was only a *displacement*: as if the de-fetishization in the 'relations between men' was paid for by the emergence of fetishism in the 'relations between things' — by commodity fetishism. The place of fetishism has just shifted from inter-subjective relations to relations 'between things': the crucial social relations, those of production, are no longer immediately transparent in the form of the interpersonal relations of domination and servitude (of the Lord and his serfs, and so on); they disguise themselves — to use Marx's accurate formula — 'under the shape of social relations between things, between the products of labour'.

This is why one has to look for the discovery of the symptom in the way Marx conceived the passage from feudalism to capitalism. With the establishment of bourgeois society, the relations of domination and servitude are *repressed*: formally, we are apparently concerned with free subjects whose interpersonal relations are discharged of all fetishism; the repressed truth — that of the persistence of domination and servitude — emerges in a symptom which subverts the ideological appearance of equality, freedom, and so on. This symptom, the point of emergence of the truth about social relations, is precisely the 'social relations between things' — in contrast to feudal society, where

> no matter what we may think of the parts played by the different classes of people themselves in this society, the social relations between individuals in the performance of their labour, appear at all events as their own mutual personal relations, and are not disguised under the shape of social relations between things, between the products of labour. (Marx, 1974, p. 82)

'Instead of appearing at all events as their own mutual relations, the social relations between individuals are disguised under the shape of social relations between things' — here we have a precise definition of the hysterical symptom, of the 'hysteria of conversion' proper to capitalism.

---

*'Lordship' and 'Bondage' are the terms used in the translation we refer to (Hegel, 1977); following Kojève, Lacan uses 'maître' and 'esclave', which are then translated as 'master' and 'slave'.

Totalitarian Laughter

Here Marx is more subversive than the majority of his contemporary critics who discard the dialectics of commodity fetishism as outdated: this dialectics can still help us to grasp the phenomenon of so-called 'totalitarianism'. Let us take as our starting point Umberto Eco's *Name of the Rose*, precisely because there is something wrong with this book. This criticism does not apply only to its ideology, which might be called — on the model of *spaghetti* Westerns — *spaghetti* structuralism: a kind of simplified, mass-culture version of structuralist and post-structuralist ideas (there is no final reality, we all live in a world of signs referring to other signs . . .). What should bother us about this book is its basic underlying thesis: the source of totalitarianism is a dogmatic attachment to the official word: the lack of laughter, of ironic detachment. An excessive commitment to Good may in itself become the greatest Evil: real Evil is any kind of fanatical dogmatism, especially that exerted in the name of the supreme Good.

This thesis is already part of the enlightened version of religious belief itself: if we become too obsessed with the Good and with a corresponding hate for the secular, our obsession with Good may itself turn into a force of Evil, a form of destructive hatred for all that fails to correspond to our idea of Good. The real Evil is the supposedly innocent gaze which perceives in the world nothing but Evil, as in *The Turn of the Screw* by Henry James, in which the real Evil is, of course, the gaze of the storyteller (the young governess) herself. . . .

First, this idea of an obsession with (a fanatical devotion to) Good turning into Evil masks the inverse experience, which is much more disquieting: how an obsessive, fanatical attachment to Evil may in itself acquire the status of an ethical position, of a position which is not guided by our egoistical interests. Consider only Mozart's Don Giovanni at the end of the opera, when he is confronted with the following choice: if he confesses his sins, he can still achieve salvation; if he persists, he will be damned for ever. From the viewpoint of the pleasure principle, the proper thing to do would be to renounce his past, but he does not, he persists in his Evil, although he knows that by persisting he will be damned for ever. Paradoxically, with his final choice of Evil, he acquires the status of an ethical hero — that is, of someone who is guided by fundamental principles 'beyond the pleasure principle' and not just by the search for pleasure or material gain.

What is really disturbing about *The Name of the Rose*, however, is the underlying belief in the liberating, anti-totalitarian force of laughter, of ironic distance. Our thesis here is almost the exact opposite of this underlying premiss of Eco's novel: in contemporary societies, democratic or totalitarian, that cynical distance, laughter, irony, are, so to speak, part of the game. The ruling ideology is not meant to be taken seriously or literally. Perhaps the greatest danger for totalitarianism is people who take its ideology literally – even in Eco's novel, poor old Jorge, the incarnation of dogmatic belief who does not laugh, is rather a tragic figure: outdated, a kind of living dead, a remnant of the past, certainly not a person representing the existing social and political powers.

What conclusion should we draw from this? Should we say that we live in a post-ideological society? Perhaps it would be better, first, to try to specify what we mean by ideology.

Cynicism as a Form of Ideology

The most elementary definition of ideology is probably the well-known phrase from Marx's *Capital*: '*Sie wissen das nicht, aber sie tun es*' – '*they do not know it, but they are doing it*'. The very concept of ideology implies a kind of basic, constitutive *naïveté*: the misrecognition of its own presuppositions, of its own effective conditions, a distance, a divergence between so-called social reality and our distorted representation, our false consciousness of it. That is why such a 'naïve consciousness' can be submitted to a critical-ideological procedure. The aim of this procedure is to lead the naïve ideological consciousness to a point at which it can recognize its own effective conditions, the social reality that it is distorting, and through this very act dissolve itself. In the more sophisticated versions of the critics of ideology – that developed by the Frankfurt School, for example – it is not just a question of seeing things (that is, social reality) as they 'really are', of throwing away the distorting spectacles of ideology; the main point is to see how the reality itself cannot reproduce itself without this so-called ideological mystification. The mask is not simply hiding the real state of things; the ideological distortion is written into its very essence.

We find, then, the paradox of a being which can reproduce itself only in so far as it is misrecognized and overlooked: the moment we see it 'as it really is', this being dissolves itself into nothingness or, more precisely, it changes into another kind of reality. That is why we must avoid the simple metaphors of demasking, of throwing away the veils which are supposed to hide the naked reality. We can see why Lacan, in his Seminar on *The Ethic of Psychoanalysis*, distances himself from the liberating gesture of saying finally that 'the emperor has no clothes'. The point is, as Lacan puts it, that the emperor is naked only beneath his clothes, so if there is an unmasking gesture of psychoanalysis, it is closer to Alphonse Allais's well-known joke, quoted by Lacan: somebody points at a woman and utters a horrified cry, 'Look at her, what a shame, under her clothes, she is totally naked' (Lacan, 1986, p.231).

But all this is already well known: it is the classic concept of ideology as 'false consciousness', misrecognition of the social reality which is part of this reality itself. Our question is: Does this concept of ideology as a naïve consciousness still apply to today's world? Is it still operating today? In the *Critique of Cynical Reason*, a great bestseller in Germany (Sloterdijk, 1983), Peter Sloterdijk puts forward the thesis that ideology's dominant mode of functioning is cynical, which renders impossible — or, more precisely, vain — the classic critical–ideological procedure. The cynical subject is quite aware of the distance between the ideological mask and the social reality, but he none the less still insists upon the mask. The formula, as proposed by Sloterdijk, would then be: 'they know very well what they are doing, but still, they are doing it'. Cynical reason is no longer naïve, but is a paradox of an enlightened false consciousness: one knows the falsehood very well, one is well aware of a particular interest hidden behind an ideological universality, but still one does not renounce it.

We must distinguish this cynical position strictly from what Sloterdijk calls *kynicism*. Kynicism represents the popular, plebeian rejection of the official culture by means of irony and sarcasm: the classical kynical procedure is to confront the pathetic phrases of the ruling official ideology — its solemn, grave tonality — with everyday banality and to hold them up to ridicule, thus exposing behind the sublime *noblesse* of the ideological phrases the egotistical interests, the violence, the brutal claims to power. This procedure, then, is more pragmatic than argumentative: it subverts the official proposition by confronting it with the situation of its enunciation; it proceeds *ad hominem* (for example when a politician preaches the duty of patriotic sacrifice, kynicism exposes the personal gain he is making from the sacrifice of others).

Cynicism is the answer of the ruling culture to this kynical subversion: it recognizes, it takes into account, the particular interest behind the ideological universality, the distance between the ideological mask and the reality, but it still finds reasons to retain the mask. This cynicism

rect position of immorality, it is more like morality itself put in
e of immorality — the model of cynical wisdom is to conceive
ntegrity, as a supreme form of dishonesty, and morals as a
supreme form of profligacy, the truth as the most effective form of a lie.
This cynicism is therefore a kind of perverted 'negation of the negation'
of the official ideology: confronted with illegal enrichment, with
robbery, the cynical reaction consists in saying that legal enrichment is a
lot more effective and, moreover, protected by the law. As Bertolt Brecht
puts it in his *Threepenny Opera*: 'what is the robbery of a bank compared
to the founding of a new bank?'

It is clear, therefore, that confronted with such cynical reason, the
traditional critique of ideology no longer works. We can no longer
subject the ideological text to 'symptomatic reading', confronting it with
its blank spots, with what it must repress to organize itself, to preserve its
consistency — cynical reason takes this distance into account in advance.
Is then the only issue left to us to affirm that, with the reign of cynical
reason, we find ourselves in the so-called post-ideological world? Even
Adorno came to this conclusion, starting from the premiss that ideology
is, strictly speaking, only a system which makes a claim to the truth —
that is, which is not simply a lie but a lie experienced as truth, a lie which
pretends to be taken seriously. Totalitarian ideology no longer has this
pretension. It is no longer meant, even by its authors, to be taken
seriously — its status is just that of a means of manipulation, purely
external and instrumental; its rule is secured not by its truth-value but by
simple extra-ideological violence and promise of gain.

It is here, at this point, that the distinction between *symptom* and
fantasy must be introduced in order to show how the idea that we live in
a post-ideological society proceeds a little too quickly: cynical reason,
with all its ironic detachment, leaves untouched the fundamental level of
ideological fantasy, the level on which ideology structures the social
reality itself.

Ideological Fantasy

If we want to grasp this dimension of fantasy, we must return to the
Marxian formula 'they do not know it, but they are doing it', and pose
ourselves a very simple question: Where is the place of ideological illusion, in the '*knowing*' or in the '*doing*' in the reality itself? At first sight,
the answer seems obvious: ideological illusion lies in the '*knowing*'. It is a

matter of a discordance between what people are effectively doing and what they think they are doing — ideology consists in the very fact that the people 'do not know what they are really doing', that they have a false representation of the social reality to which they belong (the distortion produced, of course, by the same reality). Let us take again the classic Marxian example of so-called commodity fetishism: money is in reality just an embodiment, a condensation, a materialization of a network of social relations — the fact that it functions as a universal equivalent of all commodities is conditioned by its position in the texture of social relations. But to the individuals themselves, this function of money — to be the embodiment of wealth — appears as an immediate, natural property of a thing called 'money', as if money is already in itself, in its immediate material reality, the embodiment of wealth. Here, we have touched upon the classic Marxist motive of 'reification': behind the things, the relation between things, we must detect the social relations, the relations between human subjects.

But such a reading of the Marxian formula leaves out an illusion, an error, a distortion which is already at work in the social reality itself, at the level of what the individuals are *doing*, and not only what they *think* or *know* they are doing. When individuals use money, they know very well that there is nothing magical about it — that money, in its materiality, is simply an expression of social relations. The everyday spontaneous ideology reduces money to a simple sign giving the individual possessing it a right to a certain part of the social product. So, on an everyday level, the individuals know very well that there are relations between people behind the relations between things. The problem is that in their social activity itself, in what they are *doing*, they are *acting* as if money, in its material reality, is the immediate embodiment of wealth as such. They are fetishists in practice, not in theory. What they 'do not know', what they misrecognize, is the fact that in their social reality itself, in their social activity — in the act of commodity exchange — they are guided by the fetishistic illusion.

To make this clear, let us again take the classic Marxian motive of the speculative inversion of the relationship between the Universal and the Particular. The Universal is just a property of particular objects which really exist, but when we are victims of commodity fetishism it appears as if the concrete content of a commodity (its use-value) is an expression of its abstract universality (its exchange-value) — the abstract Universal, the Value, appears as a real Substance which successively incarnates itself in a series of concrete objects. That is the basic Marxian thesis: it is already the effective world of commodities which behaves like a Hegelian subject–substance, like a Universal going through a series of particular embodiments. Marx speaks about 'commodity metaphysics', about the 'religion of everyday life'. The roots of philosophical speculative idealism are in the social reality of the world of commodities; it is this world which behaves 'idealistically' — or, as Marx puts it in the first chapter of the first edition of *Capital*:

> This *inversion* through which what is sensible and concrete counts only as a phenomenal form of what is abstract and universal, contrary to the real state of things where the abstract and the universal count only as a property of the concrete — such an inversion is characteristic of the expression of value, and it is this inversion which, at the same time, makes the understanding of this expression so difficult. If I say: Roman law and German law are both laws, it is something which goes by itself. But if, on the contrary, I say: THE Law, this abstract thing, realizes itself in Roman law and in German law, i.e. in these concrete laws, the interconnection becomes mystical. (Marx, 1977, p. 132)

The question to ask again is: Where is the illusion here? We must not forget that the bourgeois individual, in his everyday ideology, is definitely not a speculative Hegelian: he does not conceive the particular content as resulting from an autonomous movement of the universal Idea. He is, on the contrary, a good Anglo-Saxon nominalist, thinking that the Universal is a property of the Particular — that is, of really existing things. Value in itself does not exist, there are just individual things which, among other properties, have value. The problem is that in his practice, in his real activity, he acts as if the particular things (the commodities) were just so many embodiments of universal Value. To rephrase Marx: *He knows very well that Roman law and German law are just two kinds of law, but in his practice, he acts as if the Law itself, this abstract entity, realizes itself in Roman law and in German law.*

So now we have made a decisive step forward; we have established a new way to read the Marxian formula 'they do not know it, but they are doing it': the illusion is not on the side of knowledge, it is already on the side of reality itself, of what the people are doing. What they do not know is that their social reality itself, their activity, is guided by an illusion, by a fetishistic inversion. What they overlook, what they misrecognize, is not the reality but the illusion which is structuring their reality, their real social activity. They know very well how things really are, but still they are doing it as if they did not know. The illusion is therefore double: it consists in overlooking the illusion which is structuring our real, effective relationship to reality. And this overlooked, unconscious illusion is what may be called the *ideological fantasy*.

If our concept of ideology remains the classic one in which the illusion is located in knowledge, then today's society must appear post-ideological: the prevailing ideology is that of cynicism; people no longer believe in ideological truth; they do not take ideological propositions seriously. The fundamental level of ideology, however, is not of an illusion masking the real state of things but that of an (unconscious) fantasy structuring our social reality itself. And at this level, we are of course far from being post-ideological society. Cynical distance is just one way — one of many ways — to blind ourselves to the structuring power of ideological fantasy: even if we do not take things seriously, even if we keep an ironical distance, *we are still doing them.*

It is from this standpoint that we can account for the formula of cynical reason proposed by Sloterdijk: 'they know very well what they are doing, but still, they are doing it'. If the illusion were on the side of knowledge, then the cynical position would really be a post-ideological position, simply a position without illusions: 'they know what they are doing, and they are doing it'. But if the place of the illusion is in the reality of doing itself, then this formula can be read in quite another way: 'they know that, in their activity, they are following an illusion, but still, they are doing it'. For example, they know that their idea of Freedom is masking a particular form of exploitation, but they still continue to follow this idea of Freedom.

The Objectivity of Belief

From this standpoint, it would also be worth rereading the elementary Marxian formulation of so-called commodity fetishism: in a society in which the products of human labour acquire the form of commodities, the crucial relations between people take on the form of relations between things, between commodities — instead of immediate relations between people, we have social relations between things. In the 1960s and 1970s, this whole problem was discredited through Althusserian anti-humanism. The principal reproach of the Althusserians was that the Marxian theory of commodity fetishism is based on a naïve, ideological, epistemologically unfounded opposition between persons (human subjects) and things. But a Lacanian reading can give this formulation a new, unexpected twist: the subversive power of Marx's approach lies precisely in the way he uses the opposition of persons and things.

In feudalism, as we have seen, relations between people are mystified, mediated through a web of ideological beliefs and superstitions. They are the relations between the master and his servant, whereby the master exerts his charismatic power of fascination, and so forth. Although in capitalism the subjects are emancipated, perceiving themselves as free from medieval religious superstitions, when they deal with one another they do so as rational utilitarians, guided only by their selfish interests. The point of Marx's analysis, however, is that *the things (commodities) themselves believe in their place*, instead of the subjects: it is as if all their beliefs, superstitions and metaphysical mystifications, supposedly surmounted by the rational, utilitarian personality, are embodied in the 'social relations between things'. They no longer believe, *but the things themselves believe for them.*

This seems also to be a basic Lacanian proposition, contrary to the usual thesis that a belief is something interior and knowledge something exterior (in the sense that it can be verified through an external procedure). Rather, it is belief which is radically exterior, embodied in the practical, effective procedure of people. It is similar to Tibetan prayer wheels: you write a prayer on a paper, put the rolled paper into a wheel, and turn it automatically, without thinking (or, if you want to proceed according to the Hegelian 'cunning of reason', you attach it to a windmill, so that it is moved around by the wind). In this way, the wheel itself is praying for me, instead of me — or, more precisely, I myself am praying through the medium of the wheel. The beauty of it all is that in my psychological interiority I can think about whatever I want, I can yield to the most dirty and obscene fantasies, and it does not matter because — to use a good old Stalinist expression — whatever I am thinking, *objectively* I am praying.

This is how we should grasp the fundamental Lacanian proposition that psychoanalysis is not a psychology: the most intimate beliefs, even the most intimate emotions such as compassion, crying, sorrow, laughter, can be transferred, delegated to others without losing their sincerity. In his Seminar on *The Ethic of Psychoanalysis*, Lacan speaks of the role of the Chorus in classical tragedy: we, the spectators, came to the theatre worried, full of everyday problems, unable to adjust without reserve to the problems of the play, that is to feel the required fears and compassions — but no problem, there is the Chorus, who feels the sorrow and the compassion instead of us — or, more precisely, we feel the required emotions through the medium of the Chorus: 'You are then relieved of all worries, even if you do not feel anything, the Chorus will do so in your place' (Lacan, 1986, p. 295).

Even if we, the spectators, are just drowsily watching the show, objectively — to use again the old Stalinist expression — we are doing our duty of compassion for the heroes. In so-called primitive societies we find the same phenomenon in the form of 'weepers', women hired to cry instead of us: so, through the medium of the other, we accomplish our duty of mourning, while we can spend our time on more profitable exploits — disputing the division of the inheritance of the deceased, for example.

But to avoid the impression that this exteriorization, this transference of our most intimate feeling, is simply a characteristic of the so-called primitive stages of development, let us remind ourselves of a phenomenon quite usual in popular television shows or serials: 'canned laughter'. After some supposedly funny or witty remark, you can hear the laughter and applause included in the soundtrack of the show itself — here we have the exact counterpart of the Chorus in classical tragedy; it is here that we have to look for 'living Antiquity'. That is to say, why this laughter? The first possible answer — that it serves to remind us when to laugh — is interesting enough, because it implies the paradox that laughter is a matter of duty and not of some spontaneous feeling; but this answer is not sufficient because we do *not* usually laugh. The only correct answer would be that the Other — embodied in the television set — is relieving us even of our duty to laugh — is laughing instead of us. So even if, tired from a hard day's stupid work, all evening we did nothing but gaze drowsily into the television screen, we can say afterwards that objectively, through the medium of the other, we had a really good time.

If we do not take into account this objective status of belief, we might finish like the fool from a well-known joke who thought he was a grain of corn. After some time in a mental hospital, he was finally cured: now he knew that he was not a grain but a man. So they let him out; but soon afterwards he came running back, saying: 'I met a hen and I was afraid she would eat me.' The doctors tried to calm him: 'But what are you afraid of? Now you know that you are not a grain but a man.' The fool answered: 'Yes, of course, I know that, but does the *hen* know that I am no longer a grain?'

'Law is Law'

The lesson to be drawn from this concerning the social field is above all that belief, far from being an 'intimate', purely mental state, is always *materialized* in our effective social activity: belief supports the fantasy which regulates social reality. Let us take the case of Kafka: it is usually said that in the 'irrational' universe of his novels, Kafka has given an 'exaggerated', 'fantastic', 'subjectively distorted' expression to modern bureaucracy and the fate of the individual within it. In saying this we overlook the crucial fact that it is this very 'exaggeration' which articulates the fantasy regulating the libidinal functioning of the 'effective', 'real' bureaucracy itself.

The so-called 'Kafka's universe' is not a 'fantasy-image of social reality' but, on the contrary, the *mise en scène of the fantasy which is at work in the midst of social reality itself*: we all know very well that bureaucracy is not all-powerful, but our 'effective' conduct in the presence of bureaucratic machinery is already regulated by a belief in its almightiness. . . . In contrast to the usual 'criticism of ideology' trying to deduce the ideological form of a determinate society from the conjunction of its effective social relations, the analytical approach aims above all at the ideological fantasy efficient in social reality itself.

What we call 'social reality' is in the last resort an ethical construction; it is supported by a certain *as if* (we act *as if* we believe in the almightiness of bureaucracy, *as if* the President incarnates the Will of the People, *as if* the Party expresses the objective interest of the working class . . .). As soon as the belief (which, let us remind ourselves again, is definitely not to be conceived at a 'psychological' level: it is embodied, materialized, in the effective functioning of the social field) is lost, the very texture of the social field disintegrates. This was already articulated by Pascal, one of Althusser's principal points of reference in his attempt to develop the concept of 'Ideological State Apparatuses'. According to Pascal, the interiority of our reasoning is determined by the external, nonsensical 'machine' — automatism of the signifier, of the symbolic network in which the subjects are caught:

> For we must make no mistake about ourselves: we are as much automaton as mind. . . . Proofs only convince the mind; habit provides the strongest proofs and those that are most believed. It inclines the automaton, which leads the mind unconsciously along with it. (Pascal, 1966, p. 274)

Here Pascal produces the very Lacanian definition of the unconscious: 'the automaton (i.e. the dead, senseless letter), which leads the mind unconsciously [sans le savoir] with it'. It follows, from this constitutively senseless character of the Law, that we must obey it not because it is just, good or even beneficial, but simply *because it is the law* — this tautology articulates the vicious circle of its authority, the fact that the last foundation of the Law's authority lies in its process of enunciation:

> Custom is the whole of equity for the sole reason that it is accepted. That is the mystic basis of its authority. Anyone who tries to bring it back to its first principle destroys it. (ibid., p. 46)

The only real obedience, then, is an 'external' one: obedience out of conviction is not real obedience because it is already 'mediated' through our subjectivity — that is, we are not really obeying the authority but simply following our judgement, which tells us that the authority deserves to be obeyed in so far as it is good, wise, beneficent. ... Even more than for our relation to 'external' social authority, this inversion applies to our obedience to the internal authority of belief: it was Kierkegaard who wrote that to believe in Christ because we consider him wise and good is a dreadful blasphemy — it is, on the contrary, only the act of belief itself which can give us an insight into his goodness and wisdom. Certainly we must search for rational reasons which can substantiate our belief, our obedience to the religious command, but the crucial religious experience is that these reasons reveal themselves only to those who already believe — we find reasons attesting our belief because we already believe; we do not believe because we have found sufficient good reasons to believe.

'External' obedience to the Law is thus not submission to external pressure, to so-called non-ideological 'brute force', but obedience to the Command in so far as it is 'incomprehensible', not understood; in so far as it retains a 'traumatic', 'irrational' character: far from hiding its full authority, this traumatic, non-integrated character of the Law is *a positive condition of it.* This is the fundamental feature of the psychoanalytic concept of the *superego*: an injunction which is experienced as traumatic, 'senseless' — that is, which cannot be integrated into the symbolic universe of the subject. But for the Law to function 'normally', this traumatic fact that 'custom is the whole of equity for the sole reason that it is accepted' — the dependence of the Law on its process of enunciation or, to use a concept developed by Laclau and Mouffe, its radically *contingent*

character — must be repressed into the unconscious, through the ideological, imaginary experience of the 'meaning' of the Law, of its foundation in Justice, Truth (or, in a more modern way, functionality):

> It would therefore be a good thing for us to obey laws and customs because
> they are laws.... But people are not amenable to this doctrine, and thus,
> believing that truth can be found and resides in laws and customs, they
> believe them and take their antiquity as a proof of their truth (and not just of
> their authority, without truth). (Pascal, 1966, p. 216)

It is highly significant that we find exactly the same formulation in
Kafka's *Trial*, at the end of the conversation between K. and the priest:

> 'I do not agree with that point of view,' said K., shaking his head, 'for if one
> accepts it, one must accept as true everything the door-keeper says. But you
> yourself have sufficiently proved how impossible it is to do that.' 'No,' said
> the priest, 'it is not necessary to accept everything as true, one must only
> accept it as necessary.' 'A melancholy conclusion,' said K. 'It turns lying into
> a universal principle.' (Kafka, 1985, p. 243)

What is 'repressed' then, is not some obscure origin of the Law but the
very fact that the Law is not to be accepted as true, only as necessary —
the fact that *its authority is without truth.* The necessary structural illusion
which drives people to believe that truth can be found in laws describes
precisely the mechanism of *transference*: transference is this supposition of
a Truth, of a Meaning behind the stupid, traumatic, inconsistent fact of
the Law. In other words, 'transference' names the vicious circle of belief:
the reasons why we should believe are persuasive only to those who
already believe. The crucial text of Pascal here is the famous fragment
233 on the necessity of the wager; the first, largest part of it demonstrates
at length why it is rationally sensible to 'bet on God', but this argument is
invalidated by the following remark of Pascal's imaginary partner in
dialogue:

> ... my hands are tied and my lips are sealed; I am being forced to wager and I
> am not free; I am being held fast and I am so made that I cannot believe.
> What do you want me to do then? — 'That is true, but at least get it into
> your head that, if you are unable to believe, it is because of your passions,
> since reason impels you to believe and yet you cannot do so. Concentrate
> then not on convincing yourself by multiplying proofs of God's existence
> but by diminishing your passions. You want to find faith and you do not

know the road. You want to be cured of unbelief and you ask for the remedy: learn from those who were once bound like you and who now wager all they have. These are people who know the road you wish to follow, who have been cured of the affliction of which you wish to be cured: follow the way by which they began. They behaved just as if they did believe, taking holy water, having masses said, and so on. That will make you believe quite naturally, and will make you more docile.

'Now what harm will come to you from choosing this course? You will be faithful, honest, humble, grateful, full of good works, a sincere, true friend. . . . It is true you will not enjoy noxious pleasures, glory and good living, but will you not have others?

'I tell you that you will gain even in this life, and that at every step you take along this road you will see that your gain is so certain and your risk so negligible that in the end you will realize that you have wagered on something certain and infinite for which you have paid nothing.' (Pascal, 1966, pp. 152-3)

Pascal's final answer, then, is: leave rational argumentation and submit yourself simply to ideological ritual, stupefy yourself by repeating the meaningless gestures, act *as if* you already believe, and the belief will come by itself.

Far from being limited to Catholicism, such a procedure for obtaining ideological conversion has universal application, which is why, in a certain epoch, it was very popular among French Communists. The Marxist version of the theme of 'wager' runs as follows: the bourgeois intellectual has his hands tied and his lips sealed. Apparently he is free, bound only to the argument of his reason, but in reality he is permeated by bourgeois prejudices. These prejudices do not let him go, so he cannot believe in the sense of history, in the historical mission of the working class. So what can he do?

The answer: first, he should at least recognize his impotence, his incapacity to believe in the Sense of history; even if his reason leans towards the truth, the passions and prejudices produced by his class position prevent him from accepting it. So he should not exert himself with proving the truth of the historical mission of the working class; rather, he should learn to subdue his petty-bourgeois passions and prejudices. He should take lessons from those who were once as impotent as he is now but are ready to risk all for the revolutionary Cause. He should imitate the way they began: they behaved just as if they did believe in the mission of the working class, they became active in the Party, they collected money to help strikers, propagate the workers' movement, and so on. This stupefied them and made them believe quite naturally. And really, what harm has come to them through choosing this course? They became faithful, full of good works, sincere and noble. . . . It is true that they had to renounce a few noxious petty-bourgeois pleasures, their egocentrist intellectualist trifling, their false sense of individual freedom, but on the other hand — and notwithstanding the factual truth of their belief — they gained a lot: they live a meaningful life, free of doubts and uncertainty; all their everyday activity is accompanied by the conscious-ness that they are making their small contribution to the great and noble Cause.

What distinguishes this Pascalian 'custom' from insipid behaviourist wisdom ('the content of your belief is conditioned by your factual behaviour') is the paradoxical status of a *belief before belief*: by following a custom, the subject believes without knowing it, so that the final con-version is merely a formal act by means of which we recognize what we have already believed. In other words, what the behaviourist reading of Pascalian 'custom' misses is the crucial fact that the external custom is always a material support for the subject's unconscious. The main achievement of Marek Kaniewska's film *Another Country* is to designate, in a sensitive and delicate way, this precarious status of 'believing without knowing it' — precisely apropos of the conversion to Communism.

Another Country is a film *à clef* about the relationship between two Cambridge students, the Communist Judd (real model: John Cornford, idol of the Oxford student left, who died in 1936 in Spain) and the rich homosexual Guy Bennett, who later becomes a Russian spy and tells the story in retrospect to an English journalist who visits him in his Moscow exile (real model: Guy Burgess, of course). There is no sexual relationship between them; Judd is the only one who is not sensitive to Guy's charm ('the exception to the Bennett rule', as Guy puts it): precisely for that reason, for Guy he is the point of his transferential identification.

The action occurs in the 'public school' environment of the thirties: the patriotic empty talk, the terror of the student-heads ('gods') over ordinary students; yet in all this terror there is something non-binding, not quite serious; it has the ring of an amusing travesty concealing a universe in which enjoyment actually reigns in all its obscenity, above all in the form of a ramified network of homosexual relations — the real terror is, rather, the unbearable pressure of enjoyment. It is for *this* reason that Oxford and Cambridge in the thirties offered such a rich field for the KGB: not only because of the 'guilt complex' of rich students doing so well in the midst of the economic and social crisis, but above all because of this stuffy atmosphere of enjoyment, the very inertia of which creates an unbearable tension, a tension which could be dissolved only by a 'totalitarian' appeal to *renunciation* of the enjoyment — in Germany, it was Hitler who knew how to occupy the place of this appeal; in England, at least among the elite students, the KGB hunters were best versed in it.

The film is worth mentioning for the way it depicts Guy's conversion: its delicacy is attested by the very fact that it *does not* depict it, that it only lays all the elements for it. That is to say, the flashback to the thirties which occupies the main part of the film stops at the precise point at which Guy is already converted, although he does not yet know it — the film is delicate enough to leave out the formal act of conversion; it suspends the flashback in a situation homologous to one in which somebody is already in love but is not yet aware of it, and for this reason gives expression to his love in the form of an excessively cynical attitude and defensive agressivity towards the person with whom he is in love.

What is, then, looking closer, the denouement of the film? Two reactions to this situation of stuffy enjoyment are opposed: Judd's renunciation, his openly declared Communism (it is for this reason that he *couldn't* be a KGB agent), and on the other side Guy as a representative of the extreme, putrefied hedonism whose game, however, starts to fall apart (the 'gods' have humiliated him by a ritual beating because his personal enemy, a patriotic career seeker, has unmasked his homosexual relationship with a younger student: in this way, Guy lost a promised opportunity to become a 'god' himself the following year). At this point, Guy becomes aware of the fact that the key to the dissolution of his untenable situation lies in his transferential relationship to Judd: this is nicely indicated by two details.

First, he reproaches Judd for not himself being liberated of bourgeois prejudices — in spite of all his talk about equality and fraternity, he still thinks that 'some persons are better than others because of the way they make love' ; in short, he catches the subject on whom he has a transference in his inconsistency, in his lack. Secondly, he reveals to the naïve Judd the very mechanism of transference: Judd thinks that his belief in the truth of Communism results from his thorough study of history and the texts of Marx, to which Guy replies, 'You are not a Communist because you understand Marx, you understand Marx because you are a Communist!' — that is to say, Judd understands Marx because he presupposes in advance that Marx is the bearer of knowledge enabling access to the truth of history, like the Christian believer who does not believe in

Christ because he has been convinced by theological arguments but, on the contrary, is susceptible to theological arguments because he is already illuminated by the grace of belief.

In a first, naïve approach it could appear that because of these two features Guy is on the brink of liberating himself from his transference on Judd (he catches Judd in his inconsistency, and even unmasks the very mechanism of transference to boot), but the truth is none the less the opposite: these two features only confirm how 'those in the know are lost' [*les non-dupes errent*], as Lacan would say. Precisely as one 'in the know', Guy is caught in transference — both reproaches of Judd receive their meaning only against the background that his relationship with Judd is already a transferential one (as with the analysand who finds such pleasure in discovering small weaknesses and mistakes in the analyst precisely because the transference is already at work).

The state in which Guy finds himself immediately before his conversion, this state of extreme tension, is best rendered by his own answer to Judd's reproach that he is himself to blame for the mess he is in (if he had only proceeded with a little discretion and hidden his homosexuality instead of flaunting it in a provocative and defiant way, there would have been no unpleasant disclosure to ruin him): 'What better cover for someone like me than total indiscretion?' This is, of course, the very Lacanian definition of deception in its specifically human dimension, where we deceive the Other by means of the truth itself: in a universe in which all are looking for the true face beneath the mask, the best way to lead them astray is to wear the mask of truth itself. But it is impossible to maintain the coincidence of mask and truth: far from gaining us a kind of 'immediate contact with our fellow-men', this coincidence renders the situation unbearable; all communication is impossible because we are totally isolated through the very disclosure — the *sine qua non* of successful communication is a minimum of distance between appearance and its hidden rear.

The only door open is thus escape into belief in the transcendent 'another country' (Communism) and into conspiracy (becoming a KGB agent), which introduces a radical gap between the mask and the true face. So when, in the last scene of the flashback, Judd and Guy traverse the college courtyard, Guy is already a believer: his fate is sealed, even if he does not yet know it. His introductory words, 'Wouldn't it be wonderful if Communism were really true?', reveal his belief, which is for the time being still delegated, transferred on to another — and so we can immediately pass on to the Moscow exile decades later where the only leftover of enjoyment binding the old and crippled Guy to his country is the memory of cricket.

Kafka, Critic of Althusser

The externality of the symbolic machine ('automaton') is therefore not simply external: it is at the same time the place where the fate of our internal, most 'sincere' and 'intimate' beliefs is in advance staged and decided. When we subject ourselves to the machine of a religious ritual, we already believe without knowing it; our belief is already materialized in the external ritual; in other words, we already believe *unconsciously*, because it is from this external character of the symbolic machine that we can explain the status of the unconscious as radically external — that of a dead letter. Belief is an affair of obedience to the dead, uncomprehended letter. It is this short-circuit between the intimate belief and the external 'machine' which is the most subversive kernel of Pascalian theology.

Of course, in his theory of Ideological State Apparatuses (Althusser, 1976), Althusser gave an elaborated, contemporary version of this Pascalian 'machine'; but the weak point of his theory is that he or his school never succeeded in thinking out the link between Ideological State Apparatuses and ideological interpellation: how does the Ideological State Apparatus (the Pascalian 'machine', the signifying automatism) 'internalize' itself; how does it produce the effect of ideological belief in a Cause and the interconnecting effect of subjectivation, of recognition of one's ideological position? The answer to this is, as we have seen, that this external 'machine' of State Apparatuses exercises its force only in so far as it is experienced, in the unconscious economy of the subject, as a traumatic, senseless injunction. Althusser speaks only of the process of ideological interpellation through which the symbolic machine of ideology is 'internalized' into the ideological experience of Meaning and Truth: but we can learn from Pascal that this 'internalization', by structural necessity, never fully succeeds, that there is always a residue, a leftover, a stain of traumatic irrationality and senselessness sticking to it, and that *this leftover, far from hindering the full submission of the subject to the ideological command, is the very condition of it*: it is precisely this non-integrated surplus of senseless traumatism which confers on the Law its unconditional authority: in other words, which — in so far as it escapes ideological sense — sustains what we might call the ideological *se*, enjoyment-in-sense (enjoy-meant), proper to ideology.

And again, it was no accident that we mentioned the name of Kafka: concerning this ideological *jouis-sense* we can say that Kafka develops a kind of criticism of Althusser *avant la lettre*, in letting us see that which is constitutive of the gap between 'machine' and its 'internalization'. Is not Kafka's 'irrational' bureaucracy, this blind, gigantic, nonsensical apparatus, precisely the Ideological State Apparatus with which a subject is confronted *before* any identification, any recognition — any *subjectivation* — takes place? What, then, can we learn from Kafka?

In a first approach, the starting point in Kafka's novels is that of an interpellation: the Kafkaesque subject is interpellated by a mysterious bureaucratic entity (Law, Castle). But this interpellation has a somewhat strange look: it is, so to say, an *interpellation without identification/ subjectivation*; it does not offer us a Cause with which to identify — the Kafkaesque subject is the subject desperately seeking a trait with which to identify, he does not understand the meaning of the call of the Other.

This is the dimension overlooked in the Althusserian account of interpellation: before being caught in the identification, in the symbolic recognition/misrecognition, the subject ($) is trapped by the Other through a paradoxical object-cause of desire in the midst of it (a), through this secret supposed to be hidden in the Other: $\$ \lozenge a$ — the Lacanian formula of fantasy. What does it mean, more precisely, to say that ideological fantasy structures reality itself? Let us explain by starting from the fundamental Lacanian thesis that in the opposition between dream and reality, fantasy is on the side of reality: it is, as Lacan once said, the support that gives consistency to what we call 'reality'.

In his Seminar on the *Four Fundamental Concepts of Psychoanalysis*, Lacan develops this through an interpretation of the well-known dream about the 'burning child':

A father had been watching beside his child's sick-bed for days and nights on end. After the child had died, he went into the next room to lie down, but left the door open so that he could see from his bedroom into the room in which his child's body was laid out, with tall candles standing round it. An old man had been engaged to keep watch over it, and sat beside the body murmuring prayers. After a few hours' sleep, the father had a dream that *his child was standing beside his bed, caught him by the arm and whispered to him reproachfully: 'Father, don't you see I'm burning?'* He woke up, noticed a bright glare of light from the next room, hurried into it and found the old watchman had dropped off to sleep and that the wrappings and one of the arms of his beloved child's dead body had been burned by a lighted candle that had fallen on them. (Freud, 1977, p. 652)

The usual interpretation of this dream is based on a thesis that one of the functions of the dream is to enable the dreamer to prolong his sleep. The sleeper is suddenly exposed to an exterior irritation, a stimulus coming from reality (the ringing of an alarm clock, knocking on the door or, in this case, the smell of smoke), and to prolong his sleep he quickly, on the spot, constructs a dream: a little scene, a small story, which includes this irritating element. However, the external irritation soon becomes too strong and the subject is awakened.

The Lacanian reading is directly opposed to this. The subject does not awake himself when the external irritation becomes too strong; the logic of his awakening is quite different. First he constructs a dream, a story which enables him to prolong his sleep, to avoid awakening into reality. But the thing that he encounters in the dream, the reality of his desire, the Lacanian Real — in our case, the reality of the child's reproach to his father, 'Can't you see that I am burning?', implying the father's fundamental guilt — is more terrifying than so-called external reality itself, and that is why he awakens: to escape the Real of his desire, which announces itself in the terrifying dream. He escapes into so-called reality to be able to continue to sleep, to maintain his blindness, to elude awakening into the real of his desire. We can rephrase here the old 'hippy' motto of the 1960s: reality is for those who cannot support the dream. 'Reality' is a fantasy-construction which enables us to mask the Real of our desire (Lacan, 1979, chs 5 and 6).

It is exactly the same with ideology. Ideology is not a dreamlike illusion that we build to escape insupportable reality; in its basic dimension it is a fantasy-construction which serves as a support for our 'reality' itself: an 'illusion' which structures our effective, real social relations and thereby masks some insupportable, real, impossible kernel (conceptualized by Ernesto Laclau and Chantal Mouffe as 'antagonism': a traumatic social division which cannot be symbolized). The function of ideology is not to offer us a point of escape from our reality but to offer us the social reality itself as an escape from some traumatic, real kernel. To explain this logic, let us refer again to the *Four Fundamental Concepts of Psychoanalysis* (Lacan, 1979, ch. 6). Here Lacan mentions the well-known paradox of Zhuang Zi, who dreamt of being a butterfly, and after his awakening posed himself a question: How does he know that he is not *now* a butterfly dreaming of being Zhuang Zi? Lacan's commentary is that this question is justified, for two reasons.

First, it proves that Zhuang Zi was not a fool. The Lacanian definition of a fool is somebody who believes in his immediate identity with himself; somebody who is not capable of a dialectically mediated distance towards himself, like a king who thinks he is a king, who takes his being-a-king as his immediate property and not as a symbolic mandate imposed on him by a network of intersubjective relations of which he is a part (example of a king who was a fool thinking he was a king: Ludwig II of Bavaria, Wagner's patron).

However, this is not all; if it were, the subject could be reduced to a void, to an empty place in which his or her whole content is procured by others, by the symbolic network of intersubjective relations: I am 'in myself' a nothingness, the positive content of myself is what I am for others. In other words, if this were all, Lacan's last word would be a radical alienation of the subject. His content, 'what he is', would be determined by an exterior signifying network offering him the points of symbolic identification, conferring on him certain symbolic mandates. But Lacan's basic thesis, at least in his last works, is that there is a possibility for the subject to obtain some contents, some kind of positive consistency, also outside the big Other, the alienating symbolic network. This other possibility is that offered by fantasy: equating the subject to an object of fantasy. When he was thinking that he was a butterfly dreaming of being Zhuang Zi, Zhuang Zi was in a way correct. The butterfly was the object which constituted the frame, the backbone, of his fantasy-identity (the relationship *Zhuang Zi-butterfly* can be written $\$ \Diamond a$). In the symbolic reality he was Zhuang Zi, but in the real of his desire he was a butterfly. Being a butterfly was the whole consistency of his positive being outside the symbolic network. Perhaps it is not quite by accident that we find a kind of echo of this in Terry Gilliam's film *Brazil*, which depicts, in a disgustingly funny way, a totalitarian society: the hero finds an ambiguous point of escape from everyday reality in his dream of being a man-butterfly.

At first sight, what we have here is a simple symmetrical inversion of the so-called normal, ordinary perspective. In our everyday understanding, Zhuang Zi is the 'real' person dreaming of being a butterfly, and here we have something which is 'really' a butterfly dreaming of being Zhuang Zi. But as Lacan points out, this symmetrical relationship is an illusion: when Zhuang Zi is awakened, he can think to himself that he is Zhuang Zi who dreamed of being a butterfly, but in his dream, when he is a butterfly, he cannot ask himself if when awoken, when he thought he was Zhuang Zi, he was not this butterfly that is now dreaming Zhuang Zi. The question, the dialectical split, is possible only when we are awake. In other words, the illusion cannot be symmetrical, it cannot run both ways, because if it did we would find ourselves in a nonsensical situation described — again — by Alphonse Allais: Raoul and Marguerite, two lovers, arrange to meet at a masked ball; there they skip into a hidden corner, embrace and fondle each other. Finally, they both put down their masks, and — surprise — Raoul finds that he is embracing the wrong woman, that she is not Marguerite, and Marguerite also finds that the other person is not Raoul but some unknown stranger. . . .

Fantasy as a Support of Reality

This problem must be approached from the Lacanian thesis that it is only in the dream that we come close to the real awakening — that is, to the Real of our desire. When Lacan says that the last support of what we call 'reality' is a fantasy, this is definitely not to be understood in the sense of 'life is just a dream', 'what we call reality is just an illusion', and so forth. We find such a theme in many science-fiction stories: reality as a generalized dream or illusion. The story is usually told from the perspective of a hero who gradually makes the horrifying discovery that all the people around him are not really human beings but some kind of automatons, robots, who only look and act like real human beings; the final point of these stories is of course the hero's discovery that he himself is also such an automaton and not a real human being. Such a generalized illusion is impossible: we find the same paradox in a well-known drawing by Escher of two hands drawing each other.

The Lacanian thesis is, on the contrary, that there is always a hard kernel, a leftover which persists and cannot be reduced to a universal play of illusory mirroring. The difference between Lacan and 'naïve realism' is that for Lacan, *the only point at which we approach this hard kernel of the Real is indeed the dream*. When we awaken into reality after a dream, we usually say to ourselves 'it was just a dream', thereby blinding ourselves to the fact that in our everyday, wakening reality we are *nothing but a consciousness of this dream*. It was only in the dream that we approached the fantasy-framework which determines our activity, our mode of acting in reality itself.

It is the same with the ideological dream, with the determination of ideology as a dreamlike construction hindering us from seeing the real

state of things, reality as such. In vain do we try to break out of the ideological dream by 'opening our eyes and trying to see reality as it is', by
throwing away the ideological spectacles: as the subjects of such a post-
ideological, objective, sober look, free of so-called ideological prejudices,
as the subjects of a look which views the facts as they are, we remain
throughout 'the consciousness of our ideological dream'. The only way
to break the power of our ideological dream is to confront the Real of
our desire which announces itself in this dream.

Let us examine anti-Semitism. It is not enough to say that we must
liberate ourselves of so-called 'anti-Semitic prejudices' and learn to see
Jews as they really are — in this way we will certainly remain victims of
these so-called prejudices. We must confront ourselves with how the
ideological figure of the 'Jew' is invested with our unconscious desire,
with how we have constructed this figure to escape a certain deadlock of
our desire.

Let us suppose, for example, that an objective look would confirm —
why not? — that Jews really do financially exploit the rest of the population, that they do sometimes seduce our young daughters, that some of
them do not wash regularly. It is not clear that this has nothing to do
with the real roots of our anti-Semitism? Here, we have only to
remember the Lacanian proposition concerning the pathologically
jealous husband: even if all the facts he quotes in support of his jealousy
are true, even if his wife really is sleeping around with other men, this
does not change one bit the fact that his jealousy is a pathological, paranoid construction.

Let us ask ourselves a simple question: In the Germany of the late
1930s, what would be the result of such a non-ideological, objective
approach? Probably something like: 'The Nazis are condemning the Jews
too hastily, without proper argument, so let us take a cool, sober look
and see if they are really guilty or not; let us see if there is some truth in
the accusations against them.' Is it really necessary to add that such an
approach would merely confirm our so-called 'unconscious prejudices'
with additional rationalizations? The proper answer to anti-Semitism is
therefore not 'Jews are really not like that' but 'the anti-Semitic idea of
Jew has nothing to do with Jews; the ideological figure of a Jew is a way
to stitch up the inconsistency of our own ideological system.'

That is why we are also unable to shake so-called ideological prejudices by taking into account the pre-ideological level of everyday
experience. The basis of this argument is that the ideological construction always finds its limits in the field of everyday experience — that

it is unable to reduce, to contain, to absorb and annihilate this level. Let us again take a typical individual in Germany in the late 1930s. He is bombarded by anti-Semitic propaganda depicting a Jew as a monstrous incarnation of Evil, the great wire-puller, and so on. But when he returns home he encounters Mr Stern, his neighbour: a good man to chat with in the evenings, whose children play with his. Does not this everyday experience offer an irreducible resistance to the ideological construction?

The answer is, of course, no. If everyday experience offers such a resistance, then the anti-Semitic ideology has not yet really grasped us. An ideology is really 'holding us' only when we do not feel any opposition between it and reality — that is, when the ideology succeeds in determining the mode of our everyday experience of reality itself. How then would our poor German, if he were a good anti-Semite, react to this gap between the ideological figure of the Jew (schemer, wire-puller, exploiting our brave men and so on) and the common everyday experience of his good neighbour, Mr Stern? His answer would be to turn this gap, this discrepancy itself, into an argument for anti-Semitism: 'You see how dangerous they really are? It is difficult to recognize their real nature. They hide it behind the mask of everyday appearance — and it is exactly this hiding of one's real nature, this duplicity, that is a basic feature of the Jewish nature.' An ideology really succeeds when even the facts which at first sight contradict it start to function as arguments in its favour.

Surplus-value and Surplus-enjoyment

Herein lies the difference with Marxism: in the predominant Marxist perspective the ideological gaze is a *partial* gaze overlooking the *totality* of social relations, whereas in the Lacanian perspective ideology rather designates *a totality set on effacing the traces of its own impossibility*. This difference corresponds to the one which distinguishes the Freudian from the Marxian notion of fetishism: in Marxism a fetish conceals the positive network of social relations, whereas in Freud a fetish conceals the lack ('castration') around which the symbolic network is articulated.

In so far as we conceive the Real as that which 'always returns to the same place', we can deduce another, no less crucial difference. From the Marxist point of view, the ideological procedure *par excellence* is that of *'false' eternalization and/or universalization*: a state which depends on a concrete historical conjunction appears as an eternal, universal feature of the human condition; the interest of a particular class disguises itself as universal human interest . . . and the aim of the 'criticism of ideology' is to denounce this false universality, to detect behind man in general the bourgeois individual; behind the universal rights of man the form which renders possible capitalist exploitation; behind the 'nuclear family' as a trans-historical constant the historically specified and limited form of kinship relations, and so on.

In the Lacanian perspective, we should change the terms and designate as the most 'cunning' ideological procedure the very opposite of eternalization: an *over-rapid historicization*. Let us take one of the commonplaces of the Marxist-feminist criticism of psychoanalysis, the idea that its insistence on the crucial role of the Oedipus complex and the nuclear-family triangle transforms a historically conditioned form of patriarchal family into a feature of the universal human condition: is not this effort to historicize the family triangle precisely an attempt to *elude* the 'hard kernel' which announces itself through the 'patriarchal family' — the Real of the Law, the rock of castration? In other words, if over-rapid universalization produces a quasi-universal Image whose function is to make us blind to its historical, socio-symbolic determination, over-rapid historicization makes us blind to the real kernel which returns as the same through diverse historicizations/ symbolizations.

It is the same with a phenomenon that designates most accurately the 'perverse' obverse of twentieth-century civilization: concentration camps. All the different attempts to attach this phenomenon to a concrete image ('Holocaust', 'Gulag' . . .), to reduce it to a product of a concrete social order (Fascism, Stalinism . . .) — what are they if not so many attempts to elude the fact that we are dealing here with the 'real' of our civilization which returns as the same traumatic kernel in all social systems? (We should not forget that concentration camps were an invention of 'liberal' England, dating from the Boer War; that they were also used in the USA to isolate the Japanese population, and so on.)

Marxism, then, did not succeed in taking into account, coming to terms with, the surplus-object, the leftover of the Real eluding symbolization — a fact all the more surprising if we recall that Lacan modelled his notion of surplus-enjoyment on the Marxian notion of surplus-value. The proof that Marxian surplus-value announces effectively the logic of the Lacanian *objet petit a* as the embodiment of surplus-enjoyment is already provided by the decisive formula used by Marx, in the third volume of *Capital*, to designate the logical-historical limit of capitalism:

'the limit of capital is capital itself, i.e. the capitalist mode of production'.

This formula can be read in two ways. The first, usual historicist-evolutionist reading conceives it, in accordance with the unfortunate paradigm of the dialectics of productive forces and relations of production, as that of 'content' and 'form'. This paradigm follows roughly the metaphor of the serpent which, from time to time, sheds its skin, which has grown too tight: one posits as the last impetus of social development — as its (so to speak) 'natural', 'spontaneous' constant — the incessant growth of the productive forces (as a rule reduced to technical development); this 'spontaneous' growth is then followed, with a greater or lesser degree of delay, by the inert, dependent moment, the relationship of production. We have thus epochs in which the relation of production are in accordance with the productive forces, then those forces develop and outgrow their 'social clothes', the frame of relationships; this frame becomes an obstacle to their further development, until social revolution again co-ordinates forces and relations by replacing the old relations with new ones which correspond to the new state of forces.

If we conceive the formula of capital as its own limit from this point of view, it means simply that the capitalist relation of production which at first made possible the fast development of productive forces became at a certain point an obstacle to their further development: that these forces have outgrown their frame and demand a new form of social relations.

Marx himself is of course far from such a simplistic evolutionary idea. If we need convincing of this, we have only to look at the passages in *Capital* where he deals with the relation between formal and real subsumption of the process of production under Capital: the formal subsumption *precedes* the real one; that is, Capital first subsumes the process of production as it found it (artisans, and so on), and only subsequently does it change the productive forces step by step, shaping them in such a way as to create correspondence. Contrary to the above-mentioned simplistic idea, it is then the *form* of the relation of production which drives the development of productive forces — that is, of its 'content'.

All we have to do to render impossible the simplistic evolutionary reading of the formula 'the limit of capital is capital itself' is to ask a very simple and obvious question: How do we define, exactly, the moment — albeit only an ideal one — at which the capitalist relation of production become an obstacle to the further development of the productive forces?

Or the obverse of the same question: When can we speak of an accordance between productive forces and relation of production in the capitalist mode of production? Strict analysis leads to only one possible answer: *never.*

This is exactly how capitalism differs from other, previous modes of production: in the latter, we can speak of periods of 'accordance' when the process of social production and reproduction goes on as a quiet, circular movement, and of periods of convulsion when the contradiction between forces and relation aggravates itself; whereas in capitalism this contradiction, the discord forces/relation, *is contained in its very concept* (in the form of the contradiction between the social mode of production and the individual, private mode of appropriation). It is this internal contradiction which compels capitalism to permanent extended reproduction — to the incessant development of its own conditions of production, in contrast to previous modes of production where, at least in their 'normal' state, (re)production goes on as a circular movement.

If this is so, then the evolutionist reading of the formula of capital as its own limit is inadequate: the point is not that, at a certain moment of its development, the frame of the relation of production starts to constrict further development of the productive forces; the point is that *it is this very immanent limit, this 'internal contradiction', which drives capitalism into permanent development.* The 'normal' state of capitalism is the permanent revolutionizing of its own conditions of existence: from the very beginning capitalism 'putrifies', it is branded by a crippling contradiction, discord, by an immanent want of balance: this is exactly why it changes, develops incessantly — incessant development is the only way for it to resolve again and again, come to terms with, its own fundamental, constitutive imbalance, 'contradiction'. Far from constricting, its limit is thus the very impetus of its development. Herein lies the paradox proper to capitalism, its last resort: capitalism is capable of transforming its limit, its very impotence, in the source of its power — the more it 'putrefies', the more its immanent contradiction is aggravated, the more it must revolutionize itself to survive.

It is this paradox which defines surplus-enjoyment: it is not a surplus which simply attaches itself to some 'normal', fundamental enjoyment, because *enjoyment as such emerges only in this surplus,* because it is constitutively an 'excess'. If we subtract the surplus we lose enjoyment itself, just as capitalism, which can survive only by incessantly revolutionizing its own material conditions, ceases to exist if it 'stays the same', if it achieves an internal balance. This, then, is the homology between surplus-value — the 'cause' which sets in motion the capitalist process of production — and surplus-enjoyment, the object-cause of desire. Is not the paradoxical topology of the movement of capital, the fundamental blockage which resolves and reproduces itself through frenetic activity, *excessive* power as the very form of appearance of a fundamental *impotence* — this immediate passage, this coincidence of limit and excess, of lack and surplus — precisely that of the Lacanian *objet petit a*, of the leftover which embodies the fundamental, constitutive lack?

All this, of course, Marx 'knows very well . . . and yet': and yet, in the crucial formulation in the Preface to'the *Critique of Political Economy*, he proceeds *as if he does not know it*, by describing the very passage from capitalism to socialism in terms of the above-mentioned vulgar evolutionist dialectics of productive forces and the relation of production: when the forces surpass a certain degree, capitalist relation become an obstacle to their further development: this discord brings about the need for socialist revolution, the function of which is to co-ordinate again forces and relation; that is, to establish relations of production rendering possible the intensified development of the productive forces as the end-in-itself of the historical process.

How can we not detect in this formulation the fact that Marx failed to cope with the paradoxes of surplus-enjoyment? And the ironic vengeance of history for this failure is that today there exists a society which seems to correspond perfectly to this vulgar evolutionary dialectics of forces and relation: 'real socialism', a society which legitimizes itself by reference to Marx. Is it not already a commonplace to assert that 'real socialism' has rendered possible rapid industrialization, but that as soon as the productive forces have reached a certain level of development (usually designated by the vague term 'post-industrial society'), 'real socialist' social relationships began to constrict their further growth?

2

From Symptom to *Sinthome*

THE DIALECTICS OF SYMPTOM

Back to the Future

The only reference to the domain of science fiction in Lacan's work concerns the time paradox: in his first Seminar, Lacan uses Norbert Wiener's metaphor of the inverted direction of time to explain the symptom as a 'return of the repressed':

> Wiener posits two beings each of whose temporal dimensions moves in the opposite direction from the other. To be sure, that means nothing, and that is how things which mean nothing all of a sudden signify something, but in a quite different domain. If one of them sends a message to the other, for example a square, the being going in the opposite direction will first of all see the square vanishing, before seeing the square. That is what we see as well. The symptom initially appears to us as a trace, which will only ever be a trace, one which will continue not to be understood until the analysis has got quite a long way, and until we have realized its meaning. (Lacan, 1988, p. 159)

The analysis is thus conceived as a symbolization, a symbolic integration of meaningless imaginary traces; this conception implies a fundamentally *imaginary* character of the unconscious: it is made of 'imaginary fixations which could not have been assimilated to the symbolic development' of the subject's history; consequently, it is 'something which will be realized in the Symbolic, or, more precisely, something which, thanks to the symbolic progress which takes place in the analysis, *will have been*' (ibid., p. 158).

The Lacanian answer to the question: From where does the repressed return? is therefore, paradoxically: From the future. Symptoms are

55

meaningless traces, their meaning is not discovered, excavated from the hidden depth of the past, but constructed retroactively — the analysis produces the truth; that is, the signifying frame which gives the symptoms their symbolic place and meaning. As soon as we enter the symbolic order, the past is always present in the form of historical tradition and the meaning of these traces is not given; it changes continually with the transformations of the signifier's network. Every historical rupture, every advent of a new master-signifier, changes retroactively the meaning of all tradition, restructures the narration of the past, makes it readable in another, new way.

Thus, 'things which mean nothing all of a sudden signify something, but in a quite different domain'. What is a 'journey into the future' if not this 'overtaking' by means of which we suppose in advance the presence in the other of a certain knowledge — knowledge about the meaning of our symptoms — what is it, then, if not the *transference* itself? This knowledge is an illusion, it does not really exist in the other, the other does not really possess it, it is constituted afterwards, through our — the subject's — signifier's working; but it is at the same time a necessary illusion, because we can paradoxically elaborate this knowledge only by means of the illusion that the other already possesses it and that we are only discovering it.

If — as Lacan points out — in the symptom, the repressed content is returning from the future and not from the past, then the transference — the actualization of the reality of the unconscious — must transpose us into the future, not into the past. And what is the 'journey into the past' if not this retroactive working-through, elaboration, of the signifier itself? — a kind of hallucinatory mise-en-scène of the fact that in the field of the signifier and only in this field, we can change, we can bring about the past?

The past exists as it is included, as it enters (into) the synchronous net of the signifier — that is, as it is symbolized in the texture of the historical memory — and that is why we are all the time 'rewriting history', retroactively giving the elements their symbolic weight by including them in new textures — it is this elaboration which decides retroactively what they 'will have been'. The Oxford philosopher Michael Dummett has written two very interesting articles included in his collection of essays *Truth and Other Enigmas*: 'Can an Effect Precede its Cause?' and 'Bringing About the Past': the Lacanian answer to these two enigmas would be: yes, because the symptom as a 'return of the repressed' is precisely such an effect which precedes its cause (its hidden kernel, its meaning), and in working through the symptom we are precisely 'bringing about the past' — we are producing the symbolic reality of past, long-forgotten traumatic events.

One is therefore tempted to see in the 'time paradox' of science-fiction novels a kind of hallucinatory 'apparition in the Real' of the elementary structure of the symbolic process, the so-called internal, internally inverted eight: a circular movement, a kind of snare where we can progress only in such a manner that we 'overtake' ourselves in the transference, to find ourselves later at a point at which we have already been. The paradox consists in the fact that this superfluous detour, this supplementary snare of overtaking ourselves ('voyage into the future') and then reversing the time direction ('voyage into the past') is not just a subjective illusion/perception of an objective process taking place in so-called reality independently of these illusions. That supplementary snare is, rather, an internal condition, an internal constituent of the so-called 'objective' process itself: only through this additional detour does the past itself, the 'objective' state of things, become retroactively what it always was.

Transference is, then, an illusion, but the point is that we cannot bypass it and reach directly for the Truth: the Truth itself is constituted *through* the illusion proper to the transference — 'the Truth arises from misrecognition' (Lacan). If this paradoxical structure is not yet clear, let us take another science-fiction example, William Tenn's well-known story 'The Discovery of Morniel Mathaway'. A distinguished art historian takes a journey in a time machine from the twenty-fifth century to our day to visit and study *in vivo* the immortal Morniel Mathaway, a painter not appreciated in our time but later discovered to have been the greatest painter of the era. When he encounters him, the art historian finds no trace of a genius, just an imposter, a megalomaniac, even a swindler who steals his time machine from him and escapes into the future, so that the poor art historian stays tied to our time. The only action open to him is to assume the identity of the escaped Mathaway and to paint under his name all his masterpieces that he remembers from the future — it is himself who is really the misrecognized genius he was looking for!

This, therefore, is the basic paradox we are aiming at: the subject is confronted with a scene from the past that he wants to change, to meddle with, to intervene in; he takes a journey into the past, intervenes in the scene, and it is not that he 'cannot change anything' — quite the contrary, only through his intervention does the scene from the past *become what it always was*: his intervention was from the beginning comprised, included. The initial 'illusion' of the subject consists in simply forgetting to include in the scene his own act — that is, to over-look how 'it counts, it is counted, and the one who counts is already included in the account' (Lacan, 1979, p. 26). This introduces a relationship between truth and misrecognition/misapprehension by which the Truth, literally, arises from misrecognition, as in the well-known story about the 'appointment in Samarra' (from Somerset Maugham's play *Sheppey*):

> DEATH: There was a merchant in Bagdad who sent his servant to market to buy provisions and in a little while the servant came back, white and trem-bling, and said, Master, just now when I was in the market-place, I was jostled by a woman in the crowd and when I turned I saw it was death that jostled me. She looked at me and made a threatening gesture; now, lend me your horse, and I will ride away from this city and avoid my fate. I will go to Samarra and there death will not find me. The merchant lent him his horse, and the servant mounted it, and he dug his spurs in its flanks and as fast as the horse could gallop he went. Then the merchant went down to the market-place and he saw me standing in the crowd and he came to me and said, Why did you make a threatening gesture to my servant when you saw him this morning? That was not a threatening gesture, I said, it was only a start of surprise. I was astonished to see him in Bagdad, for I had an appoint-ment with him tonight in Samarra.

We find the same structure in the myth of Oedipus: it is *predicted* to Oedipus's father that his son will kill him and marry his mother, and the prophecy realizes itself, 'becomes true', through the father's attempt to evade it (he exposes his little son in the forest, and so Oedipus, not recog-nizing him when he encounters him twenty years later, kills him . . .). In other words, the prophecy becomes true by means of its being com-municated to the persons it affects and by means of his or her attempt to elude it: one knows in advance one's destiny, one tries to evade it, and it is by means of this very attempt that the predicted destiny realizes itself. Without the prophecy, the little Oedipus would live happily with his parents and there would be no 'Oedipus complex' . . .

Repetition in History

The time structure with which we are concerned here is such that it is mediated through subjectivity: the subjective 'mistake', 'fault', 'error', misrecognition, arrives paradoxically *before* the truth in relation to which we are designating it as 'error', because this 'truth' itself becomes true only through — or, to use a Hegelian term, by mediation of — the error. This is the logic of the unconscious 'cunning', the way the unconscious deceives us: the unconscious is not a kind of transcendent, unattainable thing of which we are unable to take cognizance, it is rather — to follow Lacan's wordplay-translation of *Unbewusste* — *une bévue*, an over-looking: we overlook the way our act is already part of the state of things we are looking at, the way our error is part of the Truth itself. This paradoxical structure in which the Truth arises from misrecognition also gives us the answer to the question: Why is the transference necessary, why must the analysis go through it? The transference is an essential illu-sion by means of which the final Truth (the meaning of a symptom) is produced.

We find the same logic of the error as an internal condition of truth with Rosa Luxemburg, with her description of the dialectics of the revolutionary process. We are alluding here to her argument against Eduard Bernstein, against his revisionist fear of seizing power 'too soon', 'prematurely', before the so-called 'objective conditions' had ripened — this was, as is well known, Bernstein's main reproach to the revolution-ary wing of social democracy: they are too impatient, they want to hasten, to outrun the objective logic of historical development. Rosa Luxemburg's answer is that the first seizures of power *are necessarily 'premature'*: the only way for the working class to reach its 'maturity', to await the arrival of the 'appropriate moment' for the seizure of power, is to form itself, to educate itself for this act of seizure, and the only pos-sible way of achieving this education is precisely the 'premature' attempts. . . . If we merely wait for the 'appropriate moment' we will never live to see it, because this 'appropriate moment' cannot arrive without the subjective conditions of the maturity of the revolutionary force (subject) being fulfilled — that is, it can arrive only after a series of 'premature', failed attempts. The opposition to the 'premature' seizure of power is thus revealed as opposition to the seizure of power *as such, in general*: to repeat Robespierre's famous phrase, the revisionists want a 'revolution without revolution'.

If we look at this closely, we perceive that what is at stake in Rosa Luxemburg's argument is precisely the impossibility of metalanguage in the revolutionary process: the revolutionary subject does not 'conduct', 'direct' this process from an objective distance, he is constituted through

this process, and because of this — because the temporality of the revolution passes through subjectivity — we cannot 'make the revolution at
the right moment' without the previous 'premature', failed attempts.
Here, in the opposition between Bernstein and Luxemburg, we have the
opposition between the obsessional (man) and the hysterical (woman):
the obsessional is delaying, putting off the act, waiting for the right
moment, while the hysteric (so to speak) overtakes herself in her act and
thus unmasks the falsity of the obsessional's position. This is also what is
at stake in Hegel's theory of the role of repetition in history: 'a political
revolution is generally sanctioned by the opinion of the people only
when it is renewed' — that is, it can succeed only as a repetition of a first
failed attempt. Why this need for repetition?

Hegel developed his theory of repetition apropos of the case of Julius
Caesar's death: when Caesar consolidated his personal power and
strengthened it to imperial proportions, he acted 'objectively' (in itself) in
accordance with historical truth, historical necessity — the Republican
form was losing its validity, the only form of government which could
save the unity of the Roman state was monarchy, a state based upon the
will of a single individual; but it was still the Republic which prevailed
formally (for itself, in the opinion of the people) — the Republic 'was still
alive only because she forgot that she was already dead', to paraphrase the
famous Freudian dream of the father who did not know he was already
dead: '*His father was alive once more and was talking to him in his usual way, but*
(the remarkable thing was that) *he had really died, only he did not know it*'
(Freud, 1977, p. 559).

To the 'opinion' which still believed in the Republic, Caesar's amassing of personal power — which was, of course, contrary to the spirit of
the Republic — appeared an arbitrary act, an expression of contingent
individual self-will: the conclusion was that if this individual (Caesar)
were to be removed, the Republic would regain its full splendour. But it
was precisely the conspirators against Caesar (Brutus, Cassius, and the
others) who — following the logic of the 'cunning of reason' — attested
the Truth (that is, the historical necessity) of Caesar: the final result, the
outcome of Caesar's murder, was the reign of Augustus, the first *caesar*.
The Truth thus arose from failure itself: in failing, in missing its express
goal, the murder of Caesar fulfilled the task which was, in a Machi-
avellian way, assigned to it by history: to exhibit the historical necessity
by denouncing its own non-truth — its own arbitrary, contingent character (Hegel, 1969a, pp. 111–3).

The whole problem of repetition is here: in this passage from Caesar (the name of an individual) to caesar (title of the Roman emperor). The murder of Caesar — historical personality — provoked, as its final result, the installation of *caesarism: Caesar-person repeats itself as caesar-title.* What is the reason, the driving force, of this repetition? At first sight the answer seems to be clear: the delay of the consciousness as to the 'objective' historical necessity. A certain act through which breaks historical necessity is perceived by the consciousness (the 'opinion of the people') as arbitrary, as something which also could not have happened; because of this perception people try to do away with its consequences, to restore the old state of things, but when 'this act repeats itself it is finally perceived as an expression of the underlying historical necessity. In other words, repetition is the way historical necessity asserts itself in the eyes of 'opinion'.

But such an idea of repetition rests upon the epistemologically naïve presupposition of an objective historical necessity, persisting independently of consciousness (of the 'opinion of the people') and asserting itself finally through repetition. What is lost in this notion is the way so-called historical necessity itself *is constituted through misrecognition,* through the initial failure of 'opinion' to recognize its true character — that is, the way truth itself arises from misrecognition. The crucial point here is the changed symbolic status of an event: when it erupts for the first time it is experienced as a contingent trauma, as an intrusion of a certain non-symbolized Real; only through repetition is this event recognized in its symbolic necessity — it finds its place in the symbolic network; it is realized in the symbolic order. But as with Moses in Freud's analysis, this recognition-through-repetition presupposes necessarily the crime, the act of murder: to realize himself in his symbolic necessity — as a power-title — Caesar has to die as an empirical, flesh-and-blood personality, precisely because the 'necessity' in question is a *symbolic* one.

It is not only that in its first form of appearance, the event (for example, Caesar's amassing of individual power) was too traumatic for the people to grasp its real signification — the misrecognition of its first advent is immediately 'internal' to its symbolic necessity, it is an immediate constituent of its final recognition. The first murder (the parricide of Caesar) opened up the guilt, and it was this guilt, this debt, which was the real driving force of the repetition. The event did not repeat itself because of some objective necessity, independent of our subjective inclination and thus irresistible, but because its repetition was a repayment of our symbolic debt.

In other words, the repetition announces the advent of the Law, of the

Name-of-the-Father in place of the dead, assassinated father: the event which repeats itself receives its law retroactively, through repetition. That is why we can grasp Hegelian repetition as a passage from a lawless series to a lawlike series, as the inclusion of a lawless series — as *a gesture of interpretation par excellence*, as a symbolic appropriation of a traumatic, non-symbolized event (according to Lacan, interpretation always proceeds under the sign of the Name-of-the-Father). Hegel was thus probably the first to articulate the *delay* which is constitutive of the act of interpretation: the interpretation always sets in too late, with some delay, when the event which is to be interpreted repeats itself; the event cannot already be lawlike in its first advent. This same delay is also formulated in the Preface to Hegel's *Philosophy of the Law*, in the famous passage about the owl of Minerva (that is, the philosophical comprehension of a certain epoch) which takes flight only in the evening, after this epoch has already come to its end.

The fast that the 'opinion of the people' saw in Caesar's action an individual contingency and not an expression of historical necessity is therefore not a simple case of 'delay of the consciousness in relation to the effectivity': the point is that this necessity itself — which was misrecognized by opinion in its first manifestation; that is, mistaken for a contingent self-will — constitutes itself, realizes itself, *through* this misrecognition. And we should not be surprised to find the same logic of repetition in the history of the psychoanalytic movement: it was necessary for Lacan to *repeat* his split with the International Psycho-Analytical Association. The first split (in 1953) was still experienced as a traumatic contingency — Lacanians were still trying to patch things up with the IPA, to regain admission — but in 1964 it also became clear to their 'opinion' that there was a necessity in this split, so they cut their links with the IPA and Lacan constituted his own School.

Hegel with Austen

Aust*e*n, not Aust*i*n: it is Jane Austen who is perhaps the only counterpart to Hegel in literature: *Pride and Prejudice* is the literary *Phenomenology of Spirit; Mansfield Park* the *Science of Logic* and *Emma* the *Encyclopaedia*. . . . No wonder, then, that we find in *Pride and Prejudice* the perfect case of this dialectic of truth arising from misrecognition. Although they belong to different social classes — he is from an extremely rich aristocratic family, she from the impoverished middle classes — Elizabeth and

Darcy feel a strong mutual attraction. Because of his pride, his love appears to Darcy as something unworthy; when he asks for Elizabeth's hand he confesses openly his contempt for the world to which she belongs and expects her to accept his proposition as an unheard-of honour. But because of her prejudice, Elizabeth sees him as ostentatious, arrogant and vain: his condescending proposal humiliates her, and she refuses him.

This double failure, this mutual misrecognition, possesses a structure of a double movement of communication where each subject receives from the other its own message in the inverse form: Elizabeth wants to present herself to Darcy as a young cultivated woman, full of wit, and she gets from him the message 'you are nothing but a poor empty-minded creature, full of false *finesse*'; Darcy wants to present himself to her as a proud gentleman, and he gets from her the message 'your pride is nothing but contemptible arrogance'. After the break in their relationship each discovers, through a series of accidents, the true nature of the other — she the sensitive and tender nature of Darcy, he her real dignity and wit — and the novel ends as it should, with their marriage.

The theoretical interest of this story lies in the fact that the failure of their first encounter, the double misrecognition concerning the real nature of the other, functions as a positive condition of the final outcome: we cannot go directly for the truth, we cannot say 'If, from the very beginning, she had recognized his real nature and he hers, their story could have ended at once with their marriage.' Let us take as a comical hypothesis that the first encounter of the future lovers was a success — that Elizabeth had accepted Darcy's first proposal. What would happen? Instead of being bound together in true love they would become a vulgar everyday couple, a liaison of an arrogant, rich man and a pretentious, empty-minded young girl. If we want to spare ourselves the painful roundabout route through the misrecognition, we miss the Truth itself: only the 'working-through' of the misrecognition allows us to accede to the true nature of the other and at the same time to overcome our own deficiency — for Darcy, to free himself of his false pride; for Elizabeth, to get rid of her prejudices.

These two movements are interconnected because Elizabeth encounters, in Darcy's pride, the inverse image of her own prejudices; and Darcy, in Elizabeth's vanity, the inverse image of his own false pride. In other words, Darcy's pride is not a simple, positive state of things existing independently of his relationship with Elizabeth, an immediate property of his nature; it takes place, it appears, *only from the perspective of her prejudices*; vice versa, Elizabeth is a pretentious empty-minded girl *only in Darcy's arrogant view*. To articulate things in Hegelian terms: in the perceived deficiency of the other, *each perceives* — without knowing it — *the falsity of his/her own subjective position*; the deficiency of the other is simply an objectification of the distortion of our own point of view.

Two Hegelian Jokes

There is a well-known, very Hegelian joke that illustrates perfectly the way truth arises from misrecognition — the way our path towards truth coincides with the truth itself. At the beginning of this century, a Pole and a Jew were sitting in a train, facing each other. The Pole was shifting nervously, watching the Jew all the time; something was irritating him; finally, unable to restrain himself any longer, he exploded: 'Tell me, how do you Jews succeed in extracting from people the last small coin and in this way accumulate all your wealth?' The Jew replied: 'OK, I will tell you, but not for nothing; first, you give me five zloty [Polish money].' After receiving the required amount, the Jew began: 'First, you take a dead fish; you cut off her head and put her entrails in a glass of water. Then, around midnight, when the moon is full, you must bury this glass in a churchyard. . . .' 'And,' the Pole interrupted him greedily, 'if I do all this, will I also become rich?' 'Not too quickly,' replied the Jew; 'this is not all you must do; but if you want to hear the rest, you must pay me another five zloty!' After receiving the money again, the Jew continued his story: soon afterwards, he again demanded more money, and so on, until finally the Pole exploded in fury: 'You dirty rascal, do you really think I did not notice what you were aiming at? There is no secret at all, you simply want to extract the last small coin from me!' The Jew answered him calmly and with resignation: 'Well, now you see how we, the Jews. . .'

Everything in this small story is susceptable to interpretation, starting with the curious, inquisitive way the Pole looks at the Jew — it means that from the very beginning the Pole is caught in a relationship of transference: that the Jew embodies for him the 'subject presumed to know' — to know the secret of extracting money from people. The point of the story is of course that the Jew has *not* deceived the Pole: he kept his promise and taught him how to extract money from people. What is crucial here is the double movement of the outcome — the distance between the moment when the Pole breaks out in fury and the Jew's final answer. When the Pole blurts out 'There is no secret at all, you simply want to extract the last small coin from me!', he is already telling the truth without knowing it — that is to say, he sees, in the Jew's manipulation, a simple deception. What he misses is that through this very deception the Jew kept his word, delivered him what he was paid for (the secret of how the Jews . . .). The Pole's error is simply his perspective: he looks forward to the 'secret' being revealed somewhere at the end; he situates the Jew's narration as a path to the final revelation of the 'secret'; but the real 'secret' is already in the narration itself: in the way the Jew, through his narration, captures the Pole's desire; in the way the Pole is absorbed in this narration and prepared to pay for it.

The Jew's 'secret' lies, then, in our own (the Pole's) desire: in the fact that the Jew knows how to take our desire into account. That is why we can say that the final turn of the story, with its double twist, corresponds to the final moment of the psychoanalytic cure, the dissolution of transference and 'going through the fantasy': when the Pole breaks out in fury he has already stepped out of transference, but he has yet to traverse his fantasy — this is achieved only by realizing how, through his deception, the Jew has kept his word. The fascinating 'secret' which drives us to follow the Jew's narration carefully is precisely the Lacanian *objet petit a*, the chimerical object of fantasy, the object causing our desire and at the same time — this is its paradox — posed retroactively by this desire; in 'going through the fantasy' we experience how this fantasy-object (the 'secret') only materializes the void of our desire.

Another well-known joke possesses exactly the same structure, but this is usually overlooked — we are referring, of course, to the joke about the Door of the Law from the ninth chapter of Kafka's *Trial*, to its final turn-around when the dying man from the country asks the door-keeper:

> Everyone strives to attain the law, how does it come about, then, that in all these years no one has come seeking admittance but me?' The door-keeper perceives that the man is at the end of his strength and his hearing is failing, so he bellows in his ear: 'No one but you could gain admittance through this door, since the door was intended only for you. I am now going to shut it.' (Kafka, 1985, p. 237)

This final twist is perfectly homologous to the one at the end of the story about the Pole and the Jew: the subject experiences how he (his desire) was part of the game from the very beginning, how the entrance was meant only for him, how the stake of the narration was only to capture his desire. We could even invent another ending for Kafka's story to bring it nearer to the joke about the Pole and the Jew: after the long wait, the man from the country breaks out in fury and begins to cry at the door-keeper: 'You dirty rascal, why do you pretend to guard the entrance to some enormous secret, when you know very well that there is no secret beyond the door, that this door is intended only for me, to capture my desire!' and the door-keeper (if he were an analyst) would answer him calmly: 'You see, now you've discovered the real secret: beyond the door is only what your desire introduces there . . .'.

In both cases, the nature of the final twist follows the Hegelian logic of surmounting, of abolishing the 'bad infinity'. That is to say, in both cases the starting point is the same: the subject is confronted with some substantial Truth, a secret from which he is excluded, which evades him *ad infinitum* — the inaccessible heart of the Law beyond the infinite series of doors; the unattainable last answer, the last secret of how the Jews extract money from us, awaiting us at the end of the Jew's narration (which could go on *ad infinitum*). And the solution is the same in both cases: the subject has to grasp how, from the very start of the game, the door concealing the secret was meant only for him, how the real secret at the end of the Jew's narration is his own desire — in short, how his external position *vis-à-vis* the Other (the fact that he experiences himself as excluded from the secret of the Other) is internal to the Other itself. Here we encounter a kind of 'reflexivity' which cannot be reduced to philosophical reflection: the very feature which seems to exclude the subject from the Other (his desire to penetrate the secret of the Other — the secret of the Law, the secret of how the Jews . . .) is already a 'reflexive determination' of the Other; precisely as excluded from the Other, we are already part of its game.

A Time Trap

The positivity proper to the misrecognition — the fact that the misrecognition functions as a 'productive' instance — is to be conceived in an even more radical way: not only is the misrecognition an immanent condition of the final advent of the truth, but it already possesses in itself, so to speak, a positive ontological dimension: it founds, it renders possible a certain positive entity. To exemplify this let us refer again to science fiction, to one of the classic science-fiction novels, *The Door into Summer* by Robert A. Heinlein.

The hypothesis of this novel (written in 1957) is that in 1970, hibernation has become an ordinary procedure, managed by numerous
agencies. The hero, a young engineer by the name of Daniel Boone
Davis, hibernates himself as a professional deception for thirty years.
After his awakening in December 2000, he encounters — among other
adventures — the old Dr Twitchell, a kind of 'mad genius' who has
constructed a time machine; Davis persuades Dr Twitchell to use this
machine on him and to transpose him back into the year 1970. There our
hero arranges his affairs (by investing his money in a company that he
knows, from his voyage to 2000, will be a great success in thirty years'
time, and even by arranging for his own wedding in 2000: he organizes
also the hibernation of his future bride) and then hibernates himself
again for thirty years; the date of his second awakening is 27 April 2001.

This way, all ends well — there is just one small detail annoying the
hero: in the year 2000, the newspaper publish, beside 'Births', 'Deaths'
and 'Marriages', also the column 'Awakenings', listing the names of all
persons roused from hibernation. His *first* stay in the years 2000 and 2001
lasted from December 2000 until June 2001; this means that Doc
Twitchell has transposed him back to the past *after* the date of his second
awakening in April 2001. In *The Times* for Saturday 28 April 2001, there
was of course his name in the list of those awakened on Friday 27 April:
'D.B. Davis'. Why did he, during his *first* stay in 2001, miss his own name
among the 'Awakenings', although he was all the time a very attentive
reader of this column? Was this an accidental oversight?

> But what would I have done if I *had* seen it? Gone there, met myself — and
> gone stark mad? No, for if I *had* seen it, I would not have done the things I
> did afterward — 'afterward' for me — which led up to it. Therefore it could
> never have happened that way. The control is a negative feedback type, with
> a built-in 'fail safe', because the very existence of that line of print depended
> on my not seeing it; the apparent possibility that I might have seen it is one
> of the excluded 'not possibles' on the basic circuit design. 'There's a divinity
> that shapes our ends, rough-hew them how we will.' Free will and pre-
> destination in one sentence and both true. (Heinlein, 1986, p. 287)

Here we have the literal definition of the 'agency of the letter in the
unconscious': the line 'the very existence of [which] depended on my not
seeing it'. If, during his first stay in 2001, the subject had perceived his
own name in the newspaper — if he had perceived during his first stay
the trace of his second stay in 2001 — he would have acted thereupon in
a different manner (he would not have travelled back into the past, and

so on): that is, *he would have acted in a way that would have prevented his name from appearing in the newspaper*. The oversight itself therefore has, so to speak, a negative ontological dimension: it is the 'condition of the possibility' of the letter that it must be overlooked, that we must not take notice of it — its very existence depends on its not being seen by the subject. Here we have a kind of inversion of the traditional *esse = percipi*: it is the *non-percipi* which is the condition of *esse*. This is perhaps the right way to conceive the 'pre-ontological' status of the unconscious (evoked by Lacan in his *Seminar XI*): the unconscious is a paradoxical letter which *insists* only in so far as it does not *exist* ontologically.

In a homologous way, we could also determine the status of knowledge in psychoanalysis. The knowledge at work here is knowledge concerning the most intimate, traumatic being of the subject, knowledge about the particular logic of his enjoyment. In his everyday attitude, the subject refers to the objects of his *Umwelt*, of the world that surrounds him, as to some given positivity; psychoanalysis brings about a dizzy experience of how this given positivity exists and retains its consistency only in so far as somewhere else (on another scene, *an einem anderen Schauplatz*) some fundamental non-knowledge insists — it brings about the terrifying experience that if we come to know too much, we may lose our very being.

Let us take, for example, the Lacanian notion of the imaginary self: this self exists only on the basis of the misrecognition of its own conditions; it is the effect of this misrecognition. So Lacan's emphasis is not on the supposed incapacity of the self to reflect, to grasp its own conditions — on its being the plaything of inaccessible unconscious forces: his point is that the subject can pay for such a reflection with the loss of his very ontological consistency. It is in this sense that the knowledge which we approach through psychoanalysis is impossible-real: we are on dangerous ground; in getting too close to it we observe suddenly how our consistency, our positivity, is dissolving itself.

In psychoanalysis, knowledge is marked by a lethal dimension: the subject must pay the approach to it with his own being. In other words, to abolish the misrecognition means at the same time to abolish, to dissolve, the 'substance' which was supposed to hide itself behind the form–illusion of misrecognition. This 'substance' — the only one recognized in psychoanalysis — is, according to Lacan, enjoyment [*jouissance*]: access to knowledge is then paid with the loss of enjoyment — enjoyment, in its stupidity, is possible only on the basis of certain non-knowledge, ignorance. No wonder, then, that the reaction of the analysand to the analyst is often paranoid: by driving him towards knowledge about his desire, the analyst wants effectively to steal from him his most intimate treasure, the kernel of his enjoyment.

SYMPTOM AS REAL

The *Titanic* as Symptom

This dialectics of overtaking ourselves towards the future and simultaneous retroactive modification of the past — dialectics by which the error is internal to the truth, by which the misrecognition possesses a positive ontological dimension — has, however, its limits; it stumbles on to a rock upon which it becomes suspended. This rock is of course the Real, that which resists symbolization: the traumatic point which is always missed but none the less always returns, although we try — through a set of different strategies — to neutralize it, to integrate it into the symbolic order. In the perspective of the last stage of Lacanian teaching, it is precisely the symptom which is conceived as such a real kernel of enjoyment, which persists as a surplus and returns through all attempts to domesticate it, to gentrify it (if we may be permitted to use this term adapted to designate strategies to domesticate the slums as 'symptoms' of our cities), to dissolve it by means of explication, of putting-into-words its meaning.

To exemplify this shift of emphasis in the concept of symptom in Lacan's teaching, let us take a case which is today again attracting public attention: the wreck of the *Titanic*. Of course, it is already a commonplace to read *Titanic* as a symptom in the sense of 'knot of meanings': the sinking of the *Titanic* had a traumatic effect, it was a shock, 'the impossible happened', the unsinkable ship had sunk; but the point is that precisely as a shock, this sinking arrived at its proper time — 'the time was waiting for it': even before it actually happened, there was already a place opened, reserved for it in fantasy-space. In had such a terrific impact on 'social imaginary' by virtue of the fact that it was expected. It was foretold in amazing detail:

> In 1898 a struggling author named Morgan Robertson concocted a novel about a fabulous Atlantic liner, far larger than any that had ever been built. Robertson loaded his ship with rich and complacent people and then wrecked it one cold April night on an iceberg. This somehow showed the

futility of everything, and in fact, the book was called *Futility* when it appeared that year, published by the firm of M.F. Mansfield.

Fourteen years later a British shipping company named the White Star Line built a steamer remarkably like the one in Robertson's novel. The new liner was 66,000 tons displacement; Robertson's was 70,000. The real ship was 882.5 feet long; the fictional one was 800 feet. Both vessels were triple screw and could make 24–25 knots. Both could carry about 3,000 people, and both had enough lifeboats for only a fraction of this number. But, then, this did not seem to matter because both were labeled 'unsinkable'.

On April 10, 1912, the real ship left Southampton on her maiden voyage to New York. Her cargo included a priceless copy of the *Rubaiyat of Omar Khayyam* and a list of passengers collectively worth two hundred and fifty million dollars. On her way over she too struck an iceberg and went down on a cold April night.

Robertson called his ship the *Titan*; the White Star Line called its ship the *Titanic*. (Lord, 1983, pp. XI–XII)

The reasons, the background for this incredible coincidence are not difficult to guess: at the turn of the century, it was already part of *Zeitgeist* that a certain age was coming to an end — the age of peaceful progress, of well-defined and stable class distinctions, and so on: that is, the long period from 1850 until the First World War. New dangers were hanging in the air (labour movements, eruptions of nationalism, anti-Semitism, the danger of war) which would soon tarnish the idyllic image of Western civilization, releasing its 'barbaric' potentials. And if there was a phenomenon which, at the turn of the century, embodied the end of this age, it was the great transatlantic liners: floating palaces, wonders of technical progress; incredibly complicated and well-functioning machines, and at the same time the meeting-place of the cream of society; a kind of microcosm of the social structure, an image of society not as it really was but seen as society wanted to be seen in order to appear likeable, as a stable totality with well-defined class distinctions, and so on — in brief: the ego-ideal of society.

In other words, the wreck of the *Titanic* made such a tremendous impact not because of the immediate material dimensions of the catastrophe but because of its symbolic overdetermination, because of the ideological meaning invested in it: it was read as a 'symbol', as a condensed, metaphorical representation of the approaching catastrophe of European civilization itself. The wreck of the *Titanic* was a form in which society lived the experience of its own death, and it is interesting to note how both the traditional rightist and leftist readings retain this same perspective, with only shifts of emphasis. From the traditional perspective, the *Titanic* is a nostalgic monument of a bygone era of gallantry lost in today's world of vulgarity; from the leftist viewpoint, it is a story about the impotence of an ossified class society.

But all these are commonplaces that could be found in any report on the *Titanic* — we can easily explain, in this way, the metaphorical over-determination which confers on the *Titanic* its symbolic weight. The problem is that this is not all. We can easily convince ourselves of this by looking at the photos of the wreck of the *Titanic* taken recently by undersea cameras — where lies the terrifying power of fascination exercised by these pictures? It is, so to speak, intuitively clear that this fascinating power cannot be explained by the symbolic overdetermination, by the metaphorical meaning of the *Titanic*: its last resort is not that of representation but that of a certain inert presence. The *Titanic* is a Thing in the Lacanian sense: the material leftover, the materialization of the terrifying, impossible *jouissance*. By looking at the wreck we gain an insight into the forbidden domain, into a space that should be left unseen: visible fragments are a kind of coagulated remnant of the liquid flux of *jouissance*, a kind of petrified forest of enjoyment.

This terrifying impact has nothing to do with meaning — or, more precisely, it is a meaning permeated with enjoyment, a Lacanian *jouis-sense*. The wreck of the *Titanic* therefore functions as a sublime object: a positive, material object elevated to the status of the impossible Thing. And perhaps all the effort to articulate the metaphorical meaning of the *Titanic* is nothing but an attempt to escape this terrifying impact of the Thing, an attempt to domesticate the Thing by reducing it to its symbolic status, by providing it with a meaning. We usually say that the fascinating presence of a Thing obscures its meaning; here, the opposite is true: the meaning obscures the terrifying impact of its presence.

From Symptom to *Sinthome*

This, then, is the symptom — and it is on the basis of this notion of the symptom that we must locate the fact that in the final years of Lacan's teaching we find a kind of universalization of the symptom: almost everything that is becomes in a way symptom, so that finally even woman is determined as the symptom of man. We can even say that 'symptom' is Lacan's final answer to the eternal philosophical question 'Why is there something instead of nothing?' — this 'something' which 'is' instead of nothing is indeed the symptom.

The general reference of the philosophical discussion is usually the triangle world — language-subject, the relation of the subject to the world of objects, mediated through language; Lacan is usually reproached for his 'absolutism of the signifier' — the reproach is that he does not take into account the objective world, that he limits his theory to the interplay of subject and language; as if the objective world does not exist, as if it is only the imaginary effect-illusion of the signifier's play. But Lacan's answer to this reproach is that not only does the world — as a given whole of objects — not exist, but that neither do language and subject exist: it is already a classic Lacanian thesis that 'the big Other [that is, the symbolic order as a consistent, closed totality] does not exist', and the subject is denoted by $\mathbf{S}$, the crossed, blocked S, a void, an empty place in the signifier's structure.

At this point we must of course ask ourselves the naïve but necessary question: If the world and language and subject do not exist, what does exist; more precisely: what confers on existing phenomena their consistency? Lacan's answer is, as we have already indicated, symptom. To this answer, we must give its whole anti-post-structuralist emphasis: the fundamental gesture of post-structuralism is to deconstruct every substantial identity, to denounce behind its solid consistency an interplay of symbolic overdetermination — briefly, to dissolve the substantial identity into a network of non-substantial, differential relations; the notion of symptom is the necessary counterpoint to it, the substance of enjoyment, the real kernel around which this signifying interplay is structured.

To seize the logic of this universalization of symptom, we must connect it with another universalization, that of foreclosure (*Verwerfung*). In his unpublished Seminar, J.-A. Miller ironically spoke of the passage from special to general theory of foreclosure (alluding, of course, to Einstein's passage from special to general theory of relativity). When Lacan introduced the notion of foreclosure in the fifties, it designated a specific phenomenon of the exclusion of a certain key-signifier (*point de capiton*, Name-of-the-Father) from the symbolic order, triggering the psychotic process; here, the foreclosure is not proper to language as such but a distinctive feature of the psychotic phenomena. And, as Lacan reformulated Freud, what was foreclosed from the Symbolic returns in the Real — in the form of hallucinatory phenomena, for example.

However, in the last years of his teaching Lacan gave universal range to this function of foreclosure: there is a certain foreclosure proper to the order of signifier as such; whenever we have a symbolic structure it is structured around a certain void, it implies the foreclosure of a certain key-signifier. The symbolic structuring of sexuality implies the lack of a signifier of the sexual relationship, it implies that 'there is no sexual relationship', that the sexual relation cannot be symbolized — that it is an impossible, 'antagonistic' relationship. And to seize the interconnection between the two universalizations, we must simply again apply the proposition 'what was foreclosed from the Symbolic returns in the Real of the symptom': woman does not exist, her signifier is originally fore-closed, and that is why she returns as a symptom of man.

Symptom as real — this seems directly opposed to the classic Lacanian thesis that the unconscious is structured like a language: is not the symptom a symbolic formation *par excellence*, a cyphered, coded message which can be dissolved through interpretation because it is already in itself a signifier? Is not the whole point of Lacan that we must detect, behind the corporeal-imaginary mask (for example, of a hysterical symptom), its symbolic overdetermination? To explain this apparent contradiction, we must take into account the different stages of Lacan's development.

We can use the concept of symptom as a kind of clue, or index, allow-ing us to differentiate the main stages of Lacan's theoretical develop-ment. At the beginning, in the early fifties, symptom was conceived as a symbolic, signifying formation, as a kind of cypher, a coded message addressed to the big Order which later was supposed to confer on it its true meaning. The symptom arises where the world failed, where the circuit of the symbolic communication was broken: it is a kind of 'pro-longation of the communication by other means'; the failed, repressed word articulates itself in a coded, cyphered form. The implication of this is that the symptom can not only be interpreted but is, so to speak, already formed with an eye to its interpretation: it is addressed to the big Other presumed to contain its meaning. In other words, there is no symptom without its addressee: in the psychoanalytic cure the symptom is always addressed to the analyst, it is an appeal to him to deliver its hidden meaning. We can also say that there is no symptom without transference, without the position of some subject presumed to know its meaning. Precisely as an enigma, the symptom, so to speak, announces its dissolution through interpretation: the aim of psychoanalysis is to re-establish the broken network of communication by allowing the patient to verbalize the meaning of his symptom: through this verbalization, the symptom is automatically dissolved. This, then, is the basic point: in its very constitution, the symptom implies the field of the big Other as consistent, complete, because its very formation is an appeal to the Other which contains its meaning.

But here the problems began: why, in spite of its interpretation, does the symptom not dissolve itself; why does it persist? The Lacanian answer is, of course, *enjoyment*. The symptom is not only a cyphered message, it is at the same time a way for the subject to organize his enjoyment — that is why, even after the completed interpretation, the subject is not prepared to renounce his symptom; that is why he 'loves his symptom more than himself'. In locating this dimension of enjoyment in the symptom, Lacan proceeded in two stages.

First, he tried to isolate this dimension of enjoyment as that of *fantasy*, and to oppose symptom and fantasy through a whole set of distinctive features: symptom is a signifying formation which, so to speak, 'overtakes itself' towards its interpretation — that is, which can be analysed; fantasy is an inert construction which cannot be analysed, which resists interpretation. Symptom implies and addresses some non-barred, consistent big Other which will retroactively confer on it its meaning; fantasy implies a crossed out, blocked, barred, non-whole, inconsistent Other — that is to say, it is filling out a void in the Other. Symptom (for example, a slip of the tongue) causes discomfort and displeasure when it occurs, but we embrace its interpretation with pleasure; we explain gladly to others the meaning of our slips; their 'intersubjective recognition' is usually a source of intellectual satisfaction. When we abandon ourselves to fantasy (for example, in daydreaming) we feel immense pleasure, but on the contrary it causes us great discomfort and shame to confess our fantasies to others.

In this way we can also articulate two stages of the psychoanalytic process: *interpretation of symptoms — going through fantasy*. When we are confronted with the patient's symptoms, we must first interpret them and penetrate through them to the fundamental fantasy as the kernel of enjoyment which is blocking the further movement of interpretation; then we must accomplish the crucial step of going through the fantasy, of obtaining distance from it, of experiencing how the fantasy-formation just masks, fills out a certain void, lack, empty place in the Other.

But here again another problem arose: how do we account for patients who have, beyond any doubt, gone through their fantasy, who have obtained distance from the fantasy-framework of their reality, but whose key symptom still persists? How do we explain this fact? What do we do with a symptom, with this pathological formation which persists not only beyond its interpretation but even beyond fantasy? Lacan tried to answer this challenge with the concept of *sinthome*, a neologism containing a set of associations (synthetic-artificial man, synthesis between symptom and fantasy, Saint Thomas, the saint . . .) (Lacan, 1988a). Symptom as *sinthome* is a certain signifying formation penetrated with enjoyment: it is a signifier as a bearer of *jouis-sense*, enjoyment-in-sense.

What we must bear in mind here is the radical ontological status of symptom: symptom, conceived as *sinthome*, is literally our only substance, the only positive support of our being, the only point that gives consistency to the subject. In other words, symptom is the way we — the subjects — 'avoid madness', the way we 'choose something (the symptom-formation) instead of nothing (radical psychotic autism, the destruction of the symbolic universe)' through the binding of our enjoyment to a certain signifying, symbolic formation which assures a minimum of consistency to our being-in-the-world.

If the symptom in this radical dimension is unbound, it means literally 'the end of the world' — the only alternative to the symptom is nothing: pure autism, a psychic suicide, surrender to the death drive even to the total destruction of the symbolic universe. That is why the final Lacanian definition of the end of the psychoanalytic process is *identification with the symptom*. The analysis achieves its end when the patient is able to recognize, in the Real of his symptom, the only support of his being. That is how we must read Freud's *wo es war, soll ich werden*: you, the subject, must identify yourself with the place where your symptom already was; in its 'pathological' particularity you must recognize the element which gives consistency to your being.

This, then, is a symptom: a particular, 'pathological', signifying formation, a binding of enjoyment, an inert stain resisting communication and interpretation, a stain which cannot be included in the circuit of discourse, of social bond network, but is at the same time a positive condition of it. Now it is perhaps clear why woman is, according to Lacan, a symptom of man — to explain this, we need only remember the well-known male chauvinist wisdom often referred to by Freud: women are impossible to bear, a source of eternal nuisance, but still, they are the best thing we have of their kind; without them, it would be even worse. So, if woman does not exist, man is perhaps simply a woman who thinks that she does exist.

'in you more than yourself'

In so far as the *sinthome* is a certain signifier which is not enchained in a network but immediately filled, penetrated with enjoyment, its status is by definition 'psychosomatic', that of a terrifying bodily mark which is merely a mute attestation bearing witness to a disgusting enjoyment, without representing anything or anyone. Is not Franz Kafka's story 'A Country Doctor' therefore the story of a *sinthome* in its pure — distilled, so to speak — form? The open wound growing luxuriantly on the child's body, this nauseous, verminous aperture — what is it if not the embodiment of vitality as such, of the life-substance in its most radical dimension of meaningless enjoyment?

> In his right side, near the hip, was an open wound as big as the palm of my hand. Rose-red, in many variations of shade, dark in the grooves, lighter at the edges, softly granulated, with irregular clots of blood, open as a surface-mine to the daylight. That was how it looked from a distance. But on a closer inspection there was another complication. I could not help a low whistle of surprise. Worms, as thick and as long as my little finger, themselves rose-red and blood-spotted as well, were wriggling from their fastness in the interior of the wound towards the light, with small white heads and many little legs. Poor young man, he was past helping. I had discovered his great wound; this blossom in his side was destroying him. (Kafka, 1978, p. 122)

'In his right side, near the hips ...' — exactly like Christ's wound, although its closest forerunner is the suffering of Amfortas in Wagner's *Parsifal*. Amfortas's problem is that as long as his wound bleeds *he cannot die*, he cannot find peace in death; his attendants insist that he must do his duty and perform the Grail's ritual, regardless of his suffering, while he desperately asks them to have mercy on him and put an end to his suffering by simply killing him — exactly like the child in 'A Country Doctor', who addresses the narrator-doctor with the desperate request: 'Doctor, let me die'.

At first sight, Wagner and Kafka are as far apart as they can be: on one hand, we have the late-Romantic revival of a medieval legend; on the other, the description of the fate of the individual in contemporary totalitarian bureaucracy ... but if we look closely we perceive that the fundamental problem of *Parsifal* is eminently a *bureaucratic* one: the incapacity, the incompetence of Amfortas in performing his ritual-bureaucratic duty. The terrifying voice of Amfortas's father Titurel, this superego-injunction of the living dead, addresses his impotent son in the first act with the words: 'Mein Sohn Amfortas, bist du am Amt?', to which we have to give all bureaucratic weight: Are you at your post? Are you ready to officiate? In a somewhat perfunctory sociological manner, we could say that Wagner's *Parsifal* is staging the historical fact that the classical Master (Amfortas) is no longer capable of reigning in the conditions of totalitarian bureaucracy and that he must be replaced by a new figure of a Leader (Parsifal).

In his film version of *Parsifal*, Hans-Jürgen Syberberg demonstrated — by a series of changes to Wagner's original — that he was well aware of this fact. First there is his manipulation of the sexual difference: at the crucial moment of inversion in the second act — after Kundry's kiss — Parsifal changes his sex: the male actor is replaced by a young, cold female; what is at stake here is no ideology of hermaphroditism but a shrewd insight into the 'feminine' nature of totalitarian power: totalitarian Law is an obscene Law, penetrated by enjoyment, a Law which has lost its formal neutrality. But what is crucial for us here is another feature of Syberberg's version: the fact that he has *externalized* Amfortas's wound — it is carried on a pillow beside him, as a nauseous partial object out of which, through an aperture resembling vaginal lips, trickles blood. Here we have the contiguity with Kafka: it is as if the child's wound from 'A Country Doctor' has externalized itself, becoming a separate object, gaining independent existence or — to use Lacan's style — ex-sistence. That is why Syberberg stages the scene where, just before the final denouement, Amfortas desperately begs his attendants to run their swords through his body and so relieve him of his unbearable torments, in a way which differs radically from the customary way:

> 'Already I feel the darkness of death enshroud me,
> and must I yet again return to life?
> Madmen! Who would force me to live?
> Could you but grant me death!
> *(He tears open his garment.)*
> Here I am — here is the open wound!
> Here flows my blood, that poisons me.
> Draw your weapons! Plunge your swords
> in deep — deep, up to the hilt!'

The wound is Amfortas's symptom — it embodies his filthy, nauseous enjoyment, it is his thickened, condensed life-substance which does not let him die. His words 'Here I am — here is the open wound!' are thus to be taken literally: all his being is in this wound; if we annihilate it, he himself will lose his positive ontological consistency and cease to exist. This scene is usually staged in accordance with Wagner's instructions: Amfortas tears open his garment and points at the bleeding wound on his body; with Syberberg, who has eternalized the wound, Amfortas points at the nauseous partial object outside himself — that is, he does not point back at himself but there outside, in the sense of 'there outside I am, in that disgusting piece of the real consists all my substance!' How should we read this externality?

The first, most obvious solution is to conceive this wound as a *symbolic* one: the wound is externalized to show that it does not concern the body as such but the symbolic network into which the body is caught. To put it simply: the real reason for Amfortas's impotence, and therewith for the decay of his kingdom, is a certain blockage, a certain snag in the network of symbolic relations. 'Something is rotten' in this country where the ruler has trespassed a fundamental prohibition (he allowed himself to be seduced by Kundry); the wound is then just a materialization of a moral-symbolic decay.

But there is another, perhaps more radical reading: in so far as it sticks out from the (symbolic and symbolized) reality of the body, the wound is 'a little piece of real', a disgusting protuberance which cannot be integrated into the totality of 'our own body', a materialization of that which is 'in Amfortas more than Amfortas' and is thereby — according to the classic Lacanian formula (Lacan, 1979, ch. XX) — destroying him. It is destroying him, but at the same time it is the only thing which gives him consistency. This is the paradox of the psychoanalytic concept of the symptom: symptom is an element clinging on like a kind of parasite and 'spoiling the game', but if we annihilate it things get even worse: we lose all we had — even the rest which was threatened but not yet destroyed by the symptom. Confronted with the symptom we are always in a position of an impossible choice; illustrated by a well-known joke about the chief editor of one of Hearst's newspapers: in spite of persuasion from Hearst, he did not want to take well-deserved leave. When Hearst asked him why he did not want to go on his holidays, the editor's answer was: 'I am afraid that if I were absent for a couple of weeks, the sales of the newspaper would fall; but I am even more afraid that in spite of my absence, the sales would *not* fall!' This is the symptom: an element which causes a great deal of trouble, but its absence would mean even greater trouble: total catastrophe.

To take, as a final example, Ridley Scott's film *Alien*: is not the disgusting parasite which jumps out of the body of poor John Hurt precisely such a symptom, is not its status precisely the same as that of Amfortas's externalized wound? The cave on the desert planet into which the space travellers enter when the computer registers signs of life in it, and where the polyp-like parasite sticks on to Hurt's face, has the status of the pre-symbolic Thing — that is, of the maternal body, of the living substance of enjoyment. The utero-vaginal associations aroused by this cave are almost too intrusive. The parasite adhering to Hurt's face is thus a kind of a 'sprout of enjoyment', a leftover of the maternal Thing which then functions as a symptom — the Real of enjoyment — of the group marooned in the wandering spaceship: it threatens them and at he same time constitutes them as a closed group. The fact that this parasitical object incessantly changes its form merely confirms its *anamorphic* status: it is a pure being of semblance. The 'alien', the eighth, supplementary passenger, is an object which, being nothing at all in itself, must none the less be added, annexed as an anamorphic surplus. It is the Real at its purest: a semblance, something which on a strictly symbolic level does not exist at all but at the same time the only thing in the whole film which actually exists, the thing against which the whole reality is utterly defenceless. One has only to remember the spine-chilling scene when the liquid pouring from the polyp-like parasite after the doctor makes an incision with a scalpel dissolves the metal floor of the space ship. . . .

From this perspective of *sinthome*, truth and enjoyment are radically incompatible: the dimension of truth is opened through our misrecognition of the traumatic Thing, embodying the impossible *jouissance*.

Ideological *Jouissance*

With the designation of an inconsistency of the socio-symbolic Other, the positive side of which is obcene enjoyment, have we not consented also to the usual 'post-modernist' anti-Enlightenment *ressentiment*? The text on the cover of the French edition of Lacan's *Écrits* already belies such an understanding: Lacan conceives there his theoretical effort explicitly as a prolongation of the old struggle of Enlightenment. The Lacanian criticism of the autonomous subject and his power of reflection, of reflexive appropriation of his objective condition, is therefore far from any affirmation of some irrational ground escaping the reach of reason. Paraphrasing the well-known Marxian formula of capital itself as the limit of capitalism, we should say that according to Lacan the limit of

Enlightenment is Enlightenment itself, its usually forgotten obverse already articulated in Descartes and Kant.

The leading motif of the Enlightenment is, of course, some variation of the injunction 'Reason autonomously!': 'Use your own head, free yourself of all prejudices, do not accept anything without questioning its rational foundations, always preserve a critical distance . . .'. But Kant had already, in his famous article 'What is Enlightenment?', added to this an unpleasant, disquieting supplement, introducing a certain fissure into the very heart of the Enlightenment project: 'Reason about whatever you want and as much as you want — but *obey!*' That is to say: as the autonomous subject of theoretical reflection, addressing the enlightened public, you can think freely, you can question all authority; but as a part of the social 'machine', as a subject in the other meaning of the word, you must obey unconditionally the orders of your superiors. This fissure is proper to the project of Enlightenment as such: we find it already with Descartes, in his *Discourse on Method*. The obverse of the *cogito* doubting everything, questioning the very existence of the world, is the Cartesian 'provisional morality', a set of rules established by Descartes to enable him to survive in the everyday existence of his philosophical journey: the very first rule emphasizes the need to accept and obey the customs and laws of the country into which we were born without questioning their authority.

The main point is to perceive how this acceptance of given empirical, 'pathological' (Kant) customs and rules is not some kind of pre-Enlightenment remnant — a remnant of the traditional authoritarian attitude — but, on the contrary, *the necessary obverse of the Enlightenment itself*: through this acceptance of the customs and rules of social life in their nonsensical, given character, through acceptance of the fact that 'Law is law', we are internally freed from its constraints — the way is open for free theoretical reflection. In other words, we render unto Caesar what is Caesar's, so that we can calmly reflect on everything. This experience of the given, non-founded character of customs and social rules entails in itself a kind of distance from them. In the traditional, pre-enlightened universe, the authority of the Law is never experienced as nonsensical and unfounded; on the contrary, the Law is always illuminated by the charismatic power of fascination. Only to the already enlightened view does the universe of social customs and rule appear as a nonsensical 'machine' that must be accepted as such.

Of course, we could say that the principal illusion of the Enlightenment consists in the idea that we can preserve a simple distance from the external 'machine' of social customs and thus keep the space of our inner reflection spotless, unblemished by the externality of customs. But this criticism does not affect Kant in so far as in his affirmation of the categorical imperative he has taken into account the traumatic, truth-less, non-sensical character of the internal, moral Law itself. The Kantian categorical imperative is precisely a Law which has a necessary, unconditional authority, without being true: it is — in Kant's own words — a kind of 'transcendental fact', a given fact the truth of which cannot be theoretically demonstrated; but its unconditional validity should nonetheless be presupposed for our moral activity to have any sense.

We can contrast this moral Law and the 'pathological', empirically given social laws through a whole set of distinctive features: social laws structure a field of social *reality*, moral Law is the *Real* of an unconditional imperative which takes no consideration of the limitations imposed on us by reality — it is an impossible injunction. 'You can, because you must! [*Du kannst, denn du sollst!*]'; social laws pacify our egotism and regulate social homeostasis; moral Law creates imbalance in this homeostasis by introducing an element of unconditional compulsion. The ultimate paradox of Kant is this priority of practical over theoretical reason: we can free ourselves of external social constraints and achieve the maturity proper to the autonomous enlightened subject precisely by submitting to the 'irrational' compulsion of the categorical imperative.

It is a commonplace of Lacanian theory to emphasize how this Kantian moral imperative conceals an obscene superego injunction: 'Enjoy!' — the voice of the Other impelling us to follow our duty for the sake of duty is a traumatic irruption of an appeal to impossible *jouissance*, disrupting the homeostasis of the pleasure principle and its prolongation, the reality principle. This is why Lacan conceives Sade as the truth of Kant: 'Kant avec Sade' (Lacan, 1966). But in what precisely does this obscenity of the moral Law consist? Not in some remnants, leftovers of the empirical 'pathological' contents sticking to the pure form of the Law and smudging it, but *in this form itself.* The moral Law is obscene in so far as it is its form itself which functions as a motivating force driving us to obey its command — that is, in so far as we obey moral Law because it is law and not because of a set of positive reasons: the obscenity of moral Law is the obverse of its formal character.

Of course, the elementary feature of Kant's ethics is to exclude all empirical, 'pathological' contents — in other words, all objects producing pleasure (or displeasure) — as the locus of our moral activity, but what remains hidden in Kant is the way this renunciation itself produces a certain surplus-enjoyment (the Lacanian *plus-de-jouir*). Let us take the case of Fascism — the Fascist ideology is based upon a purely formal imperative: Obey, because you must! In other words, renounce enjoyment, sacrifice yourself and do not ask about the meaning of it — the value of the sacrifice lies in its very meaninglessness; true sacrifice is for its own end; you must find positive fulfilment in the sacrifice itself, not in its instrumental value: it is this renunciation, this giving up of enjoyment itself, which produces a certain surplus-enjoyment.

This surplus produced through renunciation is the Lacanian *objet petit a*, the embodiment of surplus-enjoyment; here we can also grasp why Lacan coined the notion of surplus-enjoyment on the model of the Marxian notion of surplus-value — with Marx, surplus-value also implies a certain renunciation of 'pathological', empirical use-value. And Fascism is obscene in so far as it perceives directly the ideological form as its own end, as an end in itself — remember Mussolini's famous answer to the question 'How do the Fascists justify their claim to rule Italy? What is their programme?': 'Our programme is very simple: we want to rule Italy!' The ideological power of Fascism lies precisely in the feature which was perceived by liberal or leftist critics as its greatest weakness: in the utterly void, formal character of its appeal, in the fact that it demands obedience and sacrifice for their own sake. For Fascist ideology, the point is not the instrumental value of the sacrifice, it is the very form of sacrifice itself, 'the spirit of sacrifice', which is the cure against the liberal–decadent disease. It is also clear why Fascism was so terrified by psychoanalysis: psychoanalysis enables us to locate an obscene enjoyment at work in this act of formal sacrifice.

This is the hidden perverse, obscene dimension of Kantian moral formalism finally appearing in Fascism: it is here that Kantian formalism rejoins — or, more precisely, explicates — the logic of the second of Descartes's maxims of provisional morality:

> . . . that of being as firm and resolute in my actions as I could be, and not to follow less faithfully opinions the most dubious, when my mind was once made up regarding them, than if these had been beyond doubt. In this I should be following the example of travellers, who, finding themselves lost in a forest, know that they ought not to wander first to one side and then to the other, nor, still less, to stop in one place, but understand that they should continue to walk as straight as they can in one direction, not diverging for any slight reason, even though it was possibly chance alone that first deter-

mined them in their choice. By this means if they do not go exactly where they wish, they will at least arrive somewhere at the end, where probably they will be better off than in the middle of a forest. (Descartes, 1976, p. 64)

In this passage, Descartes is in a way revealing the hidden cards of ideology as such: the real aim of ideology is the attitude demanded by it, the consistency of the ideological form, the fact that we 'continue to walk as straight as we can in one direction'; the positive reasons given by ideology to justify this request — to make us obey ideological form — are there only to conceal this fact; in other words, to conceal the surplus-enjoyment proper to the ideological form as such.

Here we could refer to the notion, introduced by Jon Elster, of 'states that are essentially by-products' — that is, states that could be produced only as non-intended, as the side-effect of our activity: as soon as we aim directly at them, as soon as our activity is directly motivated by them, our procedure becomes self-defeating. From a whole series of ideological examples evoked by Elster, let us take Tocqueville's justification of the jury system: 'I do not know whether a jury is useful to the litigants, but I am sure that it is very good for those who have to decide the case. I regard it as one of the most effective means of popular education at society's disposal.' Elster's comment on this is that

> . . . a necessary condition for the jury system to have the educational effects on the jurors for which Tocqueville recommended it is their belief that they are doing something that is worthwhile and important, beyond their own personal development. (Elster, 1982, p. 96)

— in other words, as soon as the jurors become aware that the judicial effects of their work are rather null and that the real point of it is its effect on their own civic spirit — its educational value — *this educational effect is spoilt.*

It is the same with Pascal, with his argument for the religious wager: even if we are wrong in our wager, even if there is no God, my belief in God and my acting upon it will have many beneficial effects in my terrestrial life — I will lead a dignified, calm, moral, satisfying life, free of perturbations and doubts. But the point is again that I can achieve this terrestrial profit only if I really believe in God, in the religious beyond; this is probably the hidden, rather cynical logic of Pascal's argument: although the real stake of religion is the terrestrial profit achieved by the religious attitude, this gain is a 'state that is essentially a by-product' — it can be produced only as a non-intended result of our belief in a religious beyond.

It should be no surprise to us that we find exactly the same argument in Rosa Luxemburg's description of the revolutionary process: at the beginning, the first workers' struggles are doomed to fail, their direct aims cannot be achieved, but although they necessarily end in failure, their overall balance sheet is none the less positive because their main gain is educational — that is to say, they serve the formation of the working class into the revolutionary subject. And again, the point is that if we (the Party) say directly to the fighting workers: 'It does not matter if you fail, the main point of your struggle is its educational effect on you', the educational effect will be lost.

It is as if Descartes, in the quoted passage, is giving us, perhaps for the first time, the pure form of this fundamental ideological paradox: what is really at stake in ideology is its form, the fact that we continue to walk as straight as we can in one direction, that we follow even the most dubious opinions once our mind has been made up regarding them; but this ideological attitude can be achieved only as a 'state that is essentially by-product': the ideological subjects, 'travellers lost in a forest', must conceal from themselves the fact that 'it was possibly chance alone that first determined them in their choice'; they must believe that their decision is well founded, that it will lead to their Goal. As soon as they perceive that *the real goal is the consistency of the ideological attitude itself*, the effect is self-defeating. We can see how ideology works in a way exactly opposed to the popular idea of Jesuit morals: the aim here is to justify the means.

Why must this inversion of the relation of aim and means remain hidden, why is its revelation self-defeating? Because it would reveal the enjoyment which is at work in ideology, in the ideological renunciation itself. In other words, it would reveal that ideology serves only its own purpose, that it does not serve anything — which is precisely the Lacanian definition of *jouissance*.

我覺得我長大了
開始認識一些事情
表面跟事實並
不相符真是一件
可怕的事.

========================PART II========================

Lack in the Other

真相是
我們永遠講不出來的

真相也是永遠
要逃開我們
操控的.....跟以我是先的.

3

'Che Vuoi?'

IDENTITY

The Ideological 'Quilt'

What creates and sustains the *identity* of a given ideological field beyond all possible variations of its positive content? *Hegemony and Socialist Strategy* delineates what is probably the definitive answer to this crucial question of the theory of ideology: the multitude of 'floating signifiers', of proto-ideological elements, is structured into a unified field through the intervention of a certain 'nodal point' (the Lacanian *point de capiton*) which 'quilts' them, stops their sliding and fixes their meaning.

Ideological space is made of non-bound, non-tied elements, 'floating signifiers', whose very identity is 'open', overdetermined by their articulation in a chain with other elements — that is, their 'literal' signification depends on their metaphorical surplus-signification. *Ecologism*, for example: its connection with other ideological elements is not determined in advance; one can be a state-orientated ecologist (if one believes that only the intervention of a strong state can save us from catastrophe), a socialist ecologist (if one locates the source of merciless exploitation of nature in the capitalist system), a conservative ecologist (if one preaches that man must again become deeply rooted in his native soil), and so on; *feminism* can be socialist, apolitical ...; even *racism* could be elitist or populist .... The 'quilting' performs the totalization by means of which this free floating of ideological elements is halted, fixed — that is to say, by means of which they become parts of the structured network of meaning.

If we 'quilt' the floating signifiers through 'Communism', for example, 'class struggle' confers a precise and fixed signification to all other elements: to democracy (so-called 'real democracy' as opposed to 'bourgeois formal democracy' as a legal form of exploitation); to feminism (the exploitation of women as resulting from the class-conditioned division of labour); to ecologism (the destruction of natural resources as a logical consequence of profit-orientated capitalist production); to the peace movement (the principal danger to peace is adventuristic imperialism), and so on.

What is at stake in the ideological struggle is which of the 'nodal points', *points de capiton*, will totalize, include in its series of equivalences, these free-floating elements. Today, for example, the stake of the struggle between neo-conservativism and social democracy is 'freedom': neo-conservatives try to demonstrate how egalitarian democracy, embodied in the welfare state, necessarily leads to new forms of serfdom, to the dependency of the individual on the totalitarian state, while social democrats stress how individual freedom, to have any meaning at all, must be based upon democratic social life, equality of economic opportunity, and so forth.

In this way, every element of a given ideological field is part of a series of equivalences: its metaphorical surplus, through which it is connected with all other elements, determines retroactively its very identity (in a Communist perspective, to fight for peace *means* to fight against the capitalist order, and so on). But this enchainment is possible only on condition that a certain signifier — the Lacanian 'One' — 'quilts' the whole field and, by embodying it, effectuates its identity.

Let us take the Laclau/Mouffe project of radical democracy: here, we have an articulation of particular struggles (for peace, ecology, feminism, human rights, and so on), none of which pretends to be the 'Truth', the last Signified, the 'true Meaning' of all the others; but the title 'radical democracy' itself indicates how the very possibility of their articulation implies the 'nodal', determining role of a certain struggle which, precisely as a particular struggle, outlines the horizon of all the other struggles. This determining role belongs, of course, to democracy, to 'democratic invention': according to Laclau and Mouffe, all other struggles (socialist, feminist . . .) could be conceived as the gradual radicalization, extension, application of the democratic project to new domains (of economic relations, of the relations between sexes . . .). The dialectical paradox lies in the fact that the particular struggle playing a hegemonic role, far from enforcing a violent suppression of the differences, opens the very space for the relative autonomy of the particular struggles: the feminist struggle, for example, is made possible only through reference to democratic-egalitarian political discourse.

The first task of the analysis is therefore to isolate, in a given ideological field, the particular struggle which at the same time determines the horizon of its totality — to put it in Hegelian terms, the species which is its own universal kind. But this is the crucial theoretical problem: how does this determining, totalizing role of a particular struggle differ from the traditionally conceived 'hegemony' by which a certain struggle (workers' struggle in Marxism) appears as the Truth of all the others, so that all other struggles are in the last resort only forms of its expression, and victory in this struggle offers us the key to victory in other domains — or, as the usual Marxist line of argument runs: only successful socialist revolution will render possible the abolition of women's repression, the end of the destructive exploitation of nature, relief from the threat of nuclear destruction . . . . In other words: how do we formulate the determining role of a certain particular domain without falling into a trap of essentialism? My thesis is that Saul Kripke's antidescriptivism offers us the conceptual tools to solve this problem.

Descriptivism versus Antidescriptivism

We could call the basic experience upon which Kripke's antidescriptivism is founded *invasion of the body snatchers*, after the well-known fifties science-fiction film: an invasion of creatures from outer space which assume human shape — they look exactly like human beings, they have all their properties, but in some sense this makes them all the more uncannily strange. This problem is the same as anti-Semitism (and for that reason *Invasion of the Body Snatchers* can be read as a metaphor for McCarthyite anti-Communism in the fifties): Jews are 'like us'; it is difficult to recognize them, to determine at the level of positive reality that surplus, that evasive feature, which differentiates them from all other people.

The stake of the dispute between descriptivism and antidescriptivism is the most elementary one: how do names refer to the objects they denote? Why does the word 'table' refer to a table? The descriptivist answer is the obvious one: because of its meaning; every word is in the first place the bearer of a certain meaning — that is, it means a cluster of descriptive features ('table' means an object of a certain shape, serving certain purposes) and subsequently refers to objects in reality in so far as they possess properties designated by the cluster of descriptions. 'Table' means a table because a table has properties comprised in the meaning of the world 'table'. Intention thus has logical priority over extension: extension (a set of objects referred to by a word) is determined by intention (by universal properties comprised in its meaning). The antidescriptivist answer, in contrast, is that a word is connected to an object or a set of objects through an act of 'primal baptism', and this link maintains itself even if the cluster of descriptive features which initially determined the meaning of the word changes completely.

Let us take a simplified example from Kripke: if we ask the general public for an identifying description of 'Kurt Gödel', the answer would be 'the author of the proof of the incompleteness of arithmetic'; but suppose that the proof was written by another man, Schmidt, a friend of Gödel, and that Gödel murdered him and appropriated to himself the discovery of the proof mentioned; in this case, the name 'Kurt Gödel' would still refer to the same Gödel, although the identifying description would no longer apply to him. The point is that the name 'Gödel' has been linked to a certain object (person) through a 'primal baptism', and this link holds even if the original identifying description proves false (Kripke, 1980, pp. 83–5). This is the core of the dispute: descriptivists emphasize the immanent, internal 'intentional contents' of a word, while antidescriptivists regard as decisive the external causal link, the way a word has been transmitted from subject to subject in a chain of tradition.

Here, a first charge offers itself: is not the obvious answer to this dispute that we are concerned with two different types of names: with notions denoting (universal) kinds and with proper names? Is not its solution simply that descriptivism accounts for the way generic notions function and antidescriptivism for the way proper names function? If we refer to somebody as 'fat', it is clear that he must at least possess the property of being excessively corpulent, but if we refer to somebody as 'Peter', we cannot infer any of his effective properties — the name 'Peter' refers to him simply because he was baptized 'Peter'. But such a solution, in trying to get rid of a problem by a simple classificatory distinction, misses completely what is at stake in the dispute: both descriptivism and antidescriptivism aim at a *general* theory of referring functions. For descriptivism, proper names themselves are merely abbreviated or disguised definite descriptions, while for antidescriptivism the external causal chain determines reference even in the case of generic notions, at least those which designate natural kinds. Let us again take a somewhat simplified example from Kripke: at a certain point in prehistory, a certain kind of object was baptized 'gold', and this name was at that point linked to a cluster of descriptive features (a heavy glittering yellow metal which can be beautifully fashioned, and so on); over the centuries, this cluster of descriptions has been multiplying and changing according to the development of human knowledge, so that today we identify 'gold' with its specification within the periodic table and its protons, neutrons, electrons, spectra, and so forth; but let us suppose that today a scientist should discover that all the world was wrong about all properties of the object called 'gold' (the impression that it has a glittering yellow colour was produced by a universal optical illusion, and so on) — in this case, the word 'gold' would continue to refer to the same object as before — *i.e.* we would say 'gold doesn't possess the properties ascribed to it until now', not 'the object that we have until now taken for gold is not really gold.'

The same also applies to the opposite counterfactual situation: it is possible that

> there might be a substance which has all the identifying marks we commonly attributed to gold and used to identify it in the first place, but which is not the same kind of thing, which is not the same substance. We would say of such a thing that though it has all the appearances we initially used to identify gold, it is not gold. (Kripke, 1980, p. 119)

Why? Because this substance is not linked to the name 'gold' through a causal chain which reaches back to the 'primal baptism' establishing the reference of 'gold'. For the same reason it must be said that

> even if archaeologists or geologists were to discover tomorrow some fossils conclusively showing the existence of animals in the past satisfying everything we know about unicorns from the myth of the unicorn, that would not show that there were unicorns. (Ibid, p. 24)

In other words, even if these quasi-unicorns correspond perfectly to the cluster of descriptive features comprised by the meaning of the word 'unicorn', we cannot be sure that it was they who were the original reference of the mythical notion of 'unicorn' — that is, the object to which the word 'unicorn' was fastened in the 'primal baptism'. . . . How could we overlook the libidinal contents of these propositions of Kripke? What is at stake here is precisely the problem of the 'fulfilment of desire': when we encounter in reality an object which has all the properties of the fantasized object of desire, we are nevertheless necessarily somewhat disappointed; we experience a certain 'this is not it'; it becomes evident that the finally found real object is not the reference of desire even

though it possesses all the required properties. It is perhaps no accident
that Kripke selects as examples objects with an extreme libidinal connotation, objects which already embody desire in common mythology:
gold, unicorn. . . .

The Two Myths

Bearing in mind how the very terrain of the dispute between descriptivism and antidescriptivism is thus permeated by an undercurrent of the
economy of desire, it should come as no surprise that Lacanian theory
can help us to clarify the terms of this dispute, not in the sense of any
quasi-dialectical 'synthesis' between the two opposing views but, on the
contrary, by pointing out how both descriptivism and antidescriptivism
miss the same crucial point — the radical contingency of naming. The proof
of this is that to defend their solution, both positions have to resort to a
myth, to invent a myth: a myth of a primitive tribe in Searle, a myth of
'omniscient observer of history' in Donnellan. To refute antidescriptivism, Searle invents a primitive hunter-gatherer community with a
language containing proper names:

> Imagine that everybody in the tribe knows everybody else and that newborn
> members of the tribe are baptized at ceremonies attended by the entire tribe.
> Imagine, furthermore, that as the children grow up they learn the names of
> people as well as the local names of mountains, lakes, streets, houses, etc., by
> ostension. Suppose also that there is a strict taboo in this tribe against speak-
> ing of the dead, so that no one's name is ever mentioned after his death.
> Now the point of the fantasy is simply this: As I have described it, this tribe
> has an institution of proper names used for reference in exactly the same
> way that our names are used for reference, but *there is not a single use of a name
> in the tribe that satisfies the causal chain of communication theory.* (Searle, 1984,
> p. 240)

In other words, in this tribe every use of the name satisfies the descriptivist claim: the reference is determined exclusively by a cluster of descriptive features. Searle knows, of course, that such a tribe never existed; his
point is only that the way naming functions in this tribe is *logically
primordial*: that all the counter-examples used by antidescriptivists are
logically secondary, they are 'parasitic', they imply prior 'descriptivist'
functioning. When all we know about somebody is that his name is
Smith — when the only intentional content of 'Smith' is 'the person

others refer to as Smith' — such a condition logically presupposes the existence of at least one other subject who knows a lot more about Smith — to whom the name 'Smith' is connected with a whole cluster of descriptive features (an old fat gentleman giving a course on the history of pornography . . .). In other words, the case offered by antidescriptivism as 'normal' (the transmission of the reference through an external causal chain) is only an 'external' description (a description leaving out of consideration the intentional content) of a functioning which is 'parasitic' — that is, logically secondary.

To refute Searle, we have to demonstrate that his primitive tribe, in which language functions exclusively in a descriptive way, is not only empirically but also logically impossible. The Derridean procedure would, of course, be to show how the 'parasitic' use always corrodes, and has from the very start corroded, the purely descriptive functioning: how Searle's myth of a primitive tribe presents just another version of a totally transparent community in which referring is not blurred by any absence, by any lack.

The Lacanian approach would emphasize another feature: there is simply something missing in Searle's description of his tribe. If we are really concerned with language in a strict sense, with language as a social network in which meaning exists only in so far as it is intersubjectively recognized — with language which, by definition, cannot be 'private' — then it must be part of the meaning of each name that it refers to a certain object *because this is its name*, because others use this name to designate the object in question: every name, in so far as it is part of common language, implies this self-referential, circular moment. 'Others', of course, cannot be reduced to empirical others; they rather point to the Lacanian 'big Other', to the symbolic order itself.

Here we encounter the dogmatic stupidity proper to a signifier as such, the stupidity which assumes the shape of a tautology: a name refers to an object *because this object is called that* — this impersonal form ('it is called') announces the dimension of the 'big Other' beyond other subjects. The example evoked by Searle as an epitome of parasitism — the example of speakers who know nothing about the object of which they are speaking and whose 'only intentional content might be that they are using the name to refer to what others are using it to refer to' (Searle, 1984, p. 259) — indicates, on the contrary, a necessary constituent of every 'normal' use of names in language as a social bond — and this tautological constituent is the Lacanian master-signifier, the 'signifier without signified'.

The ironic part of it is that this lack is actually inscribed in Searle's description in the form of a prohibition ('. . . there is a strict taboo in this tribe against speaking of the dead'): Searle's mythical tribe is thus a tribe of psychotics which — because of the taboo concerning names of dead persons — forecloses the function of the Name-of-the-Father — that is to say, prevents the transformation of the dead father into the rule of his Name. If, consequently, Searle's descriptivism misses the dimension of the *big Other*, antidescriptivism — at least in its predominant version — misses the *small other*, the dimension of the object as real in the Lacanian sense: the distinction real/reality. This is why it looks for that X, for the feature guaranteeing the identity of a reference through all changes of its descriptive properties, in the reality itself; this is why it must invent its own myth, a kind of counterpoint to Searle's primitive tribe, Donnellan's myth of an 'omniscient observer of history'. Donnellan has constructed the following ingenious counterfactual example:

> Suppose that all that a certain speaker knows or thinks he knows about Thales is that he is the Greek philosopher who said that all is water. But suppose there never was a Greek philosopher who said such a thing. Suppose that Aristotle and Herodotus were referring to a well digger who said, 'I wish all were water so I wouldn't have to dig these damned wells'. In such a case, when the speaker uses the name 'Thales' he is referring to that well digger. Furthermore, suppose there was a hermit who never had any dealings with anyone, who actually held that all was water. Still, when we say 'Thales' we are plainly not referring to that hermit. (Searle, 1984, p. 252)

Today, the original reference, the starting point of a causal chain — the poor well digger — is unknown to us; but an 'omniscient observer of history' capable of following the causal chain to the act of 'primal baptism' would know how to restore the original link connecting the word 'Thales' to its reference. Why is this myth, this antidescriptivist version of the Lacanian 'subject presumed to know', necessary?

The basic problem of antidescriptivism is to determine what constitutes the identity of the designated object beyond the ever-changing cluster of descriptive features — what makes an object identical-to-itself even if all its properties have changed; in other words, how to conceive the objective correlative to the 'rigid designator', to the name in so far as it denotes the same object in all possible worlds, in all counterfactual situations. What is overlooked, at least in the standard version of anti-descriptivism, is that this guaranteeing the identity of an object in all counterfactual situations — through a change of all its descriptive features — is *the retroactive effect of naming itself*: it is the name itself, the signifier, which supports the identity of the object. That 'surplus' in the object which stays the same in all possible worlds is 'something in it more than itself', that is to say the Lacanian *objet petit a*: we search in vain for it in positive reality because it has no positive consistency — because it is just an objectification of a void, of a discontinuity opened in reality by the emergence of the signifier. It is the same with gold: we search in vain in its positive, physical features for that X which makes of it the embodiment of richness; or, to use an example from Marx, it is the same with a commodity: we search in vain among its positive properties for the feature which constitutes its value (and not only its use-value). What is missed by the antidescriptivist idea of an external causal chain of communication through which reference is transmitted is therefore the radical contingency of naming, the fact that naming itself retroactively constitutes its reference. Naming is necessary but it is, so to speak, necessary afterwards, retroactively, once we are already 'in it'.

The role of the myth of the 'omniscient observer of history' therefore corresponds exactly to that of Searle's myth of the primitive tribe: in both cases, its function is to limit, to restrain the radical contingency of naming — to construct an agency guaranteeing its necessity. In the first instance, the reference is guaranteed by the 'intentional content' immanent to the name; in the second, it is guaranteed by the causal chain which brings us to the 'primal baptism' linking the word to the object. If, in this dispute between descriptivism and antidescriptivism, the 'truth' lies, for all that, in antidescriptivism, it is because antidescriptivism's error is of another kind: in its myth, antidescriptivism blinds itself to its own result, to what it 'has produced without knowing it'. The main achievement of antidescriptivism is to enable us to conceive *objet a* as the real–impossible correlative of the 'rigid designator' — that is, of the *point de capiton* as 'pure' signifier.

Rigid Designator and *objet a*

If we maintain that the *point de capiton* is a 'nodal point', a kind of knot of meanings, this does not imply that it is simply the 'richest' word, the word in which is condensed all the richness of meaning of the field it 'quilts': the *point de capiton* is rather the word which, *as a word*, on the level of the signifier itself, unifies a given field, constitutes its identity: it is, so to speak, the word to which 'things' themselves refer to recognize themselves in their unity. Let us take the case of the famous advertisement for Marlboro: the picture of the bronzed cowboy, the wide prairie plains, and so on — all this 'connotes', of course, a certain image of America (the land of hard, honest people, of limitless horizons . . .) but the effect of 'quilting' occurs only when a certain inversion takes place; it does not occur until 'real' Americans start to identify themselves (in their ideological self-experience) with the image created by the Marlboro advertisement — until America itself is experienced as 'Marlboro country'.

It is the same for all so-called 'mass-media symbols' of America — Coca-Cola, for example: the point is not that Coca-Cola 'connotes' a certain ideological experience-vision of America (the freshness of its sharp, cold taste, and so on); the point is that this vision of America itself achieves its identity by identifying itself with the signifier 'Coke' — 'America, this is Coke!' could be the wording of an imbecile publicity device. The crucial point to grasp is that this device — 'America [the ideological vision of a land in all its diversity], this is Coke [this signifier]!' — could not be inverted as 'Coke [this signifier], this is [this means] America!' The only possible answer to the question 'What is Coke?' is already given in the advertisements: it is the impersonal 'it' ('Coke, this is it!') — 'the real thing', the unattainable X, the object-cause of desire.

Precisely because of this surplus-X, the operation of 'quilting' is not circular-symmetrical — we cannot say that we gain nothing from it because Coke first connotes 'the spirit of America', and this 'spirit of America' (the cluster of features supposed to express it) is then condensed in Coke as its signifier, its signifying representative: what we gain from this simple inversion is precisely the surplus-X, the object-cause of desire, that 'unattainable something' which is 'in Coke more than Coke' and which, according to the Lacanian formula, could suddenly change into excrement, into undrinkable mud (it is enough for Coke to be served warm and stale).

The logic of this inversion producing a surplus could be made clear apropos of anti-Semitism: at first, 'Jew' appears as a signifier connoting a cluster of supposedly 'effective' properties (intriguing spirit, greedy for gain, and so on), but this is not yet anti-Semitism proper. To achieve that, we must *invert* the relation and say: they are like that (greedy, intriguing . . .) *because they are Jews*. This inversion seems at first sight purely tautological — we could retort: of course it is so, because 'Jewish' means precisely greedy, intriguing, dirty . . . . But this appearance of tautology is false: 'Jew' in 'because they are Jews' does not connote a series of effective properties, it refers again to that unattainable X, to what is 'in Jew more than Jew' and what Nazism tried so desperately to seize, measure, change into a positive property enabling us to identify Jews in an objective-scientific way.

The 'rigid designator' aims, then, at that impossible-real kernel, at what is 'in an object more than the object', at this surplus produced by the signifying operation. And the crucial point to grasp is the connection between the radical contingency of naming and the logic of emergence of the 'rigid designator' through which a given object achieves its identity. The radical contingency of naming implies an irreducible gap between the Real and modes of its symbolization: a certain historical constellation can be symbolized in different ways; the Real itself contains no necessary mode of its symbolization.

Let us take the defeat of France in 1940: the key to Pétain's success was that his symbolization of the trauma of defeat ('the defeat is a result of a long degenerated tradition of democracy and Jewish antisocial influence; as such, it has a sobering effect in offering France a new chance to build its social body on new, corporatist, organic foundations . . .') prevailed. In this way, what had been experienced a moment ago as traumatic, incomprehensible loss became readable, obtained meaning. But the point is that this symbolization was not inscribed in the Real itself: never do we reach the point at which 'the circumstances themselves begin to speak', the point at which language starts to function immediately as 'language of the Real': the predominance of Pétain's symbolization was a result of a struggle for ideological hegemony.

It is because the Real itself offers no support for a direct symbolization of it — because every symbolization is in the last resort contingent — that the only way the experience of a given historic reality can achieve its unity is through the agency of a signifier, through reference to a 'pure' signifier. It is not the real object which guarantees as the point of reference the unity and identity of a certain ideological experience — on the contrary, it is the reference to a 'pure' signifier which gives unity and identity to our experience of historical reality itself. Historical reality is of course always symbolized; the way we experience it is always mediated through different modes of symbolization: all Lacan adds to this phenomenological common wisdom is the fact that the unity of a given 'experience of meaning', itself the horizon of an ideological field of meaning, is supported by some 'pure', meaningless 'signifier without the signified'.

The Ideological Anamorphosis

We can now see how the Kripkean theory of 'rigid designator' — of a certain pure signifier which designates, and at the same time constitutes, the identity of a given object beyond the variable cluster of its descriptive properties — offers a conceptual apparatus enabling us to conceive precisely the status of Laclau's 'anti-essentialism'. Let us take, for example, notions like 'democracy', 'socialism', 'Marxism': the essentialist illusion consists in the belief that it is possible to determine a definite cluster of features, of positive properties, however minimal, which defines the permanent essence of 'democracy' and similar terms — every phenomenon which pretends to be classified as 'democratic' should fulfil the condition of possessing this cluster of features. In contrast to this 'essentialist illusion', Laclau's anti-essentialism compels us to conclude that it is impossible to define any such essence, any cluster of positive properties which would remain the same in 'all possible worlds' — in all counterfactual situations.

In the last resort, the only way to define 'democracy' is to say that it contains all political movements and organizations which legitimize, designate themselves as 'democratic'; the only way to define 'Marxism' is to say that this term designates all movements and theories which legitimize themselves through reference to Marx, and so on. In other words, the only possible definition of an object in its identity is that this is the object which is always designated by the same signifier — tied to the same signifier. It is the signifier which constitutes the kernel of the object's 'identity'.

Let us return again to 'democracy': is there — on the level of positive, descriptive features — really anything in common between the liberal-individualist notion of democracy and the real-socialist theory, according to which the basic feature of 'real democracy' is the leading role of the Party representing the true interests of the people and thus assuring their effective rule?

Here we should not be misled by the obvious but false solution that the real-socialist notion of democracy is simply wrong, degenerated, a kind of perverse travesty of true democracy — in the final analysis, 'democracy' is defined not by the positive content of this notion (its signified) but only by its positional-relational identity — by its opposition, its differential relation to 'non-democratic' — whereas the concrete content can vary in the extreme: to mutual exclusion (for real socialist Marxists, the term 'democratic' designates the very phenomena which, for a traditional liberalist, are the embodiment of anti-democratic totalitarianism).

This then is the fundamental paradox of the *point de capiton*: the 'rigid designator', which totalizes an ideology by bringing to a halt the metonymic sliding of its signified, is not a point of supreme density of Meaning, a kind of Guarantee which, by being itself excepted from the differential interplay of elements, would serve as a stable and fixed point of reference. On the contrary, it is the element which represents the agency of the signifier within the field of the signified. In itself it is nothing but a 'pure difference': its role is purely structural, its nature is purely performative — its signification coincides with its own act of enunciation; in short, it is a 'signifier without the signified'. The crucial step in the analysis of an ideological edifice is thus to detect, behind the dazzling splendour of the element which holds it together ('God', 'Country', 'Party', 'Class' . . .) this self-referential, tautological, performative operation. A 'Jew', for example, is in the last resort one who is stigmatized with the signifier 'Jew'; all the phantasmic richness of the traits supposed to characterize Jews (avidity, the spirit of intrigue, and so on) is here to conceal not the fact that 'Jews are really not like that', not the empirical reality of Jews, but the fact that in the anti-Semitic construction of a 'Jew', we are concerned with a purely structural function.

The properly 'ideological' dimension is therefore the effect of a certain 'error of perspective': the element which represents within the field of Meaning, the agency of pure signifier — the element through which the signifier's non-sense erupts in the midst of Meaning — is perceived as a point of extreme saturation of Meaning, as the point which 'gives meaning' to all the others and thus totalizes the field of (ideological) meaning. The element which represents, in the structure of the utterance, the immanence of its own process of enunciation is experienced as a kind of transcendent Guarantee, the element which only holds the place of a certain lack, which is in its bodily presence nothing but an embodiment of a certain lack, is perceived as a point of supreme plenitude. In short, *pure difference is perceived as Identity* exempted from the relational–differential interplay and guaranteeing its homogeneity.

We could denote this 'error of perspective' as *ideological anamorphosis*. Lacan often refers to Holbein's 'Ambassadors': if we look at what appears from the frontal view as an extended, 'erected' meaningless spot, from the right perspective we notice the contours of a skull. The criticism of ideology must perform a somewhat homologous operation: if we look at the element which holds together the ideological edifice, at this 'phallic', erected Guarantee of Meaning, from the right (or, more precisely — politically speaking — left) perspective, we are able to recognize in it the embodiment of a lack, of a chasm of non-sense gaping in the midst of ideological meaning.

IDENTIFICATION
(Lower Level of the Graph of Desire)

Retroactivity of Meaning

Now, having clarified the way the *point de capiton* functions as 'rigid designator' — as the signifier maintaining its identity through all variations of its signified — we have reached the real problem: does this totalizing of a given ideological field through the operation of 'quilting', which fixes its meaning, result in the absence of remnants; does it abolish the endless floating of signifiers without residue? If not, how do we conceive the dimension which escapes it? The answer is obtained by the Lacanian graph of desire (cf. Lacan, 1977).

Lacan articulated this graph in four successive forms; in explaining it we should not limit ourselves to the last, complete form, because the succession of the four forms cannot be reduced to a linear gradual completion; it implies the retroactive changing of preceding forms. For example, the last, complete form, containing the articulation of the upper level of the graph (the vector from $S(\emptyset)$ to $S\Diamond D^*$), can be grasped only if we read it as an elaboration of the question '*Che vuoi?*' marked by the preceding form: if we forget that this upper level is nothing but an articulation of the inner structure of a question emanating from the Other to which the subject is confronted beyond symbolic identification, we necessarily miss its point.

Let us then begin with the first form, with the 'elementary cell of desire' (see below). What we have here is simply the graphic presentation of the relation between signifier and signified. As is well known, Saussure visualized this relation as two parallel undulating lines or two surfaces of the same sheet: the linear progression of the signified runs parallel to the

---

*For propaeduetic reasons, we use in this chapter the English transcription of Lacan's mathemes (O, not A, etc.).

Graph I

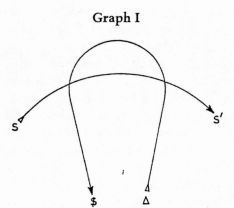

linear articulation of the signifier. Lacan structures this double movement quite differently: some mythical, pre-symbolic intention (marked Δ) 'quilts' the signifier's chain, the series of the signifier marked by the vector S-S'. The product of this quilting (what 'comes out on the other side' after the mythical — real — intention goes through the signifier and steps out of it) is the subject marked by the matheme $ (the divided, split subject, and at the same time the effaced signifier, the lack of signifier, the void, an empty space in the signifier's network). This minimal articulation already attests to the fact that we are dealing with the process of *interpellation of individuals* (this pre-symbolic, mythical entity — with Althusser, too, the 'individual' which is interpellated into subject is not conceptually defined, it is simply a hypothetical X which must be presupposed) *into subjects*. The *point de capiton* is the point through which the subject is 'sewn' to the signifier, and at the same time the point which interpellates individual into subject by addressing it with the call of a certain master-signifier ('Communism', 'God', 'Freedom', 'America') — in a word, it is the point of the subjectivation of the signifier's chain.

A crucial feature at this elementary level of the graph is the fact that the vector of the subjective intention quilts the vector of the signifier's chain backwards, in a retroactive direction: it steps out of the chain at a point *preceding* the point at which it has pierced it. Lacan's emphasis is precisely on this retroactive character of the effect of signification with respect to the signifier, on this staying behind of the signified with respect to the progression of the signifier's chain: the effect of meaning is always produced backwards, *après coup*. Signifiers which are still in a 'floating' state — whose signification is not yet fixed — follow one another. Then, at a certain point — precisely the point at which the intention pierces the signifiers's chain, traverses it — some signifier fixes retroactively the meaning of the chain, sews the meaning to the signifier, halts the sliding of the meaning.

To grasp this fully, we have only to remember the above-mentioned example of ideological 'quilting': in the ideological space float signifiers like 'freedom', 'state', 'justice', 'peace' . . . and then their chain is supplemented with some master-signifier ('Communism') which retroactively determines their (Communist) meaning: 'freedom' is effective only through surmounting the bourgeois formal freedom, which is merely a form of slavery; the 'state' is the means by which the ruling class guarantees the conditions of its rule; market exchange cannot be 'just and equitable' because the very form of equivalent exchange between labour and capital implies exploitation; 'war' is inherent to class society as such; only the socialist revolution can bring about lasting 'peace', and so forth. (Liberal-democratic 'quilting' would, of course, produce a quite different articulation of meaning; conservative 'quilting' a meaning opposed to both previous fields, and so on).

Already, at this elementary level, we can locate the logic of transference — the basic mechanism that produces the illusion proper to the phenomena of transference: transference is the obverse of the staying behind of the signified with respect to the stream of the signifiers; it consists of the illusion that the meaning of a certain element (which was retroactively fixed by the intervention of the master-signifier) was present in it from the very beginning as its immanent essence. We are 'in transference' when it appears to us that real freedom is 'in its very nature' opposed to bourgeois formal freedom, that the state is 'in its very nature' only a tool of class domination, and so on. The paradox lies, of course, in the fact that this transferential illusion is necessary, it is the very measure of success of the operation of 'quilting': the *capitonnage* is successful only in so far as it effaces its own traces.

The 'Effect of Retroversion'

This therefore is the fundamental Lacanian thesis concerning the relation between signifier and signified: instead of the linear, immanent, necessary progression according to which meaning unfolds itself from some initial kernel, we have a radically contingent process of retroactive production of meaning. In this way, we have arrived at the second form of the graph of desire — at the specification of the two points at which the intention (Δ) cuts the signifying chain: O and s(O), the big Other and the signified as its function:

Graph II

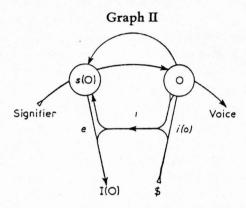

Why do we find O — that is, the big Other as the synchronous symbolic code — at the *point de capiton*? Is not the *point de capiton* precisely the One, a singular signifier occupying an exceptional place with respect to the paradigmatic network of the code? To understand this apparent incoherence, we have only to remember that the *point de capiton* fixes the meaning of the preceding elements: that is to say, it retroactively submits them to some code, it regulates their mutual relations according to this code (for example, in the case we mentioned, according to the code which regulates the Communist universe of meaning). We could say that the *point de capiton* represents, holds the place of, the big Other, the synchronous code, in the diachronic signifier's chain: a proper Lacanian paradox in which a synchronous, paradigmatic *structure* exists only in so far as it is itself again embodied in One, in an exceptional singular *element*.

From what we have just said, it is also clear why the other cross point of the two vectors is marked by s(O): at this point we find the signified, the meaning, which is a function of the big Other — which is produced as a retroactive effect of 'quilting', backwards from the point at which the relation between floating signifiers is fixed through reference to the synchronous symbolic code.

And why is the right, last part of the vector of the signifier S-S' — the part subsequent to the *point de capiton* — designated as 'voice'? To solve this enigma, we must conceive the voice in a strictly Lacanian way: not as a bearer of plenitude and self-presence of meaning (as with Derrida) but as a meaningless *object*, as an objectal remnant, leftover, of the signifying operation, of the *capitonnage*: the voice is what is left over after we subtract from the signifier the retroactive operation of 'quilting' which produces meaning. The clearest concrete embodiment of this objectal status of the voice is the hypnotic voice: when the same word is repeated to us indefinitely we become disorientated, the word loses the last traces of its meaning, all that is left is its inert presence exerting a kind of somniferous hypnotic power — this is the voice as 'object', as the objectal leftover of the signifying operation.

There is yet another feature of the second form of the graph to be explained: the change at its bottom. Instead of the mythical intention (Δ) and the subject (δ) produced when this intention traverses the signifying chain, we have at the bottom right the subject which pierces the signifying chain, and the product of this operation is now marked as I(O). So, first: why is the subject displaced from left (result) to right (starting point of the vector)? Lacan himself points out that we are dealing here with the 'effect of retroversion' — with the transferential illusion according to which the subject becomes at every stage 'what it always already was': a retroactive effect is experienced as something which was already there from the beginning. Second point: why have we now at the bottom left, as the result of the subject's vector, I(O)? Here we have finally arrived at *identification*: I(O) stands for symbolic identification, for the identification of the subject with some signifying feature, trait (I), in the big Other, in the symbolic order.

This feature is the one which, according to the Lacanian definition of the signifier, 'represents the subject for another signifier'; it assumes concrete, recognizable shape in a name or in a mandate that the subject takes upon himself and/or that is bestowed on him. This symbolic identification is to be distinguished from imaginary identification marked by a new level inserted between the vector of the signifier (S-S') and the symbolic identification: the axis connecting imaginary ego (*e*) and its imaginary other, *i(o)* — to achieve self-identity, the subject must identify himself with the imaginary other, he must alienate himself — put his identity outside himself, so to speak, into the image of his double.

The 'effect of retroversion' is based precisely upon this imaginary level — it is supported by the illusion of the self as the autonomous agent which is present from the very beginning as the origin of its acts: this imaginary self-experience is for the subject the way to misrecognize his radical dependence on the big Other, on the symbolic order as his decentred cause. But instead of repeating this thesis of the ego's constitutive alienation in its imaginary Other — the Lacanian theory of the mirror stage which is to be situated precisely on the axis *e-i(o)* — we should rather focus our attention on the crucial difference between imaginary and symbolic identification.

Image and Gaze

The relation between imaginary and symbolic identification — between the ideal ego [*Idealich*] and the ego-ideal [*Ich-Ideal*] — is — to use the distinction made by Jacques-Alain Miller (in his unpublished Seminar) — that between 'constituted' and 'constitutive' identification: to put it simply, imaginary identification is identification with the image in which we appear likeable to ourselves, with the image representing 'what we would like to be', and symbolic identification, identification with the very place *from where* we are being observed, *from where* we look at ourselves so that we appear to ourselves likeable, worthy of love.

Our predominant, spontaneous idea of identification is that of imitating models, ideals, image-makers: it is noted (usually from the condescending 'mature' perspective) how young people identify with popular heroes, pop singers, film stars, sportsmen. . . . This spontaneous notion is doubly misleading. First, the feature, the trait on the basis of which we identify with someone, is usually hidden — it is by no means necessarily a glamorous feature.

Neglecting this paradox can lead to serious political miscalculations; let us mention only the 1986 Austrian presidential campaign, with the controversial figure of Waldheim at its centre. Starting from the assumption that Waldheim was attracting voters because of his great-statesman image, leftists put the emphasis of their campaign on proving to the public that not only is Waldheim a man with a dubious past (probably involved in war crimes) but also a man who is not prepared to confront his past, a man who evades crucial questions concerning it — in short, a man whose basic feature is a refusal to 'work through' the traumatic past. What they overlooked was that it was precisely this feature with which the majority of centrist voters identified. Post-war Austria is a country whose very existence is based on a refusal to 'work through' its traumatic Nazi past — proving that Waldheim was evading confrontation with his past emphasized the exact trait-of-identification of the majority of voters.

The theoretical lesson to be learned from this is that the trait-of-identification can also be a certain failure, weakness, guilt of the other, so that by pointing out the failure we can unwittingly reinforce the identification. Rightist ideology in particular is very adroit at offering people weakness or guilt as an identifying trait: we find traces of this even with Hitler. In his public appearances, people specifically identified themselves with what were hysterical outbursts of impotent rage — that is, they 'recognized' themselves in this hysterical *acting out.*

But the second, even more serious error is to overlook the fact that imaginary identification is always identification *on behalf of a certain gaze in the Other*. So, apropos of every imitation of a model-image, apropos of every 'playing a role', the question to ask is: *for whom* is the subject enacting this role? Which *gaze* is considered when the subject identifies himself with a certain image? This gap between the way I see myself and the point from which I am being observed to appear likeable to myself is crucial for grasping hysteria (and obsessional neurosis as its subspecies) — for so-called hysterical theatre: when we take the hysterical woman in the act of such a theatrical outburst, it is of course clear that she is doing this to offer herself to the Other as the object of its desire, but concrete analysis has to discover who — which subject — embodies for her the Other. Behind an extremely 'feminine' imaginary figure, we can thus generally discover some kind of masculine, paternal identification: she is enacting fragile femininity, but on the symbolic level she is in fact identified with the paternal gaze, to which she wants to appear likeable.

This gap is brought to its extreme with the obsessional neurotic: on the 'constituted', imaginary, phenomenal level he is of course caught in the masochistic logic of his compulsive acts, he is humiliating himself, preventing his success, organizing his failure, and so on; but the crucial question is again how to locate the vicious, superego gaze for which he is humiliating himself, for which this obsessional organizing of failure procures pleasure. This gap can best be articulated with the help of the Hegelian couple 'for-the-other'/'for-itself': the hysterical neurotic is experiencing himself as somebody who is enacting a role *for the other*, his imaginary identification is his 'being-for-the-other', and the crucial break that psychoanalysis must accomplish is to induce him to realize how he is *himself* this other for whom he is enacting a role — how his being-for-the-other is his being-for-himself, because he is himself already symbolically identified with the gaze for which he is playing his role.

To make this difference between imaginary and symbolic identification clear, let us take some non-clinical examples. In his piercing analysis of Chaplin, Eisenstein exposed as a crucial feature of his burlesques a vicious, sadistic, humiliating attitude towards children: in Chaplin's films, children are not treated with the usual sweetness: they are teased, mocked, laughed at for their failures, food is scattered for them as if they were chickens, and so on. The question to ask here, however, is from which point must we look at children so that they appear to us as objects of teasing and mocking, not gentle creatures needing protection? The answer, of course, is *the gaze of the children themselves* — only children themselves treat their fellows this way; sadistic distance towards children thus implies the symbolic identification with the gaze of the children themselves.

At the opposite extreme, we find the Dickensian admiration of the 'good common people', the imaginary identification with their poor but happy, close, unspoiled world, free of the cruel struggle for power and money. But (and therein lies the falsity of Dickens) from where is the Dickensian gaze peering at the 'good common people' so that they appear likeable; from where if not from the point of view of the corrupted world of power and money? We perceive the same gap in the Brueghel's late idyllic paintings of scenes from peasant life (country festivity, reapers during midday rest, and so on): Arnold Hauser pointed out that these paintings are as far removed as possible from any real plebeian attitude, from any mingling with the working classes. Their gaze is, on the contrary, the external gaze of the aristocracy upon the peasant's idyll, not the gaze of the peasants themselves upon their life.

The same goes, of course, for the Stalinist elevation of the dignity of the socialist 'ordinary working people': this idealized image of the working class is staged for the gaze of the ruling Party bureaucracy — it serves to legitimize their rule. That is why Milos Forman's Czech films were so subversive in mocking small, ordinary people: in showing their undignified ways, the futility of their dreams ... this gesture was far more dangerous than making fun of the ruling bureaucracy. Forman did not want to destroy the bureaucrat's imaginary identification; he wisely preferred to subvert his symbolic identification by unmasking the spectacle enacted for his gaze.

From *i(o)* to I(O)

This difference between *i(o)* and I(O) — between ideal ego and ego-ideal — can be further exemplified by the way nicknames function in American and Soviet culture. Let us take two individuals, each of whom represents the supreme achievement of these two cultures: Charles 'Lucky' Luciano and Iosif Vissarionovich Dzhugashvili 'Stalin'. In the first case the nickname tends to replace the first name (we usually speak simply of 'Lucky Luciano'), while in the second it regularly replaces the family name ('Iosif Vissarionovich Stalin'). In the first case the nickname alludes to some extraordinary event which has marked the individual (Charles Luciano was 'lucky' to have survived the savage torture of his gangster enemies) — it alludes, that is, to a positive, descriptive feature which fascinates us; it marks something that sticks out on the individual, something that offers itself to our gaze, something seen, not the point from which we observe the individual.

However, in the case of Iosif Vissarionovich, it would be entirely erroneous to conclude in a homologous way that 'Stalin' (Russian for '[made] of steel') alludes to some steely, inexorable characteristic of Stalin himself: what is really inexorable and steely are the laws of the historical progress, the iron necessity of the disintegration of capitalism and of the passage to socialism in the name of which Stalin, this empirical individual, is acting — the perspective from which he is observing himself and judging his activity. We could say, then, that 'Stalin' is the ideal point from which 'Iosif Vissarionovich', this empirical individual, this person of flesh and blood, is observing himself so that he appears likeable.

We find the same split in a late writing of Rousseau, from the time of his psychotic delirium, entitled *'Jean-Jacques jugé par Rousseau'* (Jean-Jacques judged by Rousseau). It would be possible to conceive this as a draft of the Lacanian theory of forename and family name: the first name designates the ideal ego, the point of imaginary identification, while the family name comes from the father — it designates, as the Name-of-the-Father, the point of symbolic identification, the agency through which we observe and judge ourselves. The fact that should not be overlooked in this distinction is that $i(o)$ is always already subordinated to $I(O)$: it is the symbolic identification (the point from which we are observed) which dominates and determines the image, the imaginary form in which we appear to ourselves likeable. On the level of formal functioning, this subordination is attested by the fact that the nickname which marks $i(o)$ also functions as a rigid designator, not as a simple description.

To take another example from the domain of gangsters: if a certain individual is nicknamed 'Scarface', this does not signify only the simple fact that his face is full of scars; it implies at the same time that we are dealing with somebody who is designated as 'Scarface' and will remain so even if, for example, all his scars were removed by plastic surgery. Ideological designations function in the same way: 'Communism' means (in the perspective of the Communist, of course) progress in democracy and freedom, even if — on the factual, descriptive level — the political regime legitimized as 'Communist' produces extremely repressive and tyrannical phenomena. To use Kripke's terms again: 'Communism' designates in all possible worlds, in all counterfactual situations, 'democracy-and-freedom', and that is why this connection cannot be refuted empirically, through reference to a factual state of things. The analysis of ideology must then direct its attention to the points at which names which *prima facie* signify positive descriptive features already function as 'rigid designators'.

But why precisely is this difference between how we see ourselves and the point from which we are being observed the difference between imaginary and symbolic? In a first approach, we could say that in imaginary identification we imitate the other at the level of resemblance — we identify ourselves with the image of the other inasmuch as we are 'like him', while in symbolic identification we identify ourselves with the other precisely at a point at which he is inimitable, at the point which eludes resemblance. To explain this crucial distinction, let us take Woody Allen's film *Play it Again, Sam*. The movie starts with the famous final scene from *Casablanca*, but soon afterwards we notice that this was only a 'film-within-a-film' and that the real story concerns a New York hysterical intellectual whose sex life is a mess: his wife has just left him; throughout the film, a Humphrey Bogart figure appears to him: advising him, making ironic comments on his behaviour, and so on.

The end of the film resolves his relation to the Bogart figure: after spending the night with his best friend's wife, the hero has a dramatic meeting with both of them at the airport; he renounces her and lets her go with her husband, thus repeating in real life the final scene from *Casablanca* which opened the film. When his lover says of his parting words 'It's beautiful', he answers: 'It's from *Casablanca*. I waited my whole life to say it.' After this denouement the Bogart figure appears for the last time, saying that by renouncing a woman because of a friendship the hero finally 'got some style'; and no longer needs him.

How should we read this withdrawal of the Bogart figure? The most obvious reading would be the one indicated by the final words of the hero to the Bogart figure 'I guess the secret is not being you, it's being me.' In other words, as long as the hero is a weak, frail hysteric he needs an ideal ego to identify with, a figure to guide him; but as soon as he finally matures and 'gets some style' he no longer needs an external point of identification because he has achieved identity with himself — he 'has become himself', an autonomous personality. But the words that follow the quoted phrase immediately subvert such a reading: 'True, you're not too tall and kind of ugly, but what the hell, I'm short enough and ugly enough to succeed on my own.'

In other words, far from 'outgrowing identification with Bogart', it is when he becomes an 'autonomous personality' that the hero really identifies with Bogart — more precisely: he becomes an 'autonomous personality' *through* his identification with Bogart. The only difference is that now identification is no longer imaginary (Bogart as a model to imitate) but, at least in its fundamental dimension, symbolic — that is, structural: the hero realizes this identification by enacting in reality Bogart's role from *Casablanca* — by assuming a certain 'mandate', by occupying a certain place in the intersubjective symbolic network (sacrificing a woman for friendship . . .). It is this symbolic identification that dissolves the imaginary identification (makes the Bogart figure disappear) — more precisely: that radically changes its contents. On the imaginary level, the hero can now identify with Bogart through features which are repellent: his smallness, his ugliness.

BEYOND IDENTIFICATION
(Upper Level of the Graph of Desire)

'Che vuoi?'

This interplay of imaginary and symbolic identification under the domination of symbolic identification constitutes the mechanism by means of which the subject is integrated into a given socio-symbolic field — the way he/she assumes certain 'mandates', as was perfectly clear to Lacan himself:

> Lacan knew how to extract from Freud's text the difference between ideal ego, marked by him *i*, and ego-ideal, I. On the level of I, you can without difficulties introduce the social. The I of the ideal can be in a superior and legitimate way constructed as a social and ideological function. It was moreover Lacan himself who did this in his *Écrits*: he situates a certain politics in the very foundations of psychology, so that the thesis that all psychology is social can be treated as Lacanian. If not on the level at which we are examining *i*, then at least on the level at which we fix I. (Miller, 1987, p. 21)

The only problem is that this 'square of the circle' of interpellation, this circular movement between symbolic and imaginary identification, never comes out without a certain leftover. After every 'quilting' of the signifier's chain which retroactively fixes its meaning, there always remains a certain gap, an opening which is rendered in the third form of the graph by the famous '*Che vuoi?*' —'You're telling me that, but what do you want with it, what are you aiming at?':

Graph III

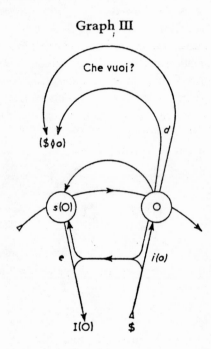

This question mark arising above the curve of 'quilting' thus indicates the persistence of a gap between utterance and its enunciation: at the level of utterance you're saying this, but what do you want to tell me with it, through it? (In the established terms of speech acts theory, we could of course denote this gap as the difference between locution and the illocutionary force of a given utterance.) And it is at this exact place of the question arising above the utterance, at the place of 'Why are you telling me this?', that we have to locate *desire* (small *d* in the graph) in its difference to demand: you demand something of me, but what do you really want, what are you aiming at through this demand? This split between demand and desire is what defines the position of the hysterical subject: according to the classic Lacanian formula, the logic of the hysterical demand is 'I'm demanding this of you, but what I'm really demanding of you is to refute my demand because this is not it!'

It is this intuition which is behind the ill-famed male chauvinist wisdom that 'woman is a whore': woman is a whore because we never really know what she means — for example, she says 'No!' to our advances, but we can never be sure that this 'No!' does not really mean a double 'Yes!' — an appeal to an even more aggressive approach; in this case, her real desire is the very opposite of her demand. In other words, 'woman is a whore' is a vulgar version of the unanswerable Freudian question '*Was will das Weib?*' ('What does the woman want?').

The same intuition is probably at work behind another common wisdom, which tells us that politics is also a whore: it is not simply that the domain of politics is corrupted, treacherous, and so on; the point is rather that every political demand is always caught in a dialectics in which it aims at something other than its literal meaning: for example, it can function as a provocation intending to be refused (in which case the best way to frustrate it is to comply with it, to consent to it without reservation). As is well known, this was Lacan's reproach to the students' revolt of 1968: that is was basically a hysterical rebellion asking for a new Master.

This '*Che vuoi?*' is perhaps best illustrated by the starting point of Hitchcock's film *North by Northwest*. To lead the Russian agents off the right track, the CIA invents a nonexistent agent named George Kaplan. Rooms are reserved for him in hotels, phone calls are made in his name, plane tickets purchased, and so on — all this to convince the Russian agents that Kaplan really exists, when in reality it is just a void, a name without a bearer. At the beginning of the film the hero, an ordinary American named Roger O. Thornhill, finds himself in the lounge of a hotel under observation by the Russians because the mysterious Kaplan is supposed to be staying there. A hotel clerk enters the lounge saying: 'Phone call for Mr Kaplan. Is Mr Kaplan here?' Exactly at that same moment, by pure coincidence, Thornhill makes a sign to this clerk, wanting to send a telegram to his mother. The Russians who are overseeing the scene mistake him for Kaplan. When he wants to leave the hotel they kidnap him, take him to a lonely villa, and ask him to tell them all about his espionage work. Of course, Thornhill knows nothing about it, but his professions of innocence pass for a double game.

Where lies the — one might call it — psychologically convincing nature of this scene, based nevertheless on an almost unbelievable coincidence? Thornhill's situation corresponds to a fundamental situation of a human being as a being-of-language (*parlêtre*, to use Lacan's condensed writing). The subject is always fastened, pinned, to a signifier which represents him for the other, and through this pinning he is loaded with a symbolic mandate, he is given a place in the intersubjective network of symbolic relations. The point is that this mandate is ultimately always arbitrary: since its nature is performative, it cannot be accounted for by reference to the 'real' properties and capacities of the subject. So, loaded with this mandate, the subject is automatically confronted with a certain '*Che vuoi?*', with a question of the Other. The Other is addressing him as if he himself possesses the answer to the question of why he has this mandate, but the question is, of course, unanswerable. The subject does not know why he is occupying this place in the symbolic network. His own answer to this '*Che vuoi?*' of the Other can only be the hysterical question 'Why am I what I'm supposed to be, why have I this mandate? Why am I . . . [a teacher, a master, a king . . . or George Kaplan]?' Briefly: '*Why am I what you [the big Other] are saying that I am?*'

And the final moment of the psychoanalytic process is, for the analysand, precisely when he gets rid of this question — that is, when he accepts his being as *non-justified by the big Other*. This is why psycho-analysis began with the interpretation of hysterical symptoms, why its 'native soil' was the experience of female hysteria: in the last resort, what is hysteria if not precisely the effect and testimony of a failed inter-pellation; what is the hysterical question if not an articulation of the incapacity of the subject to fulfil the symbolic identification, to assume fully and without restraint the symbolic mandate? Lacan formulates the hysterical question as a certain 'Why am I what you're telling me that I am?' — that is, which is that surplus-object in me that caused the Other to interpellate me, to 'hail' me as . . . [king, master, wife . . .]?' (Lacan, 1981, p. 315.) The hysterical question opens the gap of what is 'in the subject more than the subject', of the *object in subject* which resists inter-pellation — subordination of the subject, its inclusion in the symbollic network.

Perhaps the strongest artistic depiction of this moment of hysteri-cization is Rossetti's famous painting 'Ecce Ancilla Domini', showing Mary at the very moment of interpellation — when the Archangel Gabriel reveals to her her mission: to conceive immaculately and to give birth to the son of God. How does Mary react to this astonishing message, to this original 'Hail Mary'? The painting shows her frightened, with a bad conscience, withdrawing from the archangel into a corner, as if asking herself 'Why was I selected for this stupid mission? Why me?

What does this repulsive ghost really want of me?' The exhausted, pale face and the dark eyeteeth are telltale enough: we have before us a woman with a turbulent sex life, a licentious sinner — in short, an Eve-like figure; and the painting depicts 'Eve interpellated into Mary', her hysterical reaction to it.

Martin Scorsese's film *The Last Temptation of Christ* goes a step further in this direction: its theme is simply the *hystericization of Jesus Christ himself*; it shows us an ordinary, carnal, passionate man discovering gradually, with fascination and horror, that he is the son of God, bearer of the dreadful but magnificent mission to redeem humanity through his sacrifice. The problem is that he cannot come to terms with this interpellation: the meaning of his 'temptations' lies precisely in the hysterical resistance to his mandate, in his doubts about it, in his attempts to evade it even when he is already nailed to the cross.[1]

The Jew and Antigone

We come across this '*Che vuoi?*' everywhere in the political domain, including the 1988 American election struggle in which, after Jesse Jackson's first successes, the press started to ask 'What does Jackson really want?' Overtones of racism were easy to detect in this question, because it was never raised about other candidates. The conclusion that we are here dealing with racism is further confirmed by the fact that this '*Che vuoi?*' erupts most violently in the purest, so to say distilled form of racism, in anti-Semitism: in the anti-Semitic perspective, the Jew is precisely a person about whom it is never clear 'what he really wants' — that is, his actions are always suspected of being guided by some hidden motives (the Jewish conspiracy, world domination and the moral cor-ruption of Gentiles, and so on). The case of anti-Semitism also illustrates perfectly why Lacan put, at the end of the curve designating the question '*Che vuoi?*' the formula of fantasy ($\$ \lozenge o$): fantasy is an *answer* to this '*Che vuoi?*'; it is an attempt to fill out the gap of the question with an answer. In the case of anti-Semitism, the answer to 'What does the Jew want?' is a fantasy of 'Jewish conspiracy': a mysterious power of Jews to manipulate events, to pull the strings behind the scenes. The crucial point that must be made here on a theoretical level is that fantasy functions as a construction, as an imaginary scenario filling out the void, the opening of the *desire of the Other*: by giving us a definite answer to the question 'What does the Other want?', it enables us to evade the unbearable deadlock in which the Other wants something from us, but we are at the same time incapable of translating this desire of the Other into a positive interpellation, into a mandate with which to identify.

Now we can also understand why it has been the Jews who have been chosen as the object of racism *par excellence*: is not the Jewish God the purest embodiment of this '*Che vuoi?*', of the desire of the Other in its terrifying abyss, with the formal prohibition to 'make an image of God' — to fill out the gap of the Other's desire with a positive fantasy-scenario? Even when, as in the case of Abraham, this God pronounces a concrete demand (ordering Abraham to slaughter his own son), it remains quite open what he really wants with it: to say that with this horrible act Abraham must attest to his infinite trust and devotion to God is already an inadmissible simplification. The basic position of a Jewish believer is, then, that of Job: not so much lamentation as incomprehension, perplexity, even horror at what the Other (God) wants with the series of calamities that are being inflicted upon him.

This horrified perplexity marks the initial, founding relationship of the Jewish believer to God, the pact that God concluded with the Jewish people. The fact that Jews perceive themselves as the 'chosen people' has nothing to do with a belief in their superiority; they do not possess any special qualities; before the pact with God they were a people like any other, no more and no less corrupted, living their ordinary life — when suddenly, like a traumatic flash, they came to know (through Moses . . .) that the Other had chosen them. The choice was thus not at the beginning, it did not determine the 'original character' of the Jews — to use Kripkean terminology again, it has nothing to do with their descriptive features. Why were they chosen, why did they suddenly find themselves occupying the position of a debtor towards God? What does God really want from them? The answer is — to repeat the paradoxical formula of the prohibition of incest — impossible and prohibited at the same time.

In other words, the Jewish position could be denoted as a position of *God beyond — or prior to — the Holy*, in contrast to the pagan affirmation of the Holy as prior to gods. This strange god that occludes the dimension of the Holy is not the 'philosopher's god', the rational manager of the universe rendering impossible sacred ecstasy as a means of communication with him: it is simply the unbearable point of the desire of the Other, of the gap, the void in the Other concealed by the fascinating presence of the Holy. Jews persist in this enigma of the Other's desire, in this traumatic point of pure '*Che vuoi?*' which provokes an unbearable anxiety insofar as it cannot be symbolized, 'gentrified', through sacrifice or loving devotion.

It is precisely at this level that we should situate the break between Christianity and the Jewish religion — the fact that in contrast to the Jewish religion of *anxiety*, Christianity is a religion of *love*. The term 'love' is to be conceived here as articulated in Lacanian theory — that is, in its dimension of fundamental deception: we try to fill out the unbearable gap of '*Che vuoi?*', the opening of the Other's desire, by offering ourselves to the Other as the object of its desire. In this sense love is, as Lacan pointed out, an interpretation of the desire of the Other: the answer of love is 'I am what is lacking in you; with my devotion to you, with my sacrifice for you, I will fill you out, I will complete you.' The operation of love is therefore double: the subject fills in his own lack by offering himself to the other as the object filling out the lack in the Other — love's deception is that this overlapping of two lacks annuls lack as such in a mutual completion.

Christianity is therefore to be conceived as an attempt to 'gentrify' the Jewish '*Che vuoi?*' through the act of love and sacrifice. The greatest possible sacrifice, the Crucifixion, the death of the son of God, is precisely the final proof that God-Father loves us with an all-embracing, infinite love, thereby delivering us from the anxiety of '*Che vuoi?*'. The Passion of Christ, this fascinating image which cancels all other images, this fantasy-scenario which condenses all the libidinal economy of the Christian religion, acquires its meaning only against the background of the unbearable enigma of the desire of the Other (God).

We are, of course, far from implying that Christianity entails a kind of return to the pagan relationship of man to god: that this is not so is already attested by the fact that, contrary to superficial appearance, Christianity follows the Jewish religion in occluding the dimension of the Holy. What we do find in Christianity is something of quite another order: the idea of the *saint*, which is the exact opposite of the *priest* in service of the Holy. The priest is a 'functionary of the Holy'; there is no Holy without its officials, without the bureaucratic machinery supporting it, organizing its ritual, from the Aztec's official of human sacrifice to the modern sacred state or army rituals. The saint, on the contrary, occupies the place of *objet petit a*, of pure object, of somebody undergoing radical subjective destitution. He enacts no ritual, he conjures nothing, he just persists in his inert presence.

We can now understand why Lacan saw in Antigone a forerunner of Christ's sacrifice: in her persistence, Antigone is a saint, definitely not a priestess. This is why we must oppose all attempts to domesticate her, to tame her by concealing the frightening strangeness, 'inhumanity', *a-pathetic* character of her figure, making of her a gentle protectress of family and household who evokes our compassion and offers herself as a point of identification. In Sophocles' *Antigone*, the figure with which we can identify is her sister Ismene — kind, considerate, sensitive, prepared to give way and compromise, pathetic, 'human', in contrast to Antigone, who goes to the limit, who 'doesn't give way on her desire' (Lacan) and becomes, in this persistence in the 'death drive', in the being-towards-death, frighteningly ruthless, exempted from the circle of everyday feelings and considerations, passions and fears. In other words, it is Antigone herself who necessarily evokes in us, pathetic everyday compassionate creatures, the question 'What does she really want?', the question which precludes any identification with her.

In European literature, the couple Antigone-Ismene repeats itself in de Sade's work, in the shape of the couple Juliette-Justine: here, Justine is likewise a pathetic victim, as opposed to Juliette, this a-pathetic rake who also 'doesn't give way on her desire'. Finally, why should we not locate a third version of the couple Antigone-Ismene in Margaretha von Trotta's film *The Times of Plumb*, in the couple of the RAF (Red Army Fraction)-terrorist (based on the model of Gudrun Ensslin) and her pathetic-compassionate sister who 'tries to understand her' and from whose viewpoint the story is told. (The Schlöndorf episode in the omnibus film *Germany in Autumn* was based on the parallel between Antigone and Gudrun Ensslin.)

Three at first sight totally incompatible figures: the dignified Antigone sacrificing herself for her brother's memory; the promiscuous Juliette giving herself over to enjoyment beyond all limits (that is precisely beyond the limit at which enjoyment still gives pleasure); the fanatical-ascetic Gudrun wanting to awaken the world from its everyday pleasures and routines with her terrorist acts — Lacan enables us to recognize in all three the same ethical position, that of 'not giving way on one's desire'. That is why all three of them provoke the same '*Che vuoi?*', the same 'What do they really want?': Antigone with her obstinate persistence, Juliette with her a-pathetic promiscuity, Gudrun with her 'senseless' terrorist acts: all three put in question the Good embodied in the State and common morals.

Fantasy as a Screen for the Desire of the Other

Fantasy appears, then, as an answer to '*Che vuoi?*', to the unbearable enigma of the desire of the Other, of the lack in the Other; but it is at the same time fantasy itself which, so to speak, provides the co-ordinates of our desire — which constructs the frame enabling us to desire something. The usual definition of fantasy ('an imagined scenario representing the realization of desire') is therefore somewhat misleading, or at least ambiguous: in the fantasy-scene the desire is not fulfilled, 'satisfied', but constituted (given its objects, and so on) — *through fantasy, we learn 'how to desire'*. In this intermediate position lies the paradox of fantasy: it is the frame co-ordinating our desire, but at the same time a defence against '*Che vuoi?*', a screen concealing the gap, the abyss of the desire of the Other. Sharpening the paradox to its utmost — to tautology — we could say that *desire itself is a defence against desire*: the desire structured through fantasy is a defence against the desire of the Other, against this 'pure', trans-phantasmic desire (i.e. the 'death drive' in its pure form).

We can now see why the maxim of psychoanalytic ethics as formu-lated by Lacan ('not to give way on one's desire') coincides with the closing moment of the psychoanalytic process, the 'going through the fantasy': the desire with regard to which we must not 'give way' is not the desire supported by fantasy but the desire of the Other beyond fantasy. 'Not to give way on desire' implies a radical renunication of all the rich-ness of desires based upon fantasy-scenarios. In the psychoanalytic process, this desire of the Other assumes the form of the analyst's desire: the analysand tries at first to evade its abyss by means of transference — that is, by means of offering himself as the object of the analyst's love; the 'dissolution of transference' takes place when the analysand renounces filling out the void, the lack in the Other. (We find a logic homologous to the paradox of desire as defence against desire in the Lacanian thesis that the cause is always the cause of something which goes wrong, which is amiss [the French 'ça cloche': it limps]: it could be said that causality — the usual, 'normal' linear chain of causes — is a defence against the cause with which we are concerned in psychoanalysis; this cause appears precisely where 'normal' causality fails, breaks down. For example, when we make a slip of the tongue, when we say something other than what we intended to say — that is, when the causal chain regulating our 'normal' speech activity breaks down — at this point that question of the cause is imposed upon us: 'Why did it happen?')

The way fantasy functions can be explained through reference to

Kant's *Critique of Pure Reason*: the role of fantasy in the economy of desire is homologous to that of transcendental schematism in the process of knowledge (Baas, 1987). In Kant, transcendental schematism is a mediator, an intermediary agency between empirical content (contingent, inner-worldly, empirical objects of experience) and the network of transcendental categories: it is the name of the mechanism through which empirical objects are included in the network of transcendental categories which determine the way we perceive and conceive them (as substances with properties, submitted to causal links, and so on). A homologous mechanism is at work with fantasy: how does an empirical, positively given object become an object of desire; how does it begin to contain some X, some unknown quality, something which is 'in it more than it' and makes it worthy of our desire? By entering the framework of fantasy, by being included in a fantasy-scene which gives consistency to the subject's desire.

Let us take Hitchcock's *Rear Window*: the window through which James Stewart, disabled and confined to a wheelchair, gazes continually is clearly a fantasy-window — his desire is fascinated by what he can see through the window. And the problem of the unfortunate Grace Kelly is that by proposing to him she acts as an obstacle, a stain disturbing his view through the window, instead of fascinating him with her beauty. How does she succeed, finally, in becoming worthy of his desire? By literally entering the frame of his fantasy; by crossing the courtyard and appearing 'on the other side' where he can see her *through the window*. When Stewart sees her in the murderer's appartment his gaze is immediately fascinated, greedy, desirous of her: she has found her place in his fantasy-space. This would be Lacan's 'male chauvinist' lesson: man can relate to woman only in so far as she enters the frame of his fantasy.

At a certain naïve level, this is not unknown to the psychoanalytic doxa which claims that every man seeks, in a woman he chooses as his sexual partner, his mother's substitute: a man falls in love with a woman when some feature of her reminds him of his mother. The only thing Lacan adds to this traditional view is to emphasize its usually overlooked *negative* dimension: in fantasy, mother is *reduced* to a limited set of (symbolic) features; as soon as an object *too close* to the Mother-Thing — an object which is not linked with the maternal Thing only through certain reduced features but is immediately attached to it — appears in the fantasy-frame, the desire is suffocated in incestuous claustrophobia. Here we again encounter the paradoxical intermediate role of fantasy: it is a construction enabling us to seek maternal substitutes, but at the same

time a screen shielding us from getting too close to the maternal Thing
— keeping us at a distance from it. This is why it would be wrong to
conclude that any empirical, positively given object could take its place
in the fantasy-frame, thereby starting to function as an object of desire:
some objects (those which are too close to the traumatic Thing) are
definitely excluded from it; if, by any chance, they intrude into the
fantasy-space, the effect is extremely disturbing and disgusting: the
fantasy loses its fascinating power and changes into a nauseating object.

Again Hitchcock, this time in *Vertigo*, offers us an example of such a
transformation: the hero — James Stewart again — is passionately in love
with Madeleine and follows her to a museum where she admires the
portrait of Charlotte, a long-dead woman with whom Madeleine identifies: to play a practical joke on him, his everyday maternal friend, an
amateur painter, sets up an unpleasant surprise for him: she paints an
exact copy of Charlotte's portrait with white lace dress, a red bunch of
flowers in her lap, and so on, but instead of Charlotte's fatally beautiful
face she puts her own common face with spectacles . . . the effect is terrifying: depressive, broken and disgusted, Stewart leaves her. (We find the
same procedure in Hitchcock's *Rebecca*, where Joan Fontaine — to charm
her husband, whom she supposes to be still in love with his late wife,
Rebecca — appears at a formal reception in a gown Rebecca once wore
on a similar occasion — the effect is again grotesque and the husband
drives her furiously away. . . .)

It is clear, then, why Lacan developed his graph of desire apropos of
Shakespeare's *Hamlet*: is not *Hamlet*, in the last analysis, a drama of *failed
interpellation*? At the beginning we have interpellation in its pure form:
the ghost of the father-king interpellates Hamlet–individual into subject
— that is, Hamlet recognizes himself as the addressee of the imposed
mandate or mission (to revenge his father's murder); but the father's
ghost enigmatically supplements his command with the request that
Hamlet should not in any way harm his mother. And what prevents
Hamlet from acting, from accomplishing the imposed revenge, is
precisely the confrontation with the '*Che vuoi?*' of the desire of the
Other: the key scene of the whole drama is the long dialogue between
Hamlet and his mother, in which he is seized by doubt as to his mother's
desire — What does she really want? What if she really *enjoys* her filthy,
promiscuous relationship with his uncle? Hamlet is therefore hindered
not by indecision as to his own desire; it is not that 'he doesn't know
what he really wants' — he knows that very clearly: he wants to revenge
his father — what hinders him is doubt concerning the *desire of the other*,

the confrontation of a certain 'Che vuoi?' which announces the abyss of some terrifying, filthy enjoyment. If the Name-of-the-Father functions as the agency of interpellation, of symbolic identification, the mother's desire, with its fathomless 'Che vuoi?', marks a certain limit at which every interpellation necessarily fails.

The Inconsistent Other of *Jouissance*

In this way we have already reached the fourth, last, complete form of the graph of desire, because what is added in this last form is a new vector of enjoyment [*jouissance*] intersecting the vector of the symbolically structured desire:

Completed Graph

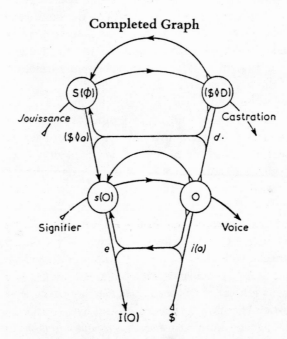

The complete graph is thus divided into two levels, which can be designated as the level of meaning and the level of enjoyment. The problem of the first (lower) level is how the intersection of the signifying chain and of a mythical intention (Δ) produces the effect of meaning, with all its internal articulation: the retroactive character of meaning in so far as it is the function of the big Other — in so far, that is, as it is conditioned by the place of the Other, the signifier's battery ($s(\mathrm{O})$); the imaginary ($i(o)$) and the symbolic (I(O)) — identification of the subject based on this retro-active production of meaning, and so on. The problem of the second (upper) level is what happens when this very field of the signifier's order, of the big Other, is perforated, penetrated by a pre-symbolic (real) stream of enjoyment — what happens when the pre-symbolic 'substance', the body as materalized, incarnated enjoyment, becomes enmeshed in the signifier's network.

Its general result is clear: by being filtered through the sieve of the signifier, the body is submitted to *castration*, enjoyment is evacuated from it, the body survives as dismembered, mortified. In other words, the order of the signifier (the big Other) and that of enjoyment (the Thing as its embodiment) are radically heterogeneous, inconsistent; any accord-ance between them is structurally impossible. This is why we find on the left-hand side of the upper level of the graph — at the first point of inter-section between enjoyment and signifier, S(Ø) — the signifier of the lack in the Other, of the inconsistency of the Other: as soon as the field of the signifier is penetrated by enjoyment it becomes inconsistent, porous, perforated — the enjoyment is what cannot be symbolized, its presence in the field of the signifier can be detected only through the holes and inconsistencies of this field, so the only possible signifier of enjoyment is the signifier of the lack in the Other, the signifier of its inconsistency.

Today, it is a commonplace that the Lacanian subject is divided, crossed-out, identical to a lack in a signifying chain. However, the most radical dimension of Lacanian theory lies not in recognizing this fact but in realizing that the big Other, the symbolic order itself, is also *barré*, crossed-out, by a fundamental impossibility, structured around an impossible/traumatic kernel, around a central lack. Without this lack in the Other, the Other would be a closed structure and the only possibility open to the subject would be his radical alienation in the Other. So it is precisely this lack in the Other which enables the subject to achieve a kind of 'de-alienation' called by Lacan *separation*: not in the sense that the subject experiences that now he is separated for ever from the object by the barrier of language, but that *the object is separated from the Other itself*, that the Other itself 'hasn't got it', hasn't got the final answer — that is to say, is in itself blocked, desiring; that there is also a desire of the Other. This lack in the Other gives the subject — so to speak — a breathing space, it enables him to avoid the total alienation in the signifier not by filling out his lack but by allowing him to identify himself, his own lack, with the lack in the Other.

The three levels of the descending vector on the left side of the graph can thus be conceived in view of the logic that regulates their succession. First, we have S(Ø): the mark of the lack of the Other, of the inconsistency of the symbolic order when it is penetrated by *jouissance*: then S◊o, the formula of fantasy: the function of fantasy is to serve as a screen concealing this inconsistency; finally s(O), the effect of the signification as dominated by fantasy: fantasy functions as 'absolute signification' (Lacan); it constitutes the frame through which we experience the world as consistent and meaningful — the a priori space within which the particular effects of signification take place.

The last point to be clarified is why we find on the other, right point of intersection between enjoyment and signifier the formula of drive ($ ◊D)? We have already said that the signifier dismembers the body, that it evacuates enjoyment from the body, but this 'evacuation' (Jacques-Alain Miller) is never fully accomplished; scattered around the desert of the symbolic Other, there are always some leftovers, oases of enjoyment, so-called 'erogenous zones', fragments still penetrated with enjoyment — and it is precisely these remnants to which Freudian drive is tied: it circulates, it pulses around them. These erogenous zones are designated with D (symbolic demand) because there is nothing 'natural', 'biological', in them: which part of the body will survive the 'evacuation of enjoyment' is determined not by physiology but by the way the body has been dissected through the signifier (as is confirmed by those hysterical symptoms in which the parts of the body from which enjoyment is 'normally' evacuated become again eroticized — neck, nose . . .).

Perhaps we should take a risk and read $◊D retroactively, from Lacan's later theoretical development, as the formula of *sinthome*: a particular signifying formation which is immediately permeated with enjoyment — that is, the impossible junction of enjoyment with the signifier. Such a reading gives us a key to the upper level, to the upper square of the graph of desire in its opposition to the lower square: instead of imaginary identification (the relation between imaginary ego and its constitutive image, its ideal ego) we have here desire (d) supported by fantasy ($◊o); the function of fantasy is to fill the opening in the Other, to conceal its inconsistency — as for instance the fascinating presence of some sexual scenario serving as a screen to mask the impossibility of the sexual relationship. Fantasy conceals the fact that the Other, the symbolic order, is structured around some traumatic impossibility, around something which cannot be symbolized — i.e. the real of *jouissance*: through fantasy, *jouissance* is domesticated, 'gentrified' — so what happens with desire after we 'traverse' fantasy? Lacan's answer, in the last pages of his

Seminar XI, is *drive*, ultimately the death drive: 'beyond fantasy' there is no yearning or some kindred sublime phenomenon, 'beyond fantasy' we find only drive, its pulsation around the *sinthome*. 'Going-through-the-fantasy' is therefore strictly correlative to identification with a *sinthome*.

'Going through' the Social Fantasy

In this way, we could read the whole upper (second) level of the graph as designating the dimension 'beyond interpellation': the impossible 'square of the circle' of symbolic and/or imaginary identification never results in the absence of any remainder; there is always a leftover which opens the space for desire and makes the Other (the symbolic order) inconsistent, with fantasy as an attempt to overcome, to conceal this inconsistency, this gap in the Other. And now we can finally return to the problematics of ideology: the crucial weakness of hitherto '(post-)structuralist' essays in the theory of ideology descending from the Althusserian theory of interpellation was to limit themselves to the lower level, to the lower square of Lacan's graph of desire — to aim at grasping the efficiency of an ideology exclusively through the mechanisms of imaginary and symbolic identification. The dimension 'beyond interpellation' which was thus left out has nothing to do with some kind of irreducible dispersion and plurality of the signifying process — with the fact that the metonymic sliding always subverts every fixation of meaning, every 'quilting' of the floating signifiers (as it would appear in a 'post-structuralist' perspective). 'Beyond interpellation' is the square of desire, fantasy, lack in the Other and drive pulsating around some unbearable surplus-enjoyment.

What does this mean for the theory of ideology? At first sight it could seem that what is pertinent in an analysis of ideology is only the way it functions as a discourse, the way the series of floating signifiers is total-ized, transformed into an unified field through the intervention of certain 'nodal points'. Briefly: the way the discursive mechanisms consti-tute the field of ideological meaning; in this perspective the enjoyment-in-signifier would be simply pre-ideological, irrelevant for ideology as a social bond. But the case of so-called 'totalitarianism' demonstrates what applies to every ideology, to ideology as such: the last support of the ideological effect (of the way an ideological network of signifiers 'holds' us) is the non-sensical, pre-ideological kernel of enjoyment. In ideology 'all is not ideology (that is, ideological meaning)', but it is this very surplus which is the last support of ideology. That is why we could say that there are also two complementary procedures of the 'criticism of ideology':

- one is *discursive*, the 'symptomal reading' of the ideological text bringing about the 'deconstruction' of the spontaneous experience of its meaning — that is, demonstrating how a given ideological field is a result of a montage of heterogeneous 'floating signifiers', of their totalization through the intervention of certain 'nodal points';

- the other aims at extracting the kernel of *enjoyment*, at articulating the way in which — beyond the field of meaning but at the same time internal to it — an ideology implies, manipulates, produces a pre-ideological enjoyment structured in fantasy.

To exemplify this necessity of supplementing the analysis of discourse with the logic of enjoyment we have only to look again at the special case of ideology, which is perhaps the purest incarnation of ideology as such: anti-semitism. To put it bluntly: 'Society doesn't exist', and the Jew is its symptom.

On the level of discourse analysis, it is not difficult to articulate the network of symbolic overdetermination invested in the figure of the Jew. First, there is displacement: the basic trick of anti-semitism is to displace social antagonism into antagonism between the sound social texture, social body, and the Jew as the force corroding it, the force of corruption. Thus it is not society itself which is 'impossible', based on antagonism — the source of corruption is located in a particular entity, the Jew. This displacement is made possible by the association of Jews with financial dealings: the source of exploitation and of class antagonism is located not in the basic relation between the working and ruling classes but in the relation between the 'productive' forces (workers, organizers of production . . .) and the merchants who exploit the 'productive' classes, replacing organic co-operation with class struggle.

This displacement is, of course, supported by condensation: the figure of the Jew condenses opposing features, features associated with lower and upper classes: Jews are supposed to be dirty *and* intellectual, voluptuous *and* impotent, and so on. What gives energy, so to speak, to the displacement is therefore the way the figure of the Jew condenses a series of heterogeneous antagonisms: economic (Jew as profiteer), political (Jew as schemer, retainer of a secret power), moral-religious (Jew as corrupt anti-Christian), sexual (Jew as seducer of our innocent girls). . . . In short,

it can easily be shown how the figure of the Jew is a symptom in the
sense of a coded message, a cypher, a disfigured representation of social
antagonism; by undoing this work of displacement/condensation, we can
determine its meaning.

But this logic of metaphoric-metonymic displacement is not sufficient to explain how the figure of the Jew captures our desire; to
penetrate its fascinating force, we must take into account the way 'Jew'
enters the framework of fantasy structuring our enjoyment. Fantasy is
basically a scenario filling out the empty space of a fundamental impossibility, a screen masking a void. 'There is no sexual relationship', and this
impossibility is filled out by the fascinating fantasy-scenario — that is
why fantasy is, in the last resort, always a fantasy of the sexual
relationship, a staging of it. As such, fantasy is not to be interpreted, only
'traversed': all we have to do is experience how there is nothing 'behind'
it, and how fantasy masks precisely this 'nothing'. (But there is a lot
behind a symptom, a whole network of symbolic overdetermination,
which is why the symptom involves its interpretation.)

It is now clear how we can use this notion of fantasy in the domain of
ideology proper: here also 'there is no class relationship', society is always
traversed by an antagonistic split which cannot be integrated into
symbolic order. And the stake of social–ideological fantasy is to construct
a vision of society which *does* exist, a society which is not split by an
antagonistic division, a society in which the relation between its parts is
organic, complementary. The clearest case is, of course, the corporatist
vision of Society as an organic Whole, a social Body in which the different classes are like extremities, members each contributing to the
Whole according to its function — we may say that 'Society as a corporate Body' is the fundamental ideological fantasy. How then do we
take account of the distance between this corporatist vision and the
factual society split by antagonistic struggles? The answer is, of course,
the Jew: an external element, a foreign body introducing corruption into
the sound social fabric. In short, 'Jew' is a fetish which simultaneously
denies and embodies the structural impossibility of 'Society': it is as if in
the figure of the Jew this impossibility had acquired a positive, palpable
existence — and that is why it marks the eruption of enjoyment in the
social field.

The notion of social fantasy is therefore a necessary counterpart to the
concept of antagonism: fantasy is precisely the way the antagonistic
fissure is masked. In other words, *fantasy is a means for an ideology to take its
own failure into account in advance.* The thesis of Laclau and Mouffe that

'Society doesn't exist', that the Social is always an inconsistent field structured around a constitutive impossibility, traversed by a central 'antagonism' — this thesis implies that every process of identification conferring on us a fixed socio-symbolic identity is ultimately doomed to fail. The function of ideological fantasy is to mask this inconsistency, the fact that 'Society doesn't exist', and thus to compensate us for the failed identification.

The 'Jew' is the means, for Fascism, of taking into account, of representing its own impossibility: in its positive presence, it is only the embodiment of the ultimate impossibility of the totalitarian project — of its immanent limit. This is why it is insufficient to designate the totalitarian project as impossible, utopian, wanting to establish a totally transparent and homogeneous society — the problem is that in a way, totalitarian ideology *knows it*, recognizes it in advance: in the figure of the 'Jew' it includes this knowledge in its edifice. The whole Fascist ideology is structured as a struggle against the element which holds the place of the immanent impossibility of the very Fascist project: the 'Jew' is nothing but a fetishistic embodiment of a certain fundamental blockage.

The 'criticism of ideology' must therefore invert the linking of causality as perceived by the totalitarian gaze: far from being the positive cause of social antagonism, the 'Jew' is just the embodiment of a certain blockage — of the impossibility which prevents the society from achieving its full identity as a closed, homogeneous totality. Far from being the positive cause of social negativity, *the 'Jew' is a point at which social negativity as such assumes positive existence*. In this way we can articulate another formula of the basic procedure of the 'criticism of ideology', supplementing the one given above: to detect, in a given ideological edifice, the element which represents within it its own impossibility. Society is not prevented from achieving its full identity because of Jews: it is prevented by its own antagonistic nature, by its own immanent blockage, and it 'projects' this internal negativity into the figure of the 'Jew'. In other words, what is excluded from the Symbolic (from the frame of the corporatist socio-symbolic order) returns in the Real as a paranoid construction of the 'Jew'.[2]

We can also see, now how 'going through' the social fantasy is likewise correlative to identification with a symptom. Jews are clearly a social symptom: the point at which the immanent social antagonism assumes a positive form, erupts on to the social surface, the point at which it becomes obvious that society 'doesn't work', that the social mechanism 'creaks'. If we look at it through the frame of (corporatist) fantasy, the 'Jew' appears as an intruder who introduces from outside disorder, decomposition and corruption of the social edifice — it appears as an outward positive cause whose elimination would enable us to restore order, stability and identity. But in 'going through the fantasy' we must in the same move identify with the symptom: we must recognize in the properties attributed to 'Jew' the necessary product of our very social system; we must recognize in the 'excesses' attributed to 'Jews' the truth about ourselves.

Precisely because of such a notion of social 'excesses', Lacan pointed out that it was Marx who invented the symptom: Marx's great achievement was to demonstrate how all phenomena which appear to everyday bourgeois consciousness as simple deviations, contingent deformations and degenerations of the 'normal' functioning of society (economic crises, wars, and so on), and as such abolishable through amelioration of the system, are necessary products of the system itself — the points at which the 'truth', the immanent antagonistic character of the system, erupts. To 'identify with a symptom' means to recognize in the 'excesses', in the disruptions of the 'normal' way of things, the key offering us access to its true functioning. This is similar to Freud's view that the keys to the functioning of the human mind were dreams, slips of the tongue, and similar 'abnormal' phenomena.

Notes

1. The other achievement of the film is the final rehabilitation of Judas as the real tragic hero of this story: he was the one whose love for Christ was the greatest, and it was for this reason that Christ considered him strong enough to fulfil the horrible mission of betraying him, thus assuring the accomplishment of Christ's destiny (the Crucifixion). The tragedy of Judas was that in the name of his dedication to the Cause, he was prepared to risk not only his life but even his 'second life', his posthumous good name: he knows very well that he will enter history as the one who betrayed our Saviour, and he is prepared to endure even that for the fulfilment of God's mission. Jesus used Judas as a means to attain his goal, knowing very well that his own suffering would be transformed into a model imitated by millions (*imitatio Christi*), while Judas's sacrifice is a pure loss without any narcissistic benefit. Perhaps he is a little like the faithful victims of the Stalinist monster trials who confessed their guilt, proclaimed themselves miserable scum, knowing that by so doing they were accomplishing the last and highest service to the Cause of the Revolution.

2. Here we could use the distinction elaborated by Kovel (Kovel, 1988), between *dominative* and *aversive* racism. In Nazi ideology, all human races form a hierarchical,

harmonious Whole (the 'destiny' of the Aryans at the top is to rule, while the Blacks, Chinese, and others have to serve) — all races *except the Jews*: they have no proper place; their very 'identity' is a fake, it consists in trespassing the frontiers, in introducing unrest, antagonism, in destabilizing the social fabric. As such, Jews plot with other races and prevent them from putting up with their proper place — they function as a hidden Master aiming at a world domination: they are a counter-image of the Aryans themselves, a kind of negative, perverted double; this is why they must be exterminated, while other races have only to be forced to occupy their proper place.

4

You Only Die Twice

Between the Two Deaths

The connection between the death drive and the symbolic order is a constant with Lacan, but we can differentiate the various stages of his teaching precisely by reference to the different modes of articulation of the death drive and the signifier:

– In the first period (the first Seminar, *The Function and the Field of Speech and Language* . . .), it is the Hegelian phenomenological idea that the word is a death, a murder of a thing: as soon as the reality is symbolized, caught in a symbolic network, the thing itself is more present in a word, in its concept, than in its immediate physical reality. More precisely, we cannot return to the immediate reality: even if we turn from the word to the thing — from the word 'table' to the table in its physical reality, for example — the appearance of the table itself is already marked with a certain lack — to know what a table really is, what it means, we must have recourse to the word which implies an absence of the thing.

– In the second period (the Lacanian reading of Poe's 'Purloined Letter'), the accent is shifted from the word, speech, to language as a synchronic structure, a senseless autonomous mechanism which produces meaning as its effect. If, in the first period, the Lacanian concept of language is still basically a phenomenological one (Lacan constantly repeats that the field of psycholanalysis is the field of meaning, *la signification*), here we have a 'structuralist' conception of language as a differential system of elements. The death drive is now identified with the symbolic order itself: in Lacan's own words, it is 'nothing but a mask of the symbolic order'. The main thing here is the opposition between the imaginary level of the experience of meaning and the meaningless signifier/signifying mechanism producing it. The imaginary level is governed by the pleasure principle, it is striving for a homeostatic balance, and the symbolic order in its blind automatism is always troubling this homeostasis: it is 'beyond the pleasure principle'. When the human being is caught in the signifier's network, this network has a mortifying effect on him; he becomes part of a strange automatic order disturbing his natural homeostatic balance (through compulsive repetition, for example).

– In the third period, in which the main accent of Lacan's teaching is put on the Real as impossible, the death drive again radically changes its signification. This change can be most easily detected through the relationship between the pleasure principle and the symbolic order.

Until the end of fifties, the pleasure principle was identified with the imaginary level: the symbolic order was conceived as the realm 'beyond the pleasure principle'. But starting from the late fifties (the Seminar on *The Ethic of Psychoanalysis*), it is, in contrast, the symbolic order itself which is identified with the pleasure principle: the unconscious 'structured like a language', its 'primary process' of metonymic-metaphoric displacement, is governed by the pleasure principle; what lies beyond is not the symbolic order but a real kernel, a traumatic core. To designate it, Lacan uses a Freudian term: *das Ding*, the Thing as an incarnation of the impossible *jouissance* (the term Thing is to be taken here with all the connotation it possesses in the domain of horror science fiction: the 'alien' from the film of the same name is a pre-symbolic, maternal Thing *par excellence*).

The symbolic order is striving for a homeostatic balance, but there is in its kernel, at its very centre, some strange, traumatic element which cannot be symbolized, integrated into the symbolic order – the Thing. Lacan coined a neologism for it: *L'extimité* – external intimacy, which served as a title for one of Jacques-Alain Miller's Seminars. And what, at this level, is the death drive? Exactly the opposite of the symbolic order: the possibility of the 'second death', the radical annihilation of the symbolic texture through which the so-called reality is constituted. The very existence of the symbolic order implies a possibility of its radical effacement, of 'symbolic death' – not the death of the so-called 'real object' in its symbol, but the obliteration of the signifying network itself.

This distinction between the different stages of Lacan's teaching is not of purely theoretical interest; it has very definite consequences for the determination of the final moment of the psychoanalytic cure:

- In the first period, in which the emphasis is on the word as a medium of the intersubjective recognition of desire, the symptoms are conceived as white spots, non-symbolized imaginary elements of the history of the subject, and the process of analysis is that of their symbolization — of their integration into the symbolic universe of the subject: the analysis gives meaning, retroactively, to what was in the beginning a meaningless trace. So the final moment of the analysis is reached when the subject is able to narrate to the Other his own history in its continuity; when his desire is integrated, recognized in 'full speech [*parole pleine*]'.

- In the second period, in which the symbolic order is conceived as having a mortifying effect on the subject, as imposing on him a traumatic loss — and the name of this loss, of this lack, is of course symbolic castration — the final moment of analysis is reached when the subject is ready to accept this fundamental loss, to consent to symbolic castration as a price to be paid for access to his desire.

- In the third period we have the big Other, the symbolic order, with a traumatic element at its very heart; and in Lacanian theory the fantasy is conceived as a construction allowing the subject to come to terms with this traumatic kernel. At this level, the final moment of the analysis is defined as 'going through the fantasy [*la traversée du fantasme*]': not its symbolic interpretation but the experience of the fact that the fantasy-object, by its fascinating presence, is merely filling out a lack, a void in the Other. There is nothing 'behind' the fantasy; the fantasy is a construction whose function is to hide this void, this 'nothing' — that is, the lack in the Other.

The crucial element of this third period of Lacan's teaching is therefore the shift of emphasis from the symbolic to the Real. To exemplify it, let us take the notion of the 'knowledge in the Real': the idea that nature knows its own laws and behaves accordingly. We all know the classical, archetypal cartoon scene: a cat approaches the edge of the precipice but she does not stop, she proceeds calmly, and although she is already hanging in the air, without ground under her feet, she does not fall — when does she fall? The moment she looks down and becomes aware of the fact that she is hanging in the air. The point of this nonsense accident is that when the cat is walking slowly in the air, it is as if the Real has for a moment forgotten its knowledge: when the cat finally looks down, she remembers that she must follow the laws of nature and falls. This is basically the same logic as in the already mentioned dream, reported in Freud's *Interpretation of Dreams*, of a father who does not know that he is dead: the point is again that because he does not know that he is dead, *he continues to live* — he must be reminded of his death or, to give this situation a comical twist, he is still living because he has forgotten to die. That is how the phrase *memento mori* should be read: don't forget to die!

This brings us back to the distinction between the two deaths: because of lack of knowledge, the father in Freud's dream is still living, although he is already dead. In a way, everybody must die twice. That is the Hegelian theory of repetition in history: when Napoleon lost for the first time and was consigned to Elba, he did not know that he was already dead, that his historical role was finished, and he had to be reminded of it through his second defeat at Waterloo — at this point, when he died for the second time, he was really dead.

The stimulus for this idea of a second death came from the Marquis de Sade: the Sadeian notion of a radical, absolute crime that liberates nature's creative force, as elaborated in the Pope's long speech in the fifth volume of *Juliette*, implies a distinction between the two deaths: natural death, which is a part of the natural cycle of generation and corruption, of nature's continual transformation, and absolute death — the destruction, the eradication, of the cycle itself, which then liberates nature from its own laws and opens the way for the creation of new forms of life *ex nihilo*. This difference between the two deaths can be linked with the Sadeian fantasy revealed by the fact that in his work his victim is, in a certain sense, indestructible: she can be endlessly tortured and can survive it; she can endure any torment and still retain her beauty. It is as though, above and beyond her natural body (a part of the cycle of generation and corruption), and thus above and beyond her natural death, she possessed another body, a body composed of some other substance, one excepted from the vital cycle — a sublime body (Božovič, 1988).

Today, we can find this same fantasy at work in various products of 'mass culture', for example in animated cartoons. Consider Tom and Jerry, cat and mouse. Each is subjected to frightful misadventures: the cat is stabbed, dynamite goes off in his pocket, he is run over by a steamroller and his body is flattened into a ribbon, and so forth; but in the next scene he appears with his normal body and the game begins again — it is as though he possessed another indestructible body. Or take the example of video games, in which we deal, literally, with the differences between the two deaths: the usual rule of such games is that the player (or, more precisely, the figure representing him in the game) possesses several lives, usually three; he is threatened by some danger — a monster who can eat him, for example, and if the monster catches him he loses a life — but if he reaches his goal very swiftly he earns one or several supplementary lives. The whole logic of such games is therefore based on the difference between the two deaths: between the death in which I lose one of my lives and the ultimate death in which I lose the game itself.

Lacan conceives this difference between the two deaths as the difference between real (biological) death and its symbolization, the 'settling of accounts', the accomplishment of symbolic destiny (deathbed confession in Catholicism, for example). This gap can be filled in various ways; it can contain either sublime beauty or fearsome monsters: in Antigone's case, her symbolic death, her exclusion from the symbolic community of the city, precedes her actual death and imbues her character with sublime beauty, whereas the ghost of Hamlet's father represents the opposite case — actual death unaccompanied by symbolic death, without a settling of accounts — which is why he returns as a frightful apparition until his debt has been repaid.

This place 'between the two deaths', a place of sublime beauty as well as terrifying monsters, is the site of *das Ding*, of the real-traumatic kernel in the midst of symbolic order. This place is opened by symbolization/historicization: the process of historicization implies an empty place, a non-historical kernel around which the symbolic network is articulated. In other words, human *history* differs from animal *evolution* precisely by its reference to this *non-historical* place, a place which cannot be symbolized, although it is retroactively produced by the symbolization itself: as soon as 'brute', pre-symbolic reality is symbolized/historicized, it 'secretes', it isolates the empty, 'indigestible' place of the Thing.

It is this reference to the empty place of the Thing which enables us to conceive the possibility of a total, global annihilation of the signifier's network: the 'second death', the radical annihilation of nature's circular movement, is conceivable only in so far as this circular movement is already symbolized/historicized, inscribed, caught in the symbolic web — absolute death, the 'destruction of the universe', is always the destruction of the *symbolic* universe. The Freudian 'death drive' is nothing but the exact theoretical concept for this Sadeian notion of the 'second death'

— the possibility of the total 'wipe-out' of historical tradition opened up by the very process of symbolization/historicization as its radical, self-destructive limit.

In the whole history of Marxism, there is probably only one point at which this non-historical 'ex-timate' kernel of history was touched — at which the reflection of history was brought to the 'death drive' as its degree zero: *Theses on the Philosophy of History*, the last text by Walter Benjamin, 'fellow-traveller' of the Frankfurt School. The reason for this is of course that it was again Benjamin who — a unique case in Marxism — conceived history as a text, as series of events which 'will have been' — their meaning, their historical dimension, is decided afterwards, through their inscription in the symbolic network.

Revolution as Repetition

These *Theses* themselves occupy an 'ex-timate' place; they are like a strange body resisting insertion not only in the frame of the Frankfurt School but in the very continuity of Benjamin's thought. That is to say, one usually conceives Benjamin's development as a gradual approach to Marxism; in this continuity, the *Theses* make a clear incision: there, at the very end of his theoretical (and physical) activity, emerges suddenly the problem of *theology*. Historical materialism can triumph only if it 'enlists the services of theology' — here is the famous first thesis:

> The story is told of an automaton constructed in such a way that it could play a winning game of chess, answering each move of an opponent with a countermove. A puppet in Turkish attire and with a hookah in its mouth sat before a chessboard placed on a large table. A system of mirrors created the illusion that this table was transparent from all sides. Actually, a little hunch-back who was an expert chess player sat inside and guided the puppet's hand by means of strings. One can imagine a philosophical counterpart to this device. The puppet called 'historical materialism' is to win all the time. It can easily be a match for anyone if it enlists the service of theology, which today, as we know, is wizened and has to keep out of sight. (Benjamin, 1969, p. 253)

What strikes the eye in this fragment is the contradiction between the allegory forming the first part of the thesis and its interpretation in the second part. In the interpretation, it is historical materialism which 'enlists the services of theology'; whereas in the allegory itself, theology ('a little hunchback') guides the puppet — 'historical materialism' — by means of strings from within. This contradiction is of course the very contradiction between allegory and its meaning, ultimately between signifier and the signified, which pretends to 'enlist the services' of the signifier as its instrument but finds itself quickly entangled in its network. The two different levels thus traverse one another: the formal structure of Benjamin's allegory functions in exactly the same way as its 'content', theology in its relationship to historical materialism, which pretends simply to enlist its services but becomes more and more entangled in its strings because — if we may permit ourselves this *Vorlust*, this forepleasure — 'theology' designates here the agency of the signifier.

But let us proceed step by step: how should we conceive the theological dimension referred to by Benjamin? 'Theology' announces here a unique experience, alluded to in the following fragment published after Benjamin's death: 'In *Eingedenken*, we make an experience which forbids us to conceive history in a fundamentally atheological way.' We cannot translate this *Eingedenken* simply by 'remembrance' or 'reminiscence'; the more literal translation, 'to transpose oneself in thoughts/into something' is also inadequate.

Although it is really a kind of 'appropriation of the past' which is at stake here, we cannot conceive *Eingedenken* in an adequate way as long as we stay within the field of hermeneutics — Benjamin's aim is quite the opposite of the fundamental guidance of hermeneutical understanding ('to locate the interpreted text into the totality of its epoch'). What Benjamin has in mind is, on the contrary, the *isolation* of a piece of the past from the continuity of history ('. . . blasting a specific life out of the era or a specific work out of the lifework' — Thesis XVII): an interpretative procedure whose opposition to hermeneutics recalls immediately the Freudian opposition between interpretation *en détail* and interpretation *en masse*: 'What we must take as the object of our attention is not the dream as a whole but the separate portions of its content' (Freud, 1977, p. 178).

This refusal of the hermeneutical approach has, to be sure, nothing whatsoever to do with a simple 'regression' to pre-hermeneutical naïveté: the point is not for us to 'accustom ourselves to the past' by abstracting our actual historical position, the place from which we are speaking. *Eingedenken* certainly is an appropriation of the past which is 'interested', biased towards the oppressed class: 'To articulate the past historically does not mean to recognize it "the way it really was" ' (Thesis VI) . . . 'Not man or men but the struggling, oppressed class itself is the depository of historical knowledge' (Thesis XIII).

We would none the less falsify the meaning of these lines by reading them in the sense of a Nietzschean historiography, of a 'will to power as interpretation', as the right of the winner to 'write his own history', to impose his 'perspective' — by seeing in them a kind of reference to the struggle between the two classes, the ruling and the oppressed, for 'who will write the history'. Perhaps it is so for the ruling class, but it is certainly not so for the oppressed class; between the two, there is a fundamental asymmetry which Benjamin designates by means of two different modes of temporality: the empty, homogeneous time of continuity (proper to the reigning, official historiography) and the 'filled' time of discontinuity (which defines historical materialism).

By confining itself to 'the way it really was', by conceiving history as a closed, homogeneous, rectilinear, continuous course of events, the traditional historiographic gaze is a priori, formally, the gaze of 'those who have won': it sees history as a closed continuity of 'progression' leading to the reign of those who rule today. It leaves out of consideration what *failed* in history, what has to be denied so that the continuity of 'what really happened' could establish itself. The reigning historiography writes a 'positive' history of great achievements and cultural treasures, whereas a historical materialist

> views them with cautious detachment. For without exception the cultural treasures he surveys have an origin which he cannot contemplate without horror. They owe their existence not only to the efforts of the great minds and talents who have created them, but also to the anonymous toil of their contemporaries. There is no document of civilization which is not at the same time a document of barbarism. (Thesis VII)

In contrast to the triumphal procession of victors exhibited by official historiography, the oppressed class appropriates the past to itself in so far as it is 'open', in so far as the 'yearning for redemption' is already at work in it — that is to say, it appropriates the past in so far as the past already contains — in the form of what failed, of what was extirpated — the dimension of the future: 'The past carries with it a temporal index by which it is referred to redemption' (Thesis II).

To accomplish the appropriation of this stifled dimension of the past in so far as it already contains the future — the future of our own revolutionary act which, by means of repetition, redeems retroactively the past ('There is a secret agreement between past generations and the present one. Our coming was expected on earth' [Thesis II]) — we have to cut through the continuous flow of historical development and make a 'tiger's leap into the past' (Thesis XIV). Only here do we arrive at the fundamental asymmetry between historiographic evolutionism describing history's continuous movement and historical materialism:

> A historical materialist cannot do without the notion of a present which is not a transition, but in which time stands still and has come to a stop. For this notion defines the present in which he himself is writing history. (Thesis XVI)

> Thinking involves not only the flow of thoughts, but their arrest as well. Where thinking suddenly stops in a configuration pregnant with tensions, it gives that configuration a shock, by which it crystallizes into a monad. A historical materialist approaches a historical subject only where he encounters it as a monad. In this structure he recognizes the sign of a Messianic cessation of happening, or, put differently, a revolutionary chance in the fight for the oppressed past. (Thesis XVII)

Here we have the first surprise: what specifies historical materialism — in contrast to the Marxist doxa according to which we must grasp events in the totality of their interconnection and in their dialectical movement — is its capacity to *arrest*, to *immobilize* historical movement and to *isolate* the detail from its historical totality.

It is this very crystallization, this 'congelation' of the movement in a monad, which announces the moment of the appropriation of the past: the monad is an actual moment to which is attached directly — bypassing the continuous line of evolution — the past: the contemporary revolutionary situation which conceives itself as a repetition of past failed situations, as their retroactive 'redemption' through the success of its own exploit. The past itself is here 'filled out with present', the moment of the revolutionary chance decides not only the lot of the actual revolution but also the lot of all past failed revolutionary attempts:

> Historical materialism wishes to retain the image of the past which unexpectedly appears to man singled out by history at a moment of danger. The danger affects both the content of the tradition and its receivers. (Thesis VI)

The risk of defeat of the actual revolution endangers the past itself because the actual revolutionary conjunction functions as a condensation of past missed revolutionary chances repeating themselves in the actual revolution:

> History is the subject of a structure whose site is not homogeneous, empty time, but time filled by the presence of the now [*Jetztzeit*]. Thus, to Robespierre ancient Rome was a past charged with the time of the now which he blasted out of the continuum of history. The French Revolution viewed itself as Rome reincarnate. It evoked ancient Rome the way fashion evokes costumes of the past. (Thesis XIV)

For those acquainted with the Freudian proposition that 'the unconscious is located outside time', all is actually said here: this 'filled-out time', this 'tiger's leap into the past' with which the revolutionary present is charged, announces the *compulsion to repeat*. The arrest of historical movement, the suspension of the temporal continuity mentioned by Benjamin, correspond precisely to the 'short-circuit' between present and past speech which characterizes the transferential situation:

> Why does the analysis become transformed the moment the transferential situation is analysed through evoking the old situation, when the subject found himself with an entirely different object, one that cannot be assimilated to the present object? Because present speech, like the old speech, is placed within a parenthesis of time, within a form of time, if I can put it that way. The modulation of time being identical, the speech of the analyst [in Benjamin: of the historical materialist] happens to have the same value as the old speech. (Lacan, 1988, p. 243)

In the monad, 'time stops' in so far as the actual constellation is directly charged with the past constellation — in other words, in so far as we have to do with a pure repetition. Repetition is 'located outside time', not in the sense of some pre-logical archaism but simply in the sense of the pure signifier's synchrony: we do not have to look for the connection between past and present constellations in the diachronous time arrow; this connection reinstates itself in the form of an immediate paradigmatic short-circuit.

The monad is thus the moment of discontinuity, of rupture, at which the linear 'flow of time' is suspended, arrested, 'coagulated', because in it resounds directly — that is to say: bypassing the linear succession of continuous time — the past which was repressed, pushed out of the continuity established by prevailing history. It is literally the point of 'suspended dialectics', of pure repetition where historical movement is placed within parentheses. And the only field in which we can speak of such an appropriation of the past that the present itself 'redeems' it retroactively — where the past itself is thus included in the present — is that of the signifier: the suspension of movement is possible only as signifier's synchrony, as the synchronization of the past with the present.

We can now see what we are dealing with in the isolation of the monad from historical continuity: *we isolate the signifier by placing within parentheses the totality of signification*. This placing of signification within parentheses is a condition *sine qua non* of the short-circuit between present and past: their synchronization occurs at the level of the autonomy of the signifier — what is synchronized, superimposed, are two signifiers' networks, not two meanings. Consequently, we should not be surprised to find that this 'insertion [*Einschluss*] of some past into the present texture' is supported by the metaphor of the text, of history as text:

> If we are prepared to consider history as a text, we can say about it what some modern author said about a literary text: the past has deposed in it images which could be compared to those retained by a photographic plate. 'Only the future disposes of developers strong enough to make appear the picture with all its details. More than one page of Marivaux or of Rousseau attests to a meaning which their contemporary readers were unable to decipher completely.' (Benjamin, 1955, p. 1238)

Here we must refer again to Lacan, who, to explain the return of the repressed, makes use of Wiener's metaphor of the inverted temporal dimension: we see the square vanishing before we see the square:

> . . . what we see in the return of the repressed is the effaced signal of something which only takes on its value in the future, through its symbolic realization, its integration into the history of the subject. Literally, it will only ever be a thing which, at the given moment of its occurrence, *will have been*. (Lacan, 1988, p. 159)

So, contrary to the misleading first impression, the actual revolutionary situation is *not* a kind of 'return of the repressed' — rather, the returns of the repressed, the 'symptoms', are past failed revolutionary attempts, forgotten, excluded from the frame of the reigning historical tradition, whereas the actual revolutionary situation presents an attempt to 'unfold' the symptom, to 'redeem' — that is, realize in the Symbolic — these past failed attempts which 'will have been' only through their repetition, at which point they become retroactively what they already were. Apropos of Benjamin's *Theses*, we can thus repeat Lacan's formula: the revolution accomplishes a 'tiger's leap into the past' not because it is in search of a kind of support in the past, in tradition, but in so far as this past which repeats itself in the revolution 'comes from the future' — was already in itself pregnant with the open dimension of the future.

The 'Perspective of the Last Judgement'

At this precise point we encounter a certain surprising congruence between Benjamin and the Stalinist notion of history: as soon as we conceive history as a text, as 'its own history', its own narration — as something which receives its signification retroactively and where this delay, this effect of *après coup*, is inscribed in the actual event itself which, literally, 'is' not but always 'will have been' — we are obliged, implicitly at least, to view the historical process from the perspective of 'Last Judgement': of a final settling of accounts, of a point of accomplished symbolization/historicization, of the 'end of history', when every event will receive retroactively its definitive meaning, its final place in the total narration. Actual history occurs, so to speak, on credit; only subsequent development will decide retroactively if the current revolutionary violence will be forgiven, legitimated, or if it will continue to exert a pressure on the shoulders of the present generation as its guilt, as its unsettled debt.

Let us recall Merleau-Ponty who, in his *Humanism and Terror*, defended the Stalinist political trials on the grounds that although their victims were undoubtedly innocent, they would be justified by the subsequent social progress rendered possible through them. Here we have the fundamental idea of this 'perspective of the Last Judgement' (the expression is Lacan's, from his Seminar on *The Ethic of Psychoanalysis*): no act, no event falls empty; there is no pure expense, no pure loss in history; everything we do is written down, registered somewhere, as a trace which for the time being remains meaningless but which, in the moment of final settling, will receive its proper place.

This is the idealism hidden in the Stalinist logic which, although it denies a personified God, none the less implies a Platonic heaven in the form of the big Other, redoubling empirical, factual history and maintaining its accountancy — that is, determining the 'objective signification' of each event and action. Without this accountancy, without this registration of events and actions in the account of the Other, it would not be possible to conceive the functioning of some of the key notions of Stalinist discourse, such as 'the objective guilt' — precisely, guilt in the eyes of the big Other of history.

At first sight, then, Benjamin is in perfect accord with Stalinism concerning this 'perspective of the Last Judgement'; but here we should follow the same advice as with 'love at first sight': take a second look. If we do, it soon becomes clear how this apparent proximity only confirms that Benjamin has touched the real nerve of the Stalinist symbolic edifice — he was the only one to question radically the very idea of 'progress' implied by the accountancy of the big Other of history and — precursor, in this respect, of the famous Lacanian formula that development 'is nothing but a hypothesis of domination' (Lacan, 1975, p. 52) — to demonstrate the uninterrupted connection between progress and domination: 'The concept of the historical progress of mankind cannot be sundered from the concept of its progression through a homogeneous, empty time' (Thesis XIII) — that is, from the temporality of the ruling class.

The Stalinist perspective is that of a *victor* whose final triumph is guaranteed in advance by the 'objective necessity of history'; which is why, in spite of the accent on ruptures, leaps, revolutions, his view on past history is *evolutionary* throughout. History is conceived as the continuous process of replacing old masters with new: each victor played a 'progressive role' in his time, then lost his purpose because of unavoidable development: yesterday, it was the capitalist who acted in accordance with the necessity of progress; today, it's our turn. . . . In Stalinist accountancy, 'objective guilt' (or contribution) is measured by a reference to the laws of historical development — of continuous evolution towards the Supreme Good (Communism). With Benjamin, in contrast, the 'perspective of the Last Judgement' is the perspective of those who have paid the price for a series of great historical triumphs; the perspective of those who had to *fail*, to miss their aim, so that the series of great historical deeds could be accomplished; the perspective of hopes deceived, of all that have left in the text of history nothing but scattered, anonymous, meaningless traces on the margin of deeds whose 'historical greatness' was attested to by the 'objective' gaze of official historiography.

This is why, for Benjamin, revolution is not part of continuous historical evolution but, on the contrary, a moment of 'stasis' when the continuity is broken, when the texture of previous history, that of the winners, is annihilated, and when, retroactively, through the success of the revolution, each abortive act, each slip, each past failed attempt which functioned in the reigning Text as an empty and meaningless trace, will be 'redeemed', will receive its signification. In this sense, revolution is strictly a *creationist* act, a radical intrusion of the 'death drive':

erasure of the reigning Text, creation *ex nihilo* of a new Text by means of which the stifled past 'will have been'.

To refer to the Lacanian reading of *Antigone*: if the Stalinist perspective is that of Creon, the perspective of the Supreme Good assuming the shape of the Common Good of the State, the perspective of Benjamin is that of Antigone — for Benjamin, revolution is an affair of life and death; more precisely: of the second, symbolic death. The alternative opened by the revolution is that between *redemption*, which will retroactively confer meaning on the 'scum of history' (to use this Stalinist expression) — on what was excluded from the continuity of Progress — and the *apocalypse* (its defeat), where even the dead will again be lost and will suffer a second death: '*even the dead* will not be safe from the enemy if he wins' (Thesis VI).

We can thus conceive the opposition between Stalinism and Benjamin as that between *evolutionary idealism* and *creationist materialism*. In his Seminar on *The Ethic of Psychoanalysis*, Lacan pointed out how the ideology of evolutionism always implies a belief in a Supreme Good, in a final Goal of evolution which guides its course from the very beginning. In other words, it always implies a hidden, disavowed teleology, whereas materialism is always creationist — it always includes a *retroactive* movement: the final Goal is not inscribed in the beginning; things receive their meaning afterwards; the sudden creation of an Order confers backward signification to the preceding Chaos.

At first sight, Benjamin's position is radically anti-Hegelian: is not dialectics the most refined and perfidious version of evolutionism, in which the very ruptures are included in the continuity of Progress, in its unavoidable logic? This was probably how Benjamin himself conceived his own position: he designated the point of rupture which cuts into the historical continuity as the point of 'suspended dialectics', as the intrusion of a pure repetition putting in parenthesis the progressive movement of *Aufhebung*. But it is at this exact juncture that we must stress Hegel's radical anti-evolutionism: the absolute negativity which 'sets in motion' dialectical movement is nothing but the intervention of the 'death drive' as radically non-historical, as the 'zero degree' of history — historical movement includes in its very heart the non-historical dimension of 'absolute negativity'. In other words, the suspension of movement is a key moment of the dialectical process: so-called 'dialectical development' consists in the incessant repetition of a beginning *ex nihilo*, in the annihilation and retroactive restructuring of the presupposed contents. The vulgar idea of 'dialectical development' as a continuous course of transformations by which the old dies and the new is born, in which all beckons in incessant movement — this idea of nature as a dynamic process of transformation, of generation and corruption, found everywhere from de Sade to Stalin — has nothing whatsoever to do with the Hegelian 'dialectical process'.

This quasi-'dialectical' vision of nature as an eternal circuit of transformations does not, however, exhaust the whole of Stalinism: what escapes it is precisely the subjective position of the Communist himself. And, to put it briefly, the place of the Stalinist Communist is exactly between the two deaths. The somewhat poetic definitions of the figure of a Communist that we find in Stalin's work are to be taken literally. When, for example, in his speech at Lenin's funeral, Stalin proclaims: 'We, the Communists, are people of a special mould. We are made of special stuff', it is quite easy to recognize the Lacanian name for this special stuff: *objet petit a*, the sublime object placed in the interspace between the two deaths.

In the Stalinist vision, the Communists are 'men of iron will', somehow excluded from the everyday cycle of ordinary human passions and weakness. It is as if they are in a way 'the living dead', still alive but already excluded from the ordinary cycle of natural forces — as if, that is, they possess another body, the sublime body beyond their ordinary physical body. (Is the fact that in Lubitch's *Ninotchka*, the role of the high Party *apparatchik* is played by Bela Lugosi, identified with the figure of Dracula, another 'living dead', expressing a presentiment of the described state of things, or is it just a happy coincidence?) The fantasy which serves as a support for the figure of the Stalinist Communist is therefore exactly the same as the fantasy which is at work in the Tom and Jerry cartoons: behind the figure of the indestructibility and invincibility of the Communist who can endure even the most terrible ordeal and survive it intact, reinforced with new strength, there is the same fantasy-logic as that of a cat whose head is blown up by dynamite and who, in the next scene, proceeds intact his pursuit of his class enemy, the mouse.

From the Master to the Leader

The problem is that we already find this notion of a sublime body located between the two deaths with the classical, pre-bourgeois Master: for example, the King — it is as if he possesses, beyond his ordinary body, a sublime, ethereal, mystical body personifying the State (Kantorowicz,

1959; Riha, 1986). Where, then, lies the difference between the classical Master and the totalitarian Leader? The transubstantiated body of the classical Master is an effect of the performative mechanism already described by la Boétie, Pascal and Marx: we, the subjects, think that we treat the king as a king because he is in himself a king, but in reality a king is a king because we treat him like one. And this fact that the charismatic power of a king is an effect of the symbolic ritual performed by his subjects must remain hidden: as subjects, we are necessarily victims of the illusion that the king is already in himself a king. That is why the classical Master must legitimize his rule with a reference to some non-social, external authority (God, nature, some mythical past event . . .) — as soon as the performative mechanism which gives him his charismatic authority is demasked, the Master loses his power.

But the problem with the totalitarian Leader is that he no longer needs this external point of reference to legitimize his rule. He is not saying to his subjects: 'You must follow me because I'm your Leader' but quite the opposite: 'In myself, I'm nothing, I am what I am only as an expression, an embodiment, an executor of your will, my strength is your strength. . . .' To put it briefly, it is as if the totalitarian Leader is addressing his subjects and legitimizing his power precisely by referring to the above-mentioned Pascalian–Marxian argument — that is, revealing to them the secret of the classical Master; basically, he is saying to them: 'I'm your Master because you treat me as your Master; it is you, with your activity, who make me your Master!'

How, then, can we subvert the position of the totalitarian Leader, if the classical Pascalian–Marxian argument no longer works? Here the basic deception consists in the fact that the Leader's point of reference, the instance to which he is referring to legitimize his rule (the People, the Class, the Nation) *does not exist* — or, more precisely, exists only through and in its fetishistic representative, the Party and its Leader. The misrecognition of the performative dimension runs here in the opposite direction: the classical Master is Master only in so far as his subjects treat him as Master, but here, the People are the 'real People' only in so far as they are embodied in their representative, the Party and its Leader.

The formula of the totalitarian misrecognition of the performative dimension would then be as follows: the Party thinks that it is the Party because it represents the People's real interests, because it is rooted in the People, expressing their will; but in reality the People are the People because — or, more precisely, in so far as — they are embodied in the Party. And by saying that the People do not exist as a support of the

Party, we do not mean the obvious fact that the majority of the people do not really support the Party rule; the mechanism is a little more complicated. The paradoxical functioning of the 'People' in the totalitarian universe can be most easily detected through analysis of phrases like 'the whole People supports the Party'. This proposition cannot be falsified because behind the form of an observation of a fact, we have a circular definition of the People: in the Stalinist universe, 'supporting the rule of the Party' is 'rigidly designated' by the term 'People' — it is, in the last analysis, *the only feature which in all possible worlds defines the People.* That is why the real member of the People is only he who supports the rule of the Party: those who work against its rule are automatically excluded from the People; they became the 'enemies of the People'. What we have here is a somewhat crueller version of a well-known joke: 'My fiancée never misses an appointment with me because the moment she misses one, she is no longer my fiancée' — the People always support the Party because any member of the People who opposes Party rule automatically excludes himself from the People.

The Lacanian definition of democracy would then be: a sociopolitical order in which the People do not exist — do not exist as a unity, embodied in their unique representative. That is why the basic feature of the democratic order is that the place of Power is, by the necessity of its structure, an empty place (Lefort, 1981). In a democratic order, sovereignty lies in the People — but what is the People if not, precisely, the collection of the *subjects* of power? Here we have the same paradox as that of a natural language which is at the same time the ultimate, the highest metalanguage. Because the People cannot immediately govern themselves, the place of Power must always remain an empty place; any person occupying it can do so only temporarily, as a kind of surrogate, a substitute for the real-impossible sovereign — 'nobody can rule innocently', as Saint-Just puts it. And in totalitarianism, the Party becomes again the very subject who, being the immediate embodiment of the People, *can* rule innocently. It is not by accident that the real-socialist countries call themselves 'people's democracies' — here, finally, 'the People' exist again.

It is against the background of this emptying of the place of Power that we can measure the break introduced by the 'democratic invention' (Lefort) in the history of institutions: 'democratic society' could be determined as a society whose institutional structure includes, as a part of its 'normal', 'regular' reproduction, the moment of dissolution of the socio-symbolic bond, the moment of irruption of the Real: elections. Lefort interprets elections (those of 'formal', 'bourgeois' democracy) as an act of symbolic dissolution of social edifice: their crucial feature is the one that is usually made the target for Marxist criticism of 'formal democracy' — the fact that we take part as abstract citizens, atomized individuals, reduced to pure Ones without further qualifications.

At the moment of elections, the whole hierarchic network of social relations is in a way suspended, put in parentheses; 'society' as an organic unity ceases to exist, it changes into a contingent collection of atomized individuals, of abstract units, and the result depends on a purely quantitative mechanism of counting, ultimately on a stochastic process: some wholly unforeseeable (or manipulated) event — a scandal which erupts a few days before an election, for example, — can add that 'half per cent' one way or the other that determines the general orientation of the country's politics over the next few years. ... In vain do we conceal this thoroughly 'irrational' character of what we call 'formal democracy': at the moment of an election, the society is delivered to a stochastic process. Only the acceptance of such a risk, only such a readiness to hand over one's fate to 'irrational' hazard, renders 'democracy' possible: it is in this sense that we should read the dictum of Winston Churchill which I have already mentioned: 'democracy is the worst of all possible political systems, the only problem is that none of the others is better'.

It is true that democracy makes possible all sorts of manipulation, corruption, the rule of demagogy, and so on, but as soon as we eliminate the possibility of such deformations, we lose democracy itself — a neat example of the Hegelian Universal which can realize itself only in impure, deformed, corrupted forms; if we want to remove these deformations and to grasp the Universal in its intact purity, we obtain its very opposite. So-called 'real democracy' is just another name for non-democracy: if we want to exclude the possibility of manipulation, we must 'verify' the candidates in advance, we must introduce the difference between the 'true interests of the People' and its contingent fluctuating opinion, subjected to all kinds of demagogy and confusion, and so on — thus finishing with what is usually called 'organized democracy', in which the effective elections take place before elections and where the ballot has only plebiscitary value. In short, 'organized democracy' is a way of excluding the irruption of the Real which characterizes 'formal' democracy: the moment of dissolution of the social edifice into a purely numerical collection of atomized individuals.

So although 'in reality' there are only 'exceptions' and 'deformations', the universal notion of 'democracy' is none the less a 'necessary fiction', a symbolic fact in the absence of which effective democracy, in all the plurality of its forms, could not reproduce itself. Here Hegel is paradoxically close to Jeremy Bentham, to his *Theory of Fictions*, one of Lacan's constant references: the Hegelian Universal is such a 'fiction' as 'exists nowhere in reality' (there, we have nothing but exceptions) but is none the less implied by 'reality' itself as a point of reference conferring on it its symbolic consistency.

PART III

The Subject

=========== 5 ===========

Which Subject of the Real?

'There is no Metalanguage'

In comprehending Lacan as 'post-structuralist', one usually overlooks the
radical break that separates him from the field of 'post-structuralism':
even the propositions common to the two fields obtain a totally different
dimension in each. 'There is no metalanguage', for example: this is a
commonplace found not only in Lacan's psychoanalysis and in post-
structuralism (Derrida) but also in contemporary hermeneutics
(Gadamer) — we usually lose from view how Lacan's theory treats this
proposition in a way that is completely incompatible with post-
structuralism, as well as hermeneutics.

Post-structuralism claims that a text is always 'framed' by its own
commentary: the interpretation of a literary text resides on the same
plane as its 'object'. Thus the interpretation is included in the literary
corpus: there is no 'pure' literary object that would not contain an
element of interpretation, of distance towards its immediate meaning. In
post-structuralism the classic opposition between the object-text and its
external interpretative reading is thus replaced by a continuity of an
infinite literary text which is always already its own reading; that is,
which sets up distance from itself. That is why the post-structuralist
procedure *par excellence* is not only to search in purely literary texts for
propositions containing a theory about their own functioning but also to
read theoretical texts themselves as 'literature' — more precisely, to put in
parentheses their claim to truth in order to expose the textual mechanisms producing the 'truth effect'. As Habermas has already pointed out,
in post-structuralism we have a kind of universalized aestheticization
whereby 'truth' itself is finally reduced to one of the style effects of the
discursive articulation (Habermas, 1985).

In contrast to this Nietzschean reference of post-structuralism, Lacan's work makes almost no references to Nietzsche. Lacan always insists on psychoanalysis as a truth-experience: his thesis that truth is structured like a fiction has nothing at all to do with a post-structuralist reduction of the truth-dimension to a textual 'truth-effect'. Actually, it was Lévi-Strauss who, in spite of his ferocious critique of 'post-structuralist fashion', opened the way to a 'deconstructivist' poeticism by reading theoretical interpretations of myths as new versions of the same myth; for example, he conceived Freud's theory of the Oedipus complex as just a new variation on the Oedipus myth.

In 'post-structuralism', metonymy obtains a clear logical pre-dominance over metaphor. The metaphorical 'cut' is conceived as an effort doomed to fail; doomed to stabilize, canalize, or dominate the metonymical dissipation of the textual stream. In this perspective, the Lacanian insistence on the primacy of metaphor over metonymy, his thesis that metonymical sliding must always be supported by a meta-phorical cut, can appear to post-structuralists only as an indication that his theory is still marked by the 'metaphysics of presence'. Post-structuralists see the Lacanian theory of the *point de capiton*, of the phallic signifier as the signifier of lack, as an effort to master and restrain the 'dissemination' of the textual process. Is it not, they say, an attempt to localize a lack in a single signifier, the One, although it is the signifier of lack itself? Derrida repeatedly reproaches Lacan for the paradoxical gesture of reducing lack through its affirmation of itself. Lack is localized in a point of exception which guarantees the consistency of all the other elements, by the mere fact that it is determined as 'symbolic castration', by the mere fact that the phallus is defined as its signifier (Derrida, 1987).

Even at the level of a naïve 'immediate' reading, it is difficult to avoid the feeling that in this post-structuralist position something is amiss — or, more precisely, that this criticism of Lacan *runs a little too smoothly*. The post-structuralist position constantly repeats that no text could be totally non-metaphysical. On the one hand, it is not possible to get rid of the metaphysical tradition by a simple gesture of taking distance, of placing oneself outside it, because the language we are obliged to use is pene-trated by metaphysics. On the other hand, however, every text, however metaphysical, always produces gaps which announce breaches in the metaphysical circle: the points at which the textual process subverts what its 'author' intended to say. Is such a position not just a little too con-venient? To put it more bluntly, the position from which the decon-structivist can always make sure of the fact that 'there is no metalanguage'; that no utterance can say precisely what it intended to say; that the process of enunciation always subverts the utterance; is *the position of metalanguage* in its purest, most radical form.

How can one not recognize, in the passionate zeal with which the post-structuralist insists that every text, his own included, is caught in a fundamental ambiguity and flooded with the 'dissemination' of the intertextual process, the signs of an obstinate *denial* (in the Freudian sense of *Verneinung*); a barely hidden acknowledgement of the fact that one is speaking from a safe position, a position not menaced by the decentred textual process? That is why post-structuralist poeticism is ultimately *affected*. The whole effort to write 'poetically', to make us feel how our own text is already caught in a decentred network of plural processes and how this textual process always subverts what we 'intended to say', the whole effort to evade the purely theoretical form of exposing our ideas and to adopt rhetorical devices usually reserved to literature, masks the annoying fact that at the root of what post-structuralists are saying there is a clearly defined theoretical position which can be articulated without difficulty in a pure and simple metalanguage.

The grand post-structuralist assumption is that the classic reduction of rhetorical devices to external means which do not concern the signified contents is illusory: the so-called stylistic devices already determine the 'inner' notional contents themselves. Yet it would appear that the post-structuralist poetic style itself — the style of continuous ironic self-commentary and self-distance, the way of constantly subverting what one was supposed to say literally — exists only to embellish some basic theoretical propositions. That is why post-structuralist commentaries often produce an effect of 'bad infinity' in the Hegelian sense: an endless quasi-poetical variation on the same theoretical assumption, a variation which does not produce anything new. The problem with deconstruction, then, is not that it renounces a strict theoretical formulation and yields to a flabby poeticism. On the contrary, it is that its position is too 'theoretical' (in the sense of a theory which excludes the truth-dimension; that is, which does not affect the place from which we speak).

The Phallic Signifier

How then, can we elude this deadlock? It is here that Lacan differs radically from post-structuralists. In *Seminar XI* he begins one of his sentences: 'But this is precisely what I want to say and what I am saying — because what I want to say is what I am saying. . . .' In a post-structuralist reading, such phrases prove that Lacan still wants to retain the position of Master: 'saying what I wanted to say' lays claim to a coincidence between what we intend to say and what we are effectively saying — is not this coincidence what defines the illusion of the Master? Is Lacan not proceeding as if his own text is exempt from the gap between what is said and what he intends to say? Is he not claiming that he can dominate the signifying effects of this text? In the Lacanian perspective it is, on the contrary, precisely such 'impossible' utterances — utterances following the logic of the paradox 'I am lying' — which keep the fundamental gap of the signifying process open and in this way prevent us from assuming a metalanguage position.

Lacan is close to Brecht here. One has only to remember the basic procedure of Brecht's 'learning plays' of the early thirties in which the *dramatis personae* pronounce an 'impossible' commentary on their own acts. An actor enters the stage and says: 'I am a capitalist whose aim is to exploit workers. Now I will try to convince one of my workers of the truth of the bourgeois ideology which legitimizes the exploitation. . . .' He then approaches the worker and does exactly what he has announced he would do. Does such a procedure — an actor commenting on his deeds from an 'objective' position of pure metalanguage — not make it clear, in an almost palpable way, the utter impossibility of occupying this position; is it not, in its very absurdity, infinitely more subversive than the poeticism which prohibits every direct, simple utterance and feels obliged always to add new comments, retreats, digressions, brackets, quotation marks . . . — so many assurances that what we are saying is not to be taken directly or literally, as identical to itself?

Metalanguage is not just an Imaginary entity. It is *Real* in the strict Lacanian sense — that is, it is impossible to *occupy* its position. But, Lacan adds, it is even more difficult simply to *avoid* it. One cannot *attain* it, but one also cannot *escape* it. That is why the only way to avoid the Real is to produce an utterance of pure metalanguage which, by its patent absurdity, materializes its own impossibility: that is, a paradoxical element which, in its very identity, embodies absolute otherness, the irreparable gap that makes it impossible to occupy a metalanguage position.

For Derrida the localization of the lack is supposed to tame the 'dissemination' of the process of writing, while for Lacan only the presence of such a paradoxical 'at least one' sustains the radical dimension of the gap. The Lacanian name of this paradoxical element is, of course, the phallus as signifier, a kind of negative version of 'truth as the index of itself'. The phallic signifier is, so to speak, an index of its own impossibility. In its very positivity it is the signifier of 'castration' — that is, of its own lack. The so-called pre-phallic objects (breasts, excrement) are lost objects, while the phallus is not simply lost but is an object which *gives body to a certain fundamental loss in its very presence. In the phallus, loss as such attains a positive existence.* Here Lacan differs from Jung, to whom has been attributed — wrongly, perhaps, but *se non e vero, e ben trovato* — the famous phrase: 'What is a penis but a phallic symbol?'

Let us also recall Otto Fenichel's interpretation of the obscene gesture called in German 'the long nose' [*die lange Nase*]. Spreading the fingers in front of the face and putting the thumb on the nose supposedly connotes the erected phallus. The message of this gesture would appear to be a simple showing-off in front of an adversary: look how big mine is; mine is bigger than yours. Instead of refuting this simplistic interpretation directly, Fenichel introduces a small displacement: the logic of insulting an adversary always involves *imitating* one of his/her features. If this is true, what, then, is so insulting in an imitation which points out that the other has a large and powerful virile member? Fenichel's solution is that one has to read this gesture as the first part of a sentence, the second part of which is omitted. The whole of it reads: 'Yours is so big and powerful, but *in spite of that, you are impotent. You cannot hurt me with it*' (Fenichel, 1928).

In this way the adversary is caught in a forced choice which, according to Lacan (1979, ch. XVI), defines the experience of castration: if he cannot, he cannot; but even if he can, any attesting to his power is doomed to function as a denial — that is, as a masking of his fundamental impotence, as a mere showing-off which just confirms, in a negative way, that he cannot do anything. The more he reacts, the more he shows his power, the more his impotence is confirmed.

It is in this precise sense that the phallus is the signifier of castration. This is the logic of the phallic inversion which sets in when the demonstration of power starts to function as a confirmation of a fundamental impotence. This is also the logic of so-called political provocation addressed against a totalitarian power structure. The punk imitating the 'sadomasochistic' power ritual is not to be conceived as a case of the victim's identification with the aggressor (as it is usually interpreted). The message to the power structure is, on the contrary, the negation implied in the positive act of imitation: You are so powerful, *but for all that, you are impotent. You cannot really hurt me!* In this way, the power structure is caught in the same trap. The more violent its reaction, the more it confirms its fundamental impotence.

'Lenin in Warsaw' as Object

To articulate more precisely the way in which the Lacanian phallic sig-nifier entails the impossibility of metalanguage, let us return to the post-structuralist understanding of the idea that 'there is no metalanguage'. Its starting point is the fact that the zero level of all metalanguages — natural, ordinary language — is simultaneously the last interpretative framework of all of them: it is the ultimate metalanguage. Ordinary language is its own metalanguage. It is self-referential; the place of an incessant auto-reflexive movement. In this conceptualization one does not mention the object too much. Usually, one gets rid of it simply by pointing out how 'reality' is already structured through the medium of language. In this way post-structuralists can calmly abandon themselves to the infinite self-interpretative play of language. 'There is no metalan-guange' is actually taken to mean *its exact opposite: that there is no pure object-language*, any language that would function as a purely transparent medium for the designation of pre-given reality. Every 'objective' statement about things includes some kind of self-distance, a rebounding of the signifier from its 'literal meaning'. In short, language is always saying, more or less, *something other* than what it means to say.

In Lacan's teaching, however, the proposition 'there is no meta-language' is to be taken literally. It means that all language is in a way an object-language: *there is no language without object*. Even when the language is apparently caught in a web of self-referential movement, even when it is apparently speaking only about itself, there is an objective, non-signifying 'reference' to this movement. The Lacanian mark of it is, of course, the *objet petit a*. The self-referential movement of the signifier is not that of a closed circle, but an elliptical movement around a certain void. And the *objet petit a*, as the original lost object which in a way coin-cides with its own loss, is precisely the embodiment of this void.

This 'internal exclusion' of the object from the Other of the symbolic network also allows us to expose the confusion upon which the Derridean assumption of the 'title-address of the letter' [*le titre de la lettre*] rests: that is, the criticism of Lacanian theory in which, according to Derrida, the letter always possesses its title-address, always reaches its destination. This is supposed to attest to the 'closed economy' of the

Lacanian concept of the Symbolic: the central point of reference (the signifier of lack) allegedly precludes the possibility that a letter could go astray, lose its circular-teleological path and miss its address (Nancy and Lacoue-Labarthe, 1973).

Where does the misunderstanding in this criticism lie? It is true that in Lacanian theory 'every letter has its title', but this title is definitely not some kind of *telos* of its trajectory. The Lacanian 'title of the letter' is closer to the title of a picture; for example, that described in a well-known joke about 'Lenin in Warsaw'. At an art exhibition in Moscow, there is a picture showing Nadezhda Krupskaya, Lenin's wife, in bed with a young member of the Komsomol. The title of the picture is 'Lenin in Warsaw'. A bewildered visitor asks a guide: 'But where is Lenin?' The guide replies quietly and with dignity: 'Lenin is in Warsaw'.

If we put aside Lenin's position as the absent Third, the bearer of the prohibition of the sexual relationship, we could say that 'Lenin in Warsaw' is, in a strict Lacanian sense, the object of this picture. The title names the object which is lacking in the field of what is depicted. That is to say, in this joke, the trap in which the visitor was caught could be defined precisely as the metalanguage trap. The visitor's mistake is to establish the same distance between the picture and the title as between the sign and the denoted object, as if the title is speaking *about* the picture from a kind of 'objective distance', and then to look for its positive correspondence in the picture. Thus the visitor poses a question: 'Where is the object indicated by its title depicted?' But the whole point is, of course, that in this case the relation between the picture and its title is not the usual one whereby the title corresponds simply to what is depicted ('Landscape', 'Self-portrait'). Here the title is, so to speak, on the same surface. It is part of the same continuity as the picture itself. Its distance from the picture is strictly internal, making an incision into the picture. That is why something must fall (out) from the picture: not its title, but the object which is replaced by the title.

In other words, the title of this picture functions as the Freudian *Vorstellungsrepräsentanz*: the representative, the substitute of some representation, the signifying element filling out the vacant place of the missing representation (of the depiction, that is, of Lenin himself). The field of representation [*Vorstellung*] is the field of what is positively depicted, but the problem is that everything cannot be depicted. Something must necessarily fall out, 'Lenin must be in Warsaw', and the title takes the place of this void, of this missing, 'originally repressed' representation: its exclusion functions as a positive condition for the emergence of what is being depicted (because, to put it bluntly, if Lenin were not in Warsaw, Nadezhda Krupskaya could not . . .). If we take the word 'subject' in the sense of 'content', we can say that what we have here is precisely *the difference subject/object*. 'Nadezhda Krupskaya in bed with a young Komsomol member' is the *subject* of the picture; 'Lenin in Warsaw' is its *object*.

We can take this as a joke about *Vorstellungsrepräsentanz*, and now we can also understand why the signifier as such has the status of the *Vorstellungsrepräsentanz* in Lacan. It is no longer the simple Saussurean material representative of the signified, of the mental representation-idea, but the substitute filling out the void of some originally missing representation: it does not bring to mind any representation, it represents its *lack*. The misunderstanding in the post-structuralist criticism of Lacan is ultimately a misunderstanding about the nature of *Vorstellungsrepräsentanz*. This criticism misses the fact that the *Vorstellungsrepräsentanz* (the pure, reflexive signifier incarnating the lack itself) fills out the void of the lost object. As soon as the *Vorstellungsrepräsentanz* is no longer connected to this hole in the Other, to the falling out of the object, it begins to function as a 'title': as a metalanguage designation, as an incision that limits, totalizes, canalizes the original dispersion of the signifying texture . . . in short, we find ourselves in a 'post-structuralist' mess.

If the joke about Lenin in Warsaw exemplifies the logic of the master-signifier, there is another joke — in a way its symmetrical inversion — which exemplifies the logic of the object: the joke about the conscript who tries to evade military service by pretending to be mad. His symptom is that he compulsively checks all the pieces of paper he can lay his hands on, constantly repeating: 'That is not it!' He is sent to the military psychiatrist, in whose office he also examines all the papers around, including those in the wastepaper basket, repeating all the time: 'That is not it!' The psychiatrist, finally convinced that he really is mad, gives him a written warrant releasing him from military service. The conscript casts a look at it and says cheerfully: 'That *is* it!'

We can say that this little piece of paper finally found — a warrant of release — has the status of an object in the Lacanian sense. Why? Because it is an object produced by the signifying texture itself. It is a kind of object that came to exist as a result of all the fuss about it. The 'mad' conscript pretends to look for something, and through his very search, through its repeated failure ('That is not it!'), he produces what he is looking for. The paradox then, is that the process of searching itself *produces* the object which *causes* it: an exact parallel to Lacanian desire which produces its own object-cause. The error of all the people around the conscript, the psychiatrist included, is that they overlook the way they are already part of the 'mad' conscript's game. They think they are examining him from an objective, metalanguage distance, like the bewildered spectator of the picture 'Lenin in Warsaw' who mistook the picture's title for a metalanguage description of its content.

Their error is therefore symmetrical. In the case of 'Lenin in Warsaw' the title is on the same level as the depicted content of the picture and is not a metalanguage designation of it. In the second example, the paper as an object is part of the actual signifying process; its product and not its external reference. First we have the paradox of a *signifier* which is a part of the *representation of reality* (filling out a void, a hole in it). Then we have the inverse paradox of an *object* which must be included in the *signifying texture*. Perhaps this double paradox offers us the final clue to the Lacanian propositon: 'There is no metalanguage'.

Antagonism as Real

To grasp this logic of an object included in the signifying texture, we must bear in mind the paradoxical character of the Lacanian Real. It is usually conceived as a hard kernel resisting symbolization, dialecticization, persisting in its place, always returning to it. There is a well-known science-fiction story ('Experiment' by Fredric Brown) that illustrates this point perfectly: Professor Johnson has developed a small-scale experimental model of a time machine. Small articles placed on it can be sent into the past or the future. He first demonstrates to his two colleagues a five-minute time travel into the future, by setting the future dial and placing a small brass cube on the machine's platform. It instantly vanishes and reappears five minutes later. The next experiment, five minutes into the past, is a little trickier. Johnson explains that having set the past dial at five minutes, he will place the cube on the platform at exactly three o'clock. But since time is now running backwards, it should vanish from his hand and appear on the platform at five minutes to three — that is, five minutes before he places it there. One of his colleagues asks the obvious question: 'How can you place it there, then?' Johnson explains that at three o'clock the cube will vanish from the platform and appear in his hand, to be placed on the machine. This is exactly what happens. The second colleague wants to know what would happen if, after the cube has appeared on the platform (five minutes before being

placed there), Johnson were to change his mind and *not* put it there at
three o'clock. Would this not create a paradox?

> 'An interesting idea,' Professor Johnson said. 'I had not thought of it and it
> will be interesting to try. Very well, I shall *not. . .*'
> There was no paradox at all. The cube remained.
> But the entire rest of the Universe, professors and all, vanished.

So, even if all symbolic reality dissolves itself, disappears into nothing,
the Real — the small cube — will return to its place. This is what Lacan
means when he says that the ethical imperative is the mode of the
presence of the Real in the Symbolic: *Fiat justitia, pereat mundus!* The cube
must return to its place even if all the world, all symbolic reality,
perishes.

But this is just one side of the Lacanian Real; it is the side which
predominates in the fifties when we have the *Real* — the brute, pre-
symbolic reality which always returns to its place — then the *symbolic*
order which structures our perception of reality, and finally the *Imaginary*, the level of illusory entities whose consistency is the effect of a kind
of mirror-play — that is, they have no real existence but are a mere structural effect. With the development of Lacanian teaching in the sixties
and seventies, what he calls 'the Real' approaches more and more what
he called, in the fifties, the Imaginary. Let us take the case of trauma: in
the fifties, in his first Seminar, the traumatic event is defined as an
imaginary entity which had not yet been fully symbolized, given a place
in the symbolic universe of the subject (Lacan, 1988, ch. XXII); but in the
seventies, trauma is *real* — it is a hard core resisting symbolization, but
the point is that it does not matter if it has had a place, if it has 'really
occurred' in so-called reality; the point is simply that it produces a series
of structural effects (displacements, repetitions, and so on). The Real is an
entity which must be constructed afterwards so that we can account for
the distortions of the symbolic structure.

The most famous Freudian example of such a real entity is of course
the primal parricide: it would be senseless to search for its traces in
prehistoric reality, but it must none the less be presupposed if we want to
account for the present state of things. It is the same with the primal fight
to death between the (future) master and servant in Hegel's *Phenomenology of Spirit*: it is senseless trying to determine when this event could
have taken place; the point is just that it must be presupposed, that it
constitutes a fantasy-scenario implied by the very fact that people work

— it is the intersubjective condition of the so-called 'instrumental relation to the world of objects'.

The paradox of the Lacanian Real, then, is that it is an entity which, although it does not exist (in the sense of 'really existing', taking place in reality), has a series of properties — it exercises a certain structural causality, it can produce a series of effects in the symbolic reality of subjects. That is why it can be illustrated by a multitude of well-known jokes based on the same matrix: 'Is this the place where the Duke of Wellington spoke his famous words?' — 'Yes, this is the place, but he never spoke those words' — these never-spoken words are a Lacanian Real. One can quote examples *ad infinitum*: 'Smith not only doesn't believe in ghosts, he isn't even afraid of them!' ... up to God himself who, according to Lacan, belongs to the Real: 'God has all perfections except one — he doesn't exist!' In this sense, the Lacanian *subjet supposé savoir* (the subject presumed to know) is also such a real entity: it does not exist, but it produces a decisive shift in the development of the psychoanalytic cure.

To mention the final example: the famous MacGuffin, the Hitchcockian object, the pure pretext whose sole role is to set the story in motion but which is in itself 'nothing at all' — the only significance of the MacGuffin lies in the fact that it has some significance for the characters — that it must seem to be of vital importance to them. The original anecdote is well known: two men are sitting in a train; one of them asks: 'What's that package up there in the luggage rack?' 'Oh, that's a MacGuffin.' 'What's a MacGuffin?' 'Well, it's an apparatus for trapping lions in the Scottish Highlands.' 'But there are no lions in the Scottish Highlands.' 'Well, then, that's not a MacGuffin.' There is another version which is much more to the point: it is the same as the other, with the exception of the last answer: 'Well, you see how efficient it is!' — that's MacGuffin, a pure nothing which is none the less efficient. Needless to add, the MacGuffin is the purest case of what Lacan calls *objet petit a*: a pure void which functions as the object-cause of desire.

That would be, then, the precise definition of the real object: a cause which in itself does not exist — which is present only in a series of effects, but always in a distorted, displaced way. If the Real is the impossible, it is precisely this impossibility which is to be grasped through its effects. Laclau and Mouffe were the first to develop this logic of the Real in its relevance for the social–ideological field in their concept of *antagonism*: antagonism is precisely such an impossible kernel, a certain limit which is in itself nothing; it is only to be constructed retroactively, from a series of its effects, as the traumatic point which escapes them; it prevents a closure of the social field. In this way we might reread even the classic notion of the 'class struggle': it is not the last signifier giving meaning to all social phenomena ('all social processes are in the final analysis expressions of the class struggle'), but — quite the contrary — a certain limit, a pure negativity, a traumatic limit which prevents the final totalization of the social–ideological field. The 'class struggle' is present only in its effects, in the fact that every attempt to totalize the social field, to assign to social phenomena a definite place in the social structure, is always doomed to failure.

If we define the Real as such a paradoxical, chimerical entity which, although it does not exist, has a series of properties and can produce a series of effects, it becomes clear that the Real *par excellence* is *jouissance*: *jouissance* does not exist, it is impossible, but it produces a number of traumatic effects. This paradoxical nature of *jouissance* also offers us a clue to explaining the fundamental paradox which unfailingly attests the presence of the Real: the fact of the prohibition of something which is already in itself impossible. The elementary model is, of course, the prohibition of incest; but there are many other examples — let us cite only the usual conservative attitude towards child sexuality: it does not exist, children are innocent beings, that is why we must control them strictly and fight child sexuality — not to mention the obvious fact that the most famous phrase of all analytical philosophy — the last proposition of Wittgenstein's *Tractatus* — implies the same paradox: 'Whereof one cannot speak, thereof one must be silent.' Immediately, the stupid question arises: If it is already stated that it is *impossible* to say anything about the unspeakable, why add that we *must not* speak about it? We find the same paradox in Kant: when treating the question of the origins of legitimate state power, he says directly that we *cannot* penetrate the obscure origins of power because we *should not* do so (because by doing so, we put ourselves *outside* its domain and so automatically subvert its legitimacy) — a curious variation on his basic ethical imperative *Du kannst, denn du sollst!* — You can, because you must!

The solution to this paradox — why forbid something which is already in itself impossible? — lies in the fact that the impossibility relates to the level of existence (it is impossible; that is, it doesn't exist), while the prohibition relates to the properties it predicates (*jouissance* is forbidden because of its properties).

The Forced Choice of Freedom

In this sense, we may say that the status of freedom itself is real. The usual '(post-)structuralist' approach would be to denounce 'freedom' as an imaginary experience resting on misrecognition, on a blindness to the structural causality which determines the activity of subjects. But on the basis of Lacan's teaching in the seventies, we can approach freedom from another perspective: freedom, 'free choice', as the real–impossible.

A few months ago, a Yugoslav student was called to regular military service. In Yugoslavia, at the beginning of military service, there is a certain ritual: every new soldier must solemnly swear that he is willing to serve his country and to defend it even if that means losing his life, and son on — the usual patriotic stuff. After the public ceremony, everybody must sign the solemn document. The young soldier simply refused to sign, saying that an oath depends upon free choice, that it is a matter of free decision, and he, from his free choice, did not want to give his signature to the oath. But, he was quick to add, if any of the officers present was prepared to give him a formal order to sign the oath, he would of course be prepared to do so. The perplexed officers explained to him that because the oath depended upon his free decision (an oath obtained by force is valueless), they could not give him such an order, but that, on the other hand, if he still refused to give his signature, he would be prosecuted for refusing to do his duty and condemned to prison. Needless to add, this is exactly what happened; but before going to prison, the student did succeed in obtaining from the military court of law the paradoxical decision, a formal document ordering him to sign a free oath. . . .

In the subject's relationship to the community to which he belongs, there is always such a paradoxical point of *choix forcé* — at this point, the community is saying to the subject: you have freedom to choose, but on condition that you choose the right thing; you have, for example, the freedom to choose to sign or not to sign the oath, on condition that you choose rightly — that is, to sign it. If you make the wrong choice, you lose freedom of choice itself. And it is by no means accidental that this paradox arises at the level of the subject's relationship to the community to which he belongs: the situation of the forced choice consists in the fact that the subject must freely choose the community to which he already belongs, independent of his choice — *he must choose what is already given to him.*

The point is that he is never actually in a position to choose: he is always treated *as if he had already chosen*. Moreover, contrary to the first impression that such a forced choice is a trap by means of which totalitarian Power catches its subjects, we must stress that there is nothing 'totalitarian' about it. The subject who thinks he can avoid this paradox and really have a free choice is a *psychotic* subject, one who retains a kind of distance from the symbolic order — who is not really caught in the signifying network. The 'totalitarian' subject is closer to this psychotic position: the proof would be the status of the 'enemy' in totalitarian discourse (the Jew in Fascism, the traitor in Stalinism) — precisely the subject supposed to have made a free choice and to have freely chosen the wrong side.

This is also the basic paradox of love: not only of one's country, but also of a woman or a man. If I am directly ordered to love a woman, it is clear that this does not work: in a way, love must be free. But on the other hand, if I proceed as if I really have a free choice, if I start to look around and say to myself 'Let's choose which of these women I will fall in love with', it is clear that this also does not work, that it is not 'real love'. The paradox of love is that it is a free choice, but a choice which never arrives in the present — it is always already made. At a certain moment, I can only state retroactively that *I've already chosen*.

Where, in philosophical tradition do we find the first formulation of this paradox? Late in his life, Kant conceived the choice of Evil as an a priori, transcendental act — in this way he tried to explain the sentiment we usually have when we find ourselves face to face with an evil person: our impression is that his wickedness does not simply depend upon circumstances (which are by definition extenuating) but is an integral part of his eternal nature. In other words, 'wickedness' appears to be something which is irrevocably *given*: the person in question can never change it, outgrow it via his ultimate moral development.

On the other hand, however, we have a contradictory sentiment according to which the evil person is wholly *responsible* for his wickedness, although it is integral to his nature — that is, although 'he was born like that': 'to be evil' is not the same as to be stupid, irascible, and other similar features pertaining to our psychic nature. Evil is always experienced as something pertaining to a free choice, to a decision for which the subject has to assume all responsibility. How can we resolve this contradiction between the 'natural', given character of human Evil and that same Evil as pertaining to a free choice? Kant's solution consists in conceiving the choice of Evil, the decision of Evil, as an atemporal, a priori, transcendental act: as an act which *never took place* in temporal reality but none the less constitutes the very frame of the subject's development, of his practical activity.

Lacan was thus quite justified in locating the starting point of the 'movement of ideas' which culminated in the Freudian discovery in Kant's philosophy, more specifically in his *Critique of Practical Reason* (Lacan, 1966, pp. 765–6). One of the consequences of the Kantian revolution in the domain of 'practical reason' usually passed over in silence was that with Kant, for the first time, *Evil as such acquired a proper ethical status*. That is to say, with his idea of an 'original Evil' inscribed into the atemporal character of a person, Evil becomes an affair of principle, an ethical attitude — 'ethical' in the exact sense of an impetus of the will beyond the pleasure principle (and its prolongation, the reality principle). 'Evil' is no longer a simple opportunist activity taking into account only 'pathological' motives (pleasure, profit, utility . . .), it is, on the contrary, an affair of the eternal and autonomous character of a person pertaining to his original, atemporal choice. This again confirms the paradoxical Lacanian conjunction 'Kant avec Sade', as well as the fact that in the epoch of Kant, we witness the resurgence of a series of musical and literary figures embodying Evil *qua* ethical attitude (from Mozart's Don Giovanni to the Byronesque Romantic hero).

In his *Treatise on Human Freedom* (1809), Schelling, the 'acme of German idealism' (Heidegger), radicalized the Kantian theory by introducing a crucial distinction between freedom (free choice) and consciousness: the atemporal choice by means of which the subject chooses himself as 'good' or 'evil' is an *unconscious* choice (how can we not recall, apropos of this Schellingian distinction, the Freudian thesis concerning the atemporal character of the unconscious?). Let us resume Schelling's line of reasoning. Freedom is posited as the cause of Evil — that is, Evil results from a free choice of the subject, from his decision for it. If, however, freedom is the cause of Evil, how do we account for the innumerable evils, moral and physical, which seem *not* to depend on our conscious will? The only possible solution is to presuppose some fundamental choice *preceding* our conscious choices and decisions — in other words, some unconscious choice.

This solution of Schelling is directed primarily against the subjective idealism of Fichte, who reduced the whole range of free activity to the self-reflection of consciousness. Schelling's main counter-argument consists in a delicate psychological observation: sometimes we feel responsible for a thing without any conscious decision on our part; we feel sinful without having effectively sinned; we feel guilty without

accomplishing the act. This sentiment is, of course, the so-called sentiment of 'irrational', unfounded guilt, well known in psychoanalysis: the
'excessive', 'inexplicable' guilt which masks the psychic reality of an
unconscious desire.

Schelling interprets it in the same way: this 'irrational' guilt bears
witness to an unconscious choice, to an unconscious decision for Evil. It
is as if our game is over *before* we awaken ourselves into consciousness:
the basic character of every human being — good or evil — is the result of
an original, eternal, eternally past, a priori, transcendental choice — that
is, a choice which was *always already made*, although it never took place in
temporal, everyday reality. Such a free unconscious choice *must be presupposed* to account for the sentiment that we are guilty even for things
which do not depend upon our conscious decision:

> . . . there is, in every man, a feeling that from all eternity, he has been what
> he is, i.e., that he did not become it in course of time. Irrespective of the
> undeniable necessity of all acts and in spite of the fact that every person,
> observing himself, must admit that he is not good or evil by chance or by his
> free will, the evil-doer does not feel himself forced in his acts [. . .], but
> accomplishes them *with* his will, not against it. Neither Judas himself nor
> any other creature could have changed the fact that he betrayed Christ, and
> yet he did not betray him under compulsion but willingly and with
> complete freedom . . .

> . . . he who says, as if to exculpate himself for an unjust deed: I was made like
> that, is for all that conscious of the fact that he is like that by his own fault,
> although he is also justified to say that it was not possible for him to act in
> any other way. How often it happens that already in his childhood when,
> from an empirical standpoint, we could barely attribute to him freedom and
> discernment, a man attests to such a disposition to Evil making possible for
> us to predict safely that he will not give way to any discipline and teaching,
> i.e., that when he matures this disposition will effectively bear the evil fruits
> we could perceive in their seeds; and yet nobody doubts his responsibility,
> everyone is convinced of his fault as if all his particular acts were in his
> power. This universal judgement about a disposition to Evil which is
> consciousless and even irresistible, a judgement rendering it into an act of
> freedom, points towards an act and consequently towards a life before this
> [terrestrial] life. (Schelling, 1978, pp. 78-9).

Is it necessary to point out how this Schellingian determination of an
original, atemporal choice corresponds perfectly to the Lacanian notion
of the Real as an act which never took place in reality but which must

nevertheless be presupposed, 'constructed', afterwards to account for the present state of things? We could now return to our unfortunate student: his deadlock is precisely that of the Schellingian act of freedom. Although, in the temporal reality of his life, he never chose his country, he was treated as if he had already chosen — as if, in an atemporal, eternally past act, he chose what was from the very beginning imposed on him — the allegiance to his country.

Coincidentia Oppositorum

The Real is therefore simultaneously both the hard, impenetrable kernel resisting symbolization *and* a pure chimerical entity which has in itself no ontological consistency. To use Kripkean terminology, the Real is the rock upon which every attempt at symbolization stumbles, the hard core which remains the same in all possible worlds (symbolic universes); but at the same time its status is thoroughly precarious; it is something that persists only as failed, missed, in a shadow, and dissolves itself as soon as we try to grasp it in its positive nature. As we have already seen, this is precisely what defines the notion of traumatic event: a point of failure of symbolization, but at the same time never given in its positivity — it can be constructed only backwards, from its structural effects. All its effectivity lies in the distortions it produces in the symbolic universe of the subject: the traumatic event is ultimately just a fantasy-construct filling out a certain void in a symbolic structure and, as such, the retroactive effect of this structure.

There is a series of other oppositions which define the Lacanian concept of the Real:

- We have the Real as the starting point, the basis, the foundation of the process of symbolization (that is why Lacan speaks of the 'symbolization of the Real') — that is, the Real which in a sense *precedes* the symbolic order and is subsequently structured by it when it gets caught in its network: this is the great Lacanian motif of symbolization as a process which mortifies, drains off, empties, carves the fullness of the Real of the living body. But the Real is at the same time the product, remainder, leftover, scraps of this process of symbolization, the remnants, the excess which escapes symbolization and is as such produced by the symbolization itself. In Hegelian terms, the Real is simultaneously *presupposed* and *posed* by the symbolic. In so far as the kernel of the Real is *jouissance*, this duality takes the form of a difference between *jouissance*, enjoyment, and *plus-de-jouir*, the surplus-of-enjoying: *jouissance* is the basis upon which symbolization works, the basis emptied, disembodied, structured by the symbolization, but this process produces at the same time a residue, a leftover, which is the surplus-enjoyment.

- The Real is the fullness of the inert presence, positivity; nothing is lacking in the Real — that is, the lack is introduced only by the symbolization; it is a signifier which introduces a void, an absence in the Real. But at the same time the Real is in itself a hole, a gap, an opening in the middle of the symbolic order — it is the lack around which the symbolic order is structured. The Real as a starting point, as a basis, is a positive fullness without lack; as a product, a leftover of symbolization, it is, in contrast, the void, the emptiness created, encircled by the symbolic structure. We might also approach the same pair of opposites from the perspective of negativity: the Real is something that cannot be negated, a positive inert datum which is insensitive to negation, cannot be caught in the dialectics of negativity; but we must add at once that it is so because the Real itself, in its positivity, is nothing but an embodiment of a certain void, lack, radical negativity. *It cannot be negated because it is already in itself, in its positivity, nothing but an embodiment of a pure negativity, emptiness.* That is why the real object is a sublime object in a strict Lacanian sense — an object which is just an embodiment of the lack in the Other, in the symbolic order. The sublime object is an object which cannot be approached too closely: if we get too near it, it loses its sublime features and becomes an ordinary vulgar object — it can persist only in an interspace, in an intermediate state, viewed from a certain perspective, half-seen. If we want to see it in the light of day, it changes into an everyday object, it dissipates itself, precisely because in itself it is nothing at all. Let us take a well-known scene from Fellini's *Roma*: the workers digging tunnels for a subway find the remnants of some old Roman buildings; they call the archaeologists, and when they enter the buildings together, a marvellous view awaits them: walls full of beautiful frescoes of immobile, melancholic figures — but the paintings are too fragile, they cannot withstand the open air and immediately begin to dissolve, leaving the spectators alone with the blank walls. . . .

- As Jacques-Alain Miller has already pointed out (in his unpublished seminar), the status of the Real is at the same time that of corporeal contingency and that of logical consistency. In a first approach, the Real is a shock of a contingent encounter which disrupts the automatic circulation of the symbolic mechanism; a grain of sand preventing its smooth functioning; a traumatic encounter which ruins the balance of the symbolic universe of the subject. But, as we have seen with regard to trauma, precisely as an irruption of a total contingency, the traumatic event is nowhere given in its positivity; only afterwards can it be *logically constructed* as a point which escapes symbolization.

- If we try to seize the Real from the perspective of the distinction between *quid* and *quod*, between the properties of a symbolic-universal nature attributed to an object and this object itself in its givenness, a surplus of an X escaping, in its positivity, the network of universal-symbolic determinations — that is, if we try to approach the Real through the field opened by the Kripkean criticism of the theory of descriptions — we should say, first, that the Real is the surplus of *quod* over *quid*, a pure positivity beyond the series of properties, beyond a set of descriptions; but at the same time, the example of trauma proves that the Real is also the exact opposite: an entity which does not exist but has nevertheless a series of properties.

- Finally, if we try to define the Real in its relation to the function of writing (*écrit*, not the post-structuralist *écriture*), we must, of course, in a first approach state that the Real cannot be inscribed, that it escapes inscription (the Real of the sexual relation, for example); but at the same time, the Real is the writing itself as opposed to the signifier — the Lacanian *écrit* has the status of an object, not of a signifier.

This immediate coincidence of opposite or even contradictory determinations is what *defines* the Lacanian Real. We can thus differentiate between the imaginary, the symbolic and the real status of the couples of opposites. In the *imaginary* relation, the two poles of opposition are complementary; together they build a harmonious totality; each gives the other what the other lacks — each fills out the lack in the other (the fantasy of the fully realized sexual relationship, for example, where man and woman form a harmonious whole). The *symbolic* relation is, on the contrary, differential: the identity of each of the moments consists in its difference to the opposite moment. A given element does not fill in the lack in the other, it is not complementary to the other but, on the contrary, *takes the place of the lack in the other*, embodies what is lacking in the other: its positive presence is nothing but an objectification of a lack in its opposite element. The opposites, the poles of the symbolic relation, each in a way returns to the other its own lack; they are united on the basis of their common lack.

That would also be the definition of symbolic communication: what circulates between the subjects is above all a certain void; the subjects pass to each other a common lack. In this perspective a woman is not complementary to a man, but she embodies his lack (which is why Lacan can say that a beautiful woman is a perfect incarnation of man's castration). Finally, the *Real* is defined as a point of the immediate coincidence of the opposite poles: each pole passes immediately into its opposite; each is already in itself its own opposite. The only philosophical counterpart here is Hegelian dialectics: at the very beginning of his *Logic*, Being and Nothingness are not complementary, neither is Hegel's point that each of them obtains its identity through its difference from the other. The point is that Being in itself, when we try to grasp it 'as it is', in its pure abstraction and indeterminacy, without further specification, reveals itself to be Nothingness.

Another example, perhaps closer to the Lacanian Real, would be Hegel's criticism of Kant's Thing-in-itself [*das Ding-an-sich*]. Hegel tries to show how this famous Thing-in-itself, this pure surplus of objectivity which cannot be reached by thought, this transcending entity, is effectively a pure 'Thing-of-Thought [*Gedankending*]', a pure form of Thought: the transcendence of the Thing-in-itself coincides immediately with the pure immanence of Thought. That is to say, how do we reach, how do we build the idea of a Thing-in-itself? By making an abstraction, by subtracting all the particular, concrete determinations of the objectivity which are supposed to depend upon our subjectivity – and what remains after this abstraction of all particular, determinate contents is precisely a pure, empty form of Thought.

Lacan gives the clue to this paradoxical coincidence of opposites in his Seminar *Encore* when he points out that 'the Real can be inscribed [*peut s'inscrire*] only through a deadlock of formalization' (Lacan, 1975, p. 85). The Real is of course, in a first approach, that which cannot be inscribed, which 'doesn't cease not to inscribe itself [*ne cesse pas de ne pas s'écrire*]' – the rock upon which every formalization stumbles. But it is precisely through this failure that we can in a way encircle, locate the empty place of the Real. In other words, the Real cannot be inscribed, but we can inscribe this impossibility itself, we can locate its place: a traumatic place which causes a series of failures. And Lacan's whole point is that the Real is *nothing but* this impossibility of its inscription: the Real is not a transcendent positive entity, persisting somewhere beyond the symbolic order like a hard kernel inaccessible to it, some kind of Kantian 'Thing-in-itself' — in itself it is nothing at all, just a void, an emptiness in a symbolic structure marking some central impossibility. It is in this sense that the enigmatic Lacanian phrase defining the subject as an 'answer of the Real' is to be understood: we can inscribe, encircle the void place of the subject through the failure of his symbolization, because the subject is nothing but the failure point of the process of his symbolic representation.

In the Lacanian perspective, the object as real is then, in the final analysis, just a certain limit: we can *overtake* it, leave it behind us, but we cannot *reach* it. That is the Lacanian reading of the classic paradox of Achilles and the tortoise: Achilles can of course overtake her, but he cannot reach her, catch up with her. It is like the old Brechtian paradox of happiness from the *Threepenny Opera*: you must not run too desperately after happiness, because if you do you might overtake it and happiness will remain behind you. . . . That is the Lacanian Real: a certain limit which is always missed — we always come too early or too late. And, as the late Michel Silvestre pointed out (Silvestre, 1986), the same thing also goes for so-called 'free association' in psychoanalysis: on the one hand it is impossible to reach it, we cannot really spontaneously give ourselves to it, we always manipulate, have a certain intention, and so on; but on the other hand *we cannot escape it*; whatever we say during analysis already has the status of free association. For example, I cannot, in the middle of the analysis, turn to the analyst and say: 'Now wait a minute, I want to speak to you really seriously, as person to person . . .' — even if we do this, its performative force is already suspended — that is, it already has the status of 'free association', of something that is to be interpreted, not taken at its face value.

Another Hegelian Joke

What notion of the subject is compatible with this paradoxical character of the Real? The basic feature of the Lacanian subject is, of course, its alienation in the signifier: as soon as the subject is caught in the radically external signifying network he is mortified, dismembered, divided. To get an idea of what is meant by the Lacanian division of the subject, one has only to remember Lewis Carroll's well-known paradox: 'I'm so glad I don't like asparagus,' said the small girl to a sympathetic friend, 'because, if I did, I should have to eat it — and I can't bear it!' Here we have the whole Lacanian problem of the reflexivity of desire: desire is always a desire of a desire — the question is not immediately 'What should I desire?' but 'There are a lot of things that I desire, I have a lot of desires — which of them is worth being the object of my desire? Which desire should I desire?'

This paradox is literally reproduced in the basic situation of the classic Stalinist political processes, in which the accused victim is at the same time supposed to confess his love for asparagus (the bourgeoisie, the counter-revolution) and express an attitude of disgust towards his own activity, to the point of demanding for himself the death penalty. That is why the Stalinist victim is the perfect example of the difference between the *sujet d'énoncé* (subject of the statement) and the *sujet d'énonciation* (subject of the enunciation). The demand that the Party is addressing to him is: 'At this moment, the Party needs the process to consolidate the revolutionary gains, so be a good Communist, do a last service to the Party and confess.' Here we have the division of the subject in its purest form: the only way for the accused to confirm himself as a good Communist at the level of the *sujet d'énonciation*, is to confess — to determine himself, at the level of the *sujet d'énoncé*, as a traitor. Ernesto Laclau was perhaps right when he once remarked (in a private conversation) that it is not only Stalinism which is a linguistic phenomenon, but language itself which is a Stalinist phenomenon.

Here, however, we must distinguish carefully between this Lacanian notion of the divided subject and the 'post-structuralist' notion of the subject-positions. In 'post-structuralism', the subject is usually reduced to so-called subjectivation, he is conceived as an effect of a fundamentally non-subjective process: the subject is always caught in, traversed by the pre-subjective process (of 'writing', of 'desire' and so on), and the emphasis is on the individuals' different modes of 'experiencing', 'living' their positions as 'subjects', 'actors', 'agents' of the historical process. For example, only at a certain point in European history did the author of works of art, a painter or a writer, begin to see himself as a creative individual who, in his work, gives expression to his interior subjective richness. The great master of such analysis was, of course, Foucault: one might say that the main point of his late work was to articulate the different modes by which individuals assume their subject-positions.

But with Lacan, we have quite another notion of the subject. To put it simply: if we make an abstraction, if we subtract all the richness of the different modes of subjectivation, all the fullness of experience present in the way the individuals are 'living' their subject-positions, what remains is an empty place which was filled out with this richness; this original void, this lack of symbolic structure, *is* the subject, the subject of the signifier. The *subject* is therefore to be strictly opposed to the effect of *subjectivation*: what the subjectivation masks is not a pre- or trans-subjective process of writing but a lack in the structure, a lack which is the subject.

Our predominant idea of the subject is, in Lacanian terms, that of the 'subject of the signified', the active agent, the bearer of some signification who is trying to express himself in language. Lacan's starting point is, of course, that symbolic representation always distorts the subject, that it is always a displacement, a failure — that the subject cannot find a signifier which would be 'his own', that he is always saying too little or too much: in short, *something other* than what he wanted or intended to say.

The usual conclusion from this would be that the subject is some kind of interior richness of meaning which always exceeds its symbolic articulation: 'language cannot express fully what I'm trying to say ...'. The Lacanian thesis is the opposite: this surplus of signification masks a fundamental lack. The subject of the signifier is precisely this lack, this impossibility of finding a signifier which would be 'its own': *the failure of its representation is its positive condition*. The subject tries to articulate itself in a signifying representation; the representation fails; instead of a richness we have a lack, and this void opened by the failure *is* the subject of the signifier. To put it paradoxically: the subject of the signifier is a retroactive effect of the failure of its own representation; that is why the failure of representation is the only way to represent it adequately.

Here we have a kind of dialogic economy: we articulate a proposition defining the subject, our attempt fails, we experience the absolute contradiction, the extreme negative relationship between the subject and the predicate — and this absolute discordance is the subject as absolute negativity. It is like a well-known Soviet joke about Rabinovitch, a Jew who wants to emigrate. The bureaucrat at the emigration office asks him why; Rabinovitch answers: 'There are two reasons why. The first is that I'm afraid that in the Soviet Union the Communists will lose power, there will be a counter-revolution and the new power will put all the blame for the Communist crimes on us, Jews — there will again be anti-Jewish pogroms....' 'But', interrupts the bureaucrat, 'this is pure nonsense, nothing can change in the Soviet Union, the power of the Communists will last forever!' 'Well,' responds Rabinovitch calmly, 'that's my second reason.' The logic is the same here as in the Hegelian proposition 'the spirit is a bone': the very failure of the first reading gives us the true meaning.

The Rabinovitch joke also exemplifies the logic of the ill-famed Hegelian triad: if the first reason for emigrating is the 'thesis' and the bureaucrat's objection the 'anti-thesis', then the 'synthesis' is not any kind of return to the thesis, some kind of healing of the wound made by the anti-thesis — *the 'synthesis' is exactly the same as the anti-thesis*; the only difference lies in a certain change of perspective, in a certain turn through which what was a moment ago experienced as an obstacle, as an impediment, proves itself to be a positive condition: the fact that Soviet power is eternal, which was proposed as an argument *against* emigrating, reveals itself as the real reason *for* emigrating.

This is also, in a nutshell, the logic of the 'negation of the negation': this double, self-referential negation does not entail any kind of return to positive identity, any kind of abolition, of cancellation of the disruptive force of negativity, of reducing it to a passing moment in the self-mediating process of identity; in the 'negation of the negation', the negativity preserves all its disruptive power; the whole point is just that we come to experience how this negative, disruptive power, menacing our identity is simultaneously a positive condition of it. The 'negation of the negation' does not in any way abolish the antagonism, it consists only in the experience of the fact that this immanent limit which is preventing me from achieving my full identity with myself simultaneously enables me to achieve a minimum of positive consistency, however mutilated it is. To give a most elementary example: in the anti-Semitic vision, the Jew is experienced as the embodiment of negativity, as the force disrupting stable social identity — but the 'truth' of anti-Semitism is, of course, that the very identity of our position is structured through a negative relationship to this traumatic figure of the Jew. Without the reference to the Jew who is corroding the social fabric, the social fabric itself would be dissolved. In other words, all my positive consistency is a kind of 'reaction-formation' to a certain traumatic, antagonistic kernel: if I lose this 'impossible' point of reference, my very identity dissolves.

This, then, is the 'negation of the negation': not a kind of 'superseding' of negativity but the experience of the fact that *the negativity as such has a positive function,* enables and structures our positive consistency. In simple negation, there is still the pre-given positive identity which is being negated, the movement of negativity is still conceived as the limitation of some pre-given positivity; while in the 'negation of the negation', negativity is in a way *prior to what is being negated*, it is a negative movement which opens the very place where every positive identity can be situated.

If, then, antagonism is always a kind of opening, a hole in the field of the symbolic Other, a void of an unanswered, unresolved question, the 'negation of the negation' does not bring us the final answer filling out the void of all questions: it is to be conceived more like a paradoxical twist whereby *the question itself begins to function as its own answer*: what we mistook for a question was already an answer. To explain this, let us take an example from Adorno concerning the antagonistic character of society (Adorno, 1970). Adorno starts from the fact that today it is not possible to formulate one appropriate definition of Society: as soon as we set to work, a number of opposing, mutually excluding determinations present themselves: on the one hand those which lay stress upon Society as an organic whole encompassing individuals; on the other those which conceive Society as a bond, a kind of contract between atomized individuals — in short, we find ourselves caught in the opposition between 'organicism' and 'individualism'.

In a first approach, this opposition presents itself as an epistemological obstacle, as a hindrance preventing us from grasping Society as it is in itself — making out of Society a kind of Kantian Thing-in-itself which can be approached only through partial, distorted insights: its real nature escapes us for ever. But in a dialectical approach, this contradiction which appears at first as an unresolved question is already in itself a solution: far from barring our access to the real essence of Society, the opposition between 'organicism' and 'individualism' is not only epistemological but is already at work in the 'Thing-in-itself'. In other words, the antagonism between Society as a corporate Whole transcending its members and Society as an external, 'mechanical' net connecting atomized individuals is the fundamental antagonism of contemporary society; it is in a way *its very definition*.

This is what is basically at stake in the Hegelian strategy: *the discordance, the incompatibility as such* (of the opposing determinations of Society) *makes the secret disappear* — what at first appeared to be an epistemological obstacle turns out to be the very index of the fact that we have 'touched the Truth', we are in the heart of the 'Thing-in-itself' *by the very trait which appeared to bar our access to it.* The implication, of course, is that this 'Thing-in-itself' is already mutilated, split, marked by a radical lack, structured around an antagonistic kernel.

This Hegelian strategy of transposing an epistemological impotence (the way we necessarily entangle ourselves in a contradiction when we try to define Society) into an ontological impossibility (into an antagonism defining the object itself) implies the same twist as the Rabinovitch joke: what appears at first to be an obstacle reveals itself as the solution — in the very movement by which the truth escapes us, we already rejoin it: 'truth grabs error by the scruff of the neck in the mistake' (Lacan, 1988, p. 265). Such a paradoxical space, in which the very heart of a certain field immediately touches its exterior, is best exemplified by a well-known Hegelian dictum according to which the secrets of the ancient Egyptians were also secrets for the Egyptians themselves: the solution of the riddle is to redouble it.

When a subject is confronted with an enigmatic, impenetrable Other, the thing he has to grasp is that his question to the Other is already the question of the Other itself — the impenetrability of the substantial Other, the hindrance which is preventing the subject from penetrating the heart of the Other, is immediately an index of the fact that this Other is already in itself hindered, structured around a certain 'indigestible' rock, resisting symbolization, symbolic integration. The subject cannot grasp Society as a close Whole, but this impotence has, so to speak, an immediate ontological status: it bears witness to the fact that Society itself does not exist, that it is marked by a radical impossibility. And it is because of this impossibility to achieve full identity with itself that the Other, Society as Substance, is already subject.

Subject as an 'Answer of the Real'

What, then, is the status of this subject before subjectivation? The Lacanian answer would be, roughly speaking, that before subjectivation as identification, before ideological interpellation, before assuming a certain subject-position, the subject is subject of a question. At first sight, it may seem that we are here again in the middle of traditional philosophical problematics: subject as a force of negativity which can question every given, objective status of things, introducing into the positivity the openness of the questioning . . . in a word, the subject is a question. But the Lacanian position is the exact opposite: the subject is not a question, it is as an *answer*, the answer of the Real to the question asked by the big Other, the symbolic order (Miller, 1987). It is not the subject which is asking the question; the subject is the void of the impossibility of answering the question of the Other.

To explain this, let us refer to an interesting book by Aron Boden-heimer: *Why? On the Obscenity of Questioning* (Bodenheimer, 1984). Its fundamental thesis is that there is something obscene in the very act of asking a question, without regard to its content. It is the form of the question as such which is obscene: the question lays open, exposes, denudes its addressee, it invades his sphere of intimacy; this is why the basic, elementary reaction to a question is shame on the bodily level, blushing and lowering our eyes, like a child whom we ask 'What were you doing?' It is clear in our everyday experience, that such a questioning of children is a priori incriminating, provoking a sensation of guilt: 'What were you doing? Where were you? What does this white spot mean?' Even if I can offer an answer which is objectively true and at the same time delivers me from guilt ('I was studying with my friend', for example), the guilt is already admitted on the level of desire; every answer is an excuse. With a prompt answer like 'I was studying with my friend' I am confirming precisely that I did not really *want* to do so, that my desire was to stroll about, or something of that nature. . . .

Questioning is the basic procedure of the totalitarian intersubjective relationship: one need not refer to such exemplary cases as police inter-rogation or religious confession; it is quite sufficient to recall the usual abuse of the enemy in the real-socialist press: how much more threaten-ing is the question 'Who is really hiding behind. . . . [the demands for the freedom of press, for democracy]? Who is really pulling the strings of the so-called new social movements? Who is really speaking through them?' than the vulgar, direct positive affirmation 'Those who demand the free-dom of the press really want to open the space for the activity of counter-socialist powers and in this way diminish the hegemony of the working class. . . .' Totalitarian power is not a dogmatism which has all the answers; it is, on the contrary, the instance which has all the questions.

The basic indecency of the question consists in its drive to put into words what should be left unspoken, as in the well-known dialogue: 'What were you doing?' 'You know what!' 'Yes, but I want *you* to tell me!' Which is the instance in the other, in its addressee, that the question is aiming at? It aims at a point at which the answer is not possible, where the word is lacking, where the subject is exposed in his impotence. We can illustrate this by the inverse type of the question, not the question of the authority to its subjects but the question of the subject-child to his father: the stake of such a question is always to catch the other who embodies authority in his impotence, in his inability, in his lack.

Bodenheimer articulates this dimension apropos of the child's question to the father: 'Father, why is the sky blue?' — the child is not really interested in the sky as such; the real stake of the question is to expose father's impotence, his helplessness in the face of the hard fact that the sky is blue, his incapacity to substantiate this fact, to present the whole chain of reasons leading to it. The blue of the sky thus becomes not only the father's problem, but in a way even his fault: 'The sky is blue, and you're just staring at it like an idiot, incapable of doing anything about it!' A question, even if it refers only to a given state of things, always makes the subject formally responsible for it, although only in a negative way — responsible, that is, for his impotence in the face of this fact.

What, then, is this point in the other at which the word fails, this point of impotence at which the question as such is aiming? The question as such creates shame because it aims at my innermost, intimate kernel called by Freud *Kern unseres Wesens* and by Lacan *das Ding*: at that strange body in my interior which is 'in me more than me', which is radically interior and the same time already exterior and for which Lacan coined a new word, *extime*. The real object of the question is what Plato, in the *Symposium*, called — through the mouth of Alcibiades — *agalma*, the hidden treasure, the essential object in me which cannot be objecti-vated, dominated. (Lacan develops this concept in his unpublished Seminar VIII on *Transference*.) The Lacanian formula for this object is of course *objet petit a*, this point of Real in the very heart of the subject which cannot be symbolized, which is produced as a residue, a remnant, a leftover of every signifying operation, a hard core embodying horri-fying *jouissance*, enjoyment, and as such an object which simultaneously attracts and repels us — which *divides* our desire and thus provokes shame.

Our thesis is that it is precisely the question in its obscene dimension, in so far as it aims at the ex-timate kernel, at what is in the subject more than subject, at the *object in subject* which is constitutive for the subject. In other words there is no subject without guilt, the subject exist only in so far as he is ashamed because of the object in himself, in its interior. This is the meaning of Lacan's thesis that the subject is originally split, divided: he is divided as to the object himself, as to the Thing, which at the same time attracts and repels him: $\$ \lozenge a$.

Let us resume: the subject is an answer of the Real (of the object, of the traumatic kernel) to the question of the Other. The question as such produces in its addressee an effect of shame and guilt, it divides, it hystericizes him, and this hystericization is the constitution of the subject: the status of the subject as such is hysterical. The subject is constituted through his own division, splitting, as to the object in him; this object, this traumatic kernel, is the dimension that we have already named as that of a 'death drive', of a traumatic imbalance, a rooting out. Man as such is 'nature sick unto death', derailed, run off the rails through a fascination with a lethal Thing.

The process of interpellation–subjectivation is precisely an attempt to elude, to avoid this traumatic kernel through identification: in assuming a symbolic mandate, in recognizing himself in the interpellation, the subject evades the dimension of the Thing. (There are, of course, other possibilities of avoiding this hysterical deadlock: the perverse position, for example, in which the subject identifies himself immediately with the object and thus relieves himself of the burden of the question. Psychoanalysis itself also de-hystericizes the subject, but in another way: at the end of the psychoanalysis the question is, so to speak, returned to the Other, the impotence of the subject displaces itself into the impossibility proper to the Other: the subject experiences the Other as blocked, failed, marked with a central impossibility — in brief, as 'antagonistic'.)

The subject, then, as an impossible answer, consubstantive with a certain guilt — the first literary association which comes to our mind is of course the work of Franz Kafka. Indeed, we might say that Kafka's achievement is to articulate this paradoxical status of the subject before subjectivation — we were speaking of shame, and the last words of *The Trial* are: '. . . it was as if he meant the shame of it to outlive him' (Kafka, 1985, p. 251).

This is why we find in Kafka's work the reverse, disquieting side of the comical aspect of the interpellation: the illusion proper to interpellation, the illusion of 'already-there', shows its negative face. The procedure of incrimination is to put the subject into the position of somebody who is *already presumed to know* (to use this Lacanian term in another context). For example, in *The Trial* Josef K. is summoned to appear before the Court on Sunday morning: the exact time of interrogation is not specified. When he finally finds the courtroom, the judge reproaches him: 'You should have been here an hour and five minutes ago' (Kafka, 1985, p. 47). Some of us probably remember the same situation from army service: the corporal incriminates us from the very beginning with the cry: 'What are you staring at like idiots? Don't you know what to do? One really has to explain things to you again and again!' — and he then proceeds to give us instructions as if they were superfluous, as if we should already know them. This, therefore, is the reverse side of the ideological 'already-there' illusion: the subject is incriminated by suddenly being thrown into a situation in which he is presumed to know what is expected of him.

S(Ⱥ), *a*, Φ

How do we specify the dimension of this 'object in subject' which causes the presumption of knowledge? That is to say, there are objects and objects — in Lacan's teaching, we have to distinguish at least three types of object. To articulate these distinctions, let us return to the MacGuffin — we must not forget that in Hitchcock's films, too, MacGuffin is just one of three types of object:

- First, then, the MacGuffin itself, 'nothing at all', an empty place, a pure pretext for setting the action in motion: the formula of the aircraft engines in *The Thirty-Nine Steps*, the secret clause of the naval treaty in *The Foreign Correspondent*, the coded melody in *The Lady Vanishes*, the uranium bottles in *Notorious*, and so on. It is a pure semblance: in itself it is totally indifferent and, by structural necessity, absent; its signification is purely auto-reflexive, it consists in the fact that it has some signification for others, for the principal characters of the story.

- But in a series of Hitchcock's films, we find another type of object which is decidedly *not* indifferent, *not* pure absence: what matters here is precisely its presence, the material presence of a fragment of reality — it is a leftover, remnants which cannot be reduced to a network of formal relations proper to the symbolic structure, but it is para-doxically, at the same time, the positive condition for the effectuation of the formal structure. We can define this object as an object of exchange circulating among subjects, serving as a kind of guarantee, pawn, on their symbolic relationship. It is the role of the key in *Notorious* and *Dial M for Murder*, the role of the wedding ring in *Shadow of a Doubt* and *Rear Window*, the role of the lighter in *Strangers on a Train*, and even the role of the child circulating between the two couples in *The Man Who Knew Too Much*. It is unique, non-specular; it has no double, it escapes the dual mirror-relation — that is why it plays a crucial role in those very films which are built on a whole series of dual relations, each element having its mirror-counterpart (*Strangers on a Train*; *Shadow of a Doubt*, where the name of the central character is already redoubled — uncle Charlie, niece Charlie): it is the one which *has no* counterpart, and that is why it must circulate between the opposite elements. The paradox of its role is that although it is a leftover of the Real, an 'excrement', it functions as a positive condition of the restoration of a symbolic structure: the structure of symbolic exchanges between the subjects can take place only in so far as it is embodied in this pure material element which acts as its guarantee — for example, in *Strangers on a Train* the murderous pact between Bruno and Guy holds only in so far as the object (the cigarette lighter) is circulating between them.

That is the basic situation in a whole series of Hitchcock's films: at the beginning we have a non-structured, pre-symbolic, imaginary homeostatic state of things, an indifferent balance in which the relations between subjects are not yet structured in a strict sense — that is, through the lack circulating between them. And the paradox is that this symbolic pact, this structural network of relations, can establish itself only in so far as it is embodied in a totally contingent material element, a little-bit-of-Real which, by its sudden irruption, disrupts the homeostatic indifference of relations between subjects. In other words, the imaginary balance changes into a symbolically structured network through a shock of the Real (Dolar, 1986). That is why Hitchcock (and with him Lacan) is no longer a 'structuralist': the basic gesture of 'structuralism' is to reduce the imaginary richness to a formal network of symbolic relations: what escapes the structuralist perspective is that this formal structure is itself tied by an umbilical cord to some radically contingent material element which, in its pure particularity, 'is' a structure, embodies it. Why? Because the big Other, the symbolic order, is always *barré*, failed, crossed-out, mutilated, and the contingent material element embodies this internal blockage, limit, of the symbolic structure.

The symbolic structure must include an element which embodies its 'stain', its own point of impossibility around which it is articulated: in a way it is the structuring of its own impossibility. The only philosophical counterpoint to this logic is again Hegelian dialectics: the greatest speculative mystery of the dialectical movement is not how the richness and diversity of reality can be reduced to a dialectical conceptual mediation, but the fact that in order to take place this dialectical structuring must itself be embodied in some totally contingent element — that, for

example, is the point of the Hegelian deduction of the role of the King:
the State as the rational totality exists effectively only in so far as it is
embodied in the inert presence of the King's body: the King, in his non-
rational, biologically determined presence, 'is' the State, it is in his body
that the State achieves its effectiveness.

Here we can use the distinction, developed by Laclau and Mouffe,
between the accidental and the contingent: an ordinary element of a
formal structure is accidental, indifferent — that is, it can be inter-
changed; but there is always an element which, paradoxically, embodies
this formal structure as such — it is not necessary but it is, in its very
contingency, the positive condition of the restoration of the structural
necessity: this necessity depends upon it, hangs on it.

– Finally, we have a third kind of object: the birds in *The Birds*, for
  example (we could also add, in *Marnie*, the body of the giant ship at the
  end of the street in which Marnie's mother lives). This object has a
  massive, oppressive material presence; it is not an indifferent void like
  the MacGuffin, but at the same time it does not circulate between the
  subjects, it is not an object of exchange, it is just a mute embodiment
  of an impossible *jouissance*.

How can we explain the logic, the consistency of these three objects? In
his Seminar *Encore*, Lacan proposes a schema of it (Lacan, 1975, p. 83):

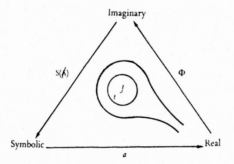

Here, we have to interpret the vector not as indicating a relation of
determination ('the Imaginary determines the Symbolic' and so on), but
more in the sense of the 'symbolization of the Imaginary'. So:

- MacGuffin is clearly the *objet petit a*, the lack, the leftover of the Real setting in motion the symbolic movement of interpretation, a void in the centre of the symbolic order, a pure semblance of the 'mystery' to be explained, interpreted;

- the birds are Φ, the impassive, imaginary objectification of the Real, an image which embodies *jouissance*;

- and finally, the circulating object of exchange is $S(\slashed{A})$, the symbolic object which cannot be reduced to imaginary mirror-play and which at the same time embodies the lack in the Other, the impossibility around which the symbolic order is structured. It is the radically contingent element through which the symbolic necessity arises. That is the greatest mystery of the symbolic order: how its necessity arises from the shock of a totally contingent encounter of the Real — like the well-known accident in the *Arabian Nights*: the hero, lost in the desert, quite by chance enters a cave; there, he finds three old wise men, awoken by his entry, who say to him: 'Finally, you have arrived! We have been waiting for you for the last three hundred years.'

The Subject Presumed To . . .

This mystery is, in the final analysis, the mystery of the *transference* itself: to *produce* new meaning, it is necessary to *presuppose* its existence in the other. That is the logic of the 'subject presumed to know' which Lacan isolated as the central axis, anchor, of the phenomenon of transference: the analyst is presumed to know in advance — what? — the meaning of the analysand's symptoms. This knowledge is of course an illusion, but it is a necessary one: in the end only through this supposition of knowledge, can some real knowledge can be produced. In the scheme above we have three versions of the object around the central nauseous protuberance of *jouissance*, the Thing in its inaccessibility; one is tempted to construct, on the same matrix, three other concepts around the subject presumed to know.

- Let us start with the *subject presumed to believe* (Močnik, 1986). Coming from Yugoslavia — that is, from a real-socialist country — the author of this book is tempted to take an example typical of 'really existing socialism' where, as is well known, there is always something lacking in the shops. Our hypothetical starting point is that there is an abundance of toilet paper on the market. But, suddenly and unexpectedly, a rumour starts to circulate that there is a shortage of toilet paper — because of this rumour, people frantically begin to buy it, and of course the result is that there is real shortage of toilet paper. At first sight this seems to be a simple mechanism of what is called self-fulfilling prophecy, but the effective way in which it functions is a little more complicated. Each participant reasons as follows: 'I'm not naïve and stupid, I know very well that there is more than enough toilet paper in the shops; but there are probably some naïve and stupid people who believe these rumours, who take them seriously and will act accordingly — they will start frantically buying toilet paper and so in the end there will be a real shortage of it, so even if I know very well that there is enough, it would be a good idea to go and buy a lot!' The crucial point is that this other presumed to believe naïvely does not have to exist effectively: to produce his effects in reality, it is enough that he is presumed by others to exist. In a definite, closed multitude of subjects, each person can play this role for all the others — the effect will be exactly the same: a real shortage of toilet paper. The one who will in the end remain without it will be precisely the one who persists in the truth: the one who says to himself, 'I know that this is only a rumour, there is enough toilet paper' and acts upon it. . . .

This concept of the subject presumed to believe also has its clinical use: it serves to mark the difference between real Freudian analysis and the revisionist cure. While in Freudian analysis the analyst plays the role of the subject presumed to know, in the revisionist tradition his role is closer to that of the subject presumed to believe; that is to say, in this case the reasoning of the patient goes as follows: 'I have some psychic problems, I'm neurotic, so I need an analyst to cure me. The problem is that I don't believe in maternal phallus, symbolic castration and all that shit — to me this is plain nonsense. But happily for me, here is an analyst who believes in it and, why not, perhaps he can cure me with his belief!' No wonder various neo-Freudian schools try to incorporate some elements of shamanism!

- The second concept in this series would be the *subject presumed to enjoy* (Dolar, 1987). His role is fundamental in obsessional neurosis: for the obsessional neurotic the traumatic point is the supposed existence, in the other, of an insupportable, limitless, horrifying *jouissance*; the stake of all his frantic activity is to protect, to save the Other from his *jouissance*, even at the price of destroying him or her (saving the woman from her corruption, for example). Again, this subject does not have to exist effectively: to produce his effects, it is enough for others to presume that he exists. This supposed *jouissance* is one of the key components of racism: the Other (Jew, Arab, Negro) is always presumed to have access to some specific enjoyment, and that is what really bothers us.

- The last concept would be, of course, that of the *subject presumed to desire*. If the subject presumed to enjoy plays a central role in obsessional neurosis, the subject presumed to desire plays such a role in hysteria. One only has to remind oneself of Freud's analysis of Dora: it is quite clear that Frau K. is playing for Dora the role — not of her object of desire, as Freud mistakenly supposed, but of the subject presumed to desire, presumed to know how to organize her desire, how to avoid its deadlock. That is why, when we are confronted with a hysteric, the question to ask is not 'What is his object of desire?' but 'Where does he desire from? Who is the other person through whom he is organizing his desire?' The problem for the hysterical subject is that he always needs to have recourse to another subject to organize his desire — that is the meaning of the Lacanian formula that hysterical desire is the desire of the other.

The Presumed Knowledge

This conceptual quartet is useful in an analysis of ideological mechanisms: in oriental despotism, the whole system pivots around the central point, the figure of the despot presumed to enjoy; in classical Stalinism, the leadership is presumed to know; and so on. But the thing to remember is that the four subjects presumed to . . . are not on the same level: the subject presumed to know is their basis, their matrix, and the function of the remaining three is precisely to disguise its troubling paradox.

The link between this presumed knowledge and the unconscious is best exemplified by a small scene from Hitchcock's *Foreign Correspondent*. The hero (played by Joel McCrea) and his friend design an elaborate plot to extort from a Nazi agent posing as a 'pacifist' (Herbert Marshall) a confession of his betrayal. The hero, already half in love with the traitor's beautiful daughter, entices her on to an all-day excursion to the countryside; meanwhile, his friend visits the traitor at his home and tells him that he and the hero have abducted his daughter — they are prepared to return her in exchange for his written confession that he is a Nazi agent. The father assents to the demand, writes something on a piece of paper — obviously the requested confession — and hands it over to the extortioner, but when the latter glances at it, he sees that it reads: 'Sorry, but I've just heard my daughter's car entering the garage'. The gallantry of the father (who, despite his treason, remains a gentleman of the old school) prevents him from simply flying into a temper after he hears the approaching car and so unmasks the extortioner's bluff: he continues calmly with his job and lets the extortioner know that he has seen through his cards *in the very form of the confession.*

What is the libidinal charge of this gesture? The treacherous father from *Foreign Correspondent* is one in the series of Hitchcockian villains gnawed by the knowledge of their own corruption: unconsciously, they desire unmasking and self-destruction; this truth emerges, articulates itself in the *form* of the confession, persisting even when the reasons for it proved invalid. This is the 'unconscious' in the Lacanian sense: a desire which articulates itself in the very gap separating the form from its content, in the autonomy of the form. Behind the ironic–gallant gesture of the father addressed to the extortioner (meaning something like: 'Here you have the confession you wanted! I'm giving you back your own cards!') there is a desperate eruption of the desire for self-purification, a desire which realizes itself towards the end of the film with the father's suicidal act.

The word 'gallantry' was not used carelessly: it has to be conceived in its precise Rococo–pre-Romantic, *Mozartian* meaning. That is to say, one of the most subversive features of Mozart's operas consists precisely in the adroit manipulation of the gap between form and content, where it is the form which articulates the 'repressed' truth of the content. Leaving aside *Don Giovanni*, which is in its entirety the embodiment of this gap (on the level of 'content', Don Giovanni runs from one fiasco to another, while the musical form emphasizes more and more his triumphalism, his mythical power), it is sufficient to recall a small detail from the finale of *Le nozze di Figaro*, the aria which follows the reconciliation between Figaro and Susanna ('Pace, pace . . .'). At first, form and content accord with each other: the elucidation of the misunderstanding (Figaro knew that the woman he was making a conquest of was not the Countess but his beloved Susanna dressed up as the Countess) is confirmed by their harmonized duet which attests to their reconciliation; this duet then changes into a trio: From the background breaks in the angry voice of the

Count looking for Susanna in the park (to entrap him, she had promised him a rendezvous).

With this emergence of a third voice, form and content split, each goes its own way: on the level of content, we have tension, disharmony, contrasting with the former spirit of reconciliation (the Count angrily asking what Susanna is up to), but what is crucial is the fact that *the Count articulates his anger in the very melody used by Figaro and Susanna to express their reconciliation* — on the level of form there is no discontinuity, no rupture, the same melodic line simply goes on. . . . In this way, all is actually said: *the reconciliation is already here*, the Count's tension is already pacified, he has already lost, he simply does not yet know it, or, more precisely — and this is the crucial point — *he does not know yet that he already knows it*, because unconsciously he does already know it, he is already pacified, resigned to the loss of Susanna. His unconscious knowledge erupts again precisely in the gap between form and content — in the form which already announces reconciliation while the Count is still full of fury.

It is because of this gap that Mozart is not yet a Romantic composer: such a gap is excluded by the very definition of 'Romantic'. From the Romantic perspective, Mozart's procedure appears 'mechanical', psychologically unconvincing, an automatic repetition of the same melodic line irrespective of the changed psychological constellation: as if Mozart has 'forgotten to change the tonality' and mechanically continued with the same melody, although the psychological truth of the situation demanded a clear break (an eruption of disharmony). Far from being simply erroneous, this impression of an 'automatism to repeat' asserting itself irrespective of the 'psychological truth' has to be interpreted on the basis of the Lacanian thesis that the status of the unconscious 'compulsion to repeat' is not psychological: the very external form of the Count's melody, its discord with its own content (the words sung), articulates the unconscious truth as yet inaccessible to him, to his psychological experience.

In Mozart, we still have the 'unconscious' as the network of external, 'non-psychological' symbolic relations which decide on the 'truth' of the subjects caught in it: in the very restraining, holding back, in preventing the subjective–psychological content from 'expressing' itself too strongly in the form, to permeate the form too directly — in this very keeping the content at a distance from the form — the 'repressed' truth of the content finds room to articulate itself. We enter the 'romantic' mode the moment the external, 'mechanical' form is experienced as 'mere form', form without its own content: hence truth is measured exclusively by the expression of the psychological subjectivity in the form. In Beethoven we find the subject as the infinite wealth of inner content which struggles to express itself in the form: the way is open for the Romantic cult of a 'genius', of a 'titanic' personality, and all the disgusting phantoms resulting therefrom.

'The fear of error is . . . the error itself'

Contrary to the usual parallel between Kant-Mozart on one side and Hegel-Beethoven on the other, we should stress that *here Hegel is Mozartian.* That is to say, this Mozartian practice of articulating the truth by the very distance of the form from its content finds its exact counterpart in Hegel's notion of the 'formal side [*das Formelle*]' articulating the truth of a given phenomenon. This, of course, introduces a dialectical relation between Truth and appearance: 'Truth' is definitely not a kind of surplus *eluding* us again and again; it appears, on the contrary, in the form of traumatic *encounters* — that is, we chance upon it where we presumed the presence of 'mere appearance': the 'shock of the truth' consists in its sudden emergence in the the midst of the realm of reassuring phenomena.

The 'unthinkable' for Kant is such an encounter, such a paradoxical point at which 'appearance' itself, without knowing it, touches the truth: what is at stake in Kant's 'obsessional' economy is precisely the avoidance of the traumatic encounter of the Truth. That is to say, his 'transcendental' procedure of limiting our possible experience to the world of phenomena and of excluding from it the 'Thing-in-itself' apparently expresses an aspiration to truth — the fear of falling into error by illegitimately taking phenomena for the Thing-in-itself. However, as Hegel puts it, this fear of error, of a confusion between phenomena and the Thing-in-itself, conceals its opposite, the fear of Truth — it announces a desire to elude, at any price, an encounter with the Truth:

> . . . if the fear of falling into error sets up a mistrust of Science, which in the absence of such scruples gets on with the work itself, and actually cognizes something, it is hard to see why we should not turn round and mistrust this very mistrust. Should we not be concerned as to whether this fear of error is not just the error itself? (Hegel, 1977, p. 47)

The relation between appearance and Truth should thus be conceived in a dialectically reflexive way: the most radical illusion consists not in accepting as Truth, as the 'Thing-in-itself', what is effectively a mere deceptive illusion, but rather in a refusal to recognize the presence of the Truth — in pretending that we are still dealing with a fictitious appearance, when Truth is already here.

Sydney Pollack's film *Three Days of the Condor* exemplifies perfectly this paradoxical, self-reflexive character of the illusion. A small branch of the CIA is occupied with reading all espionage and detective novels in search of ideas which could perhaps be applied in real espionage work. Suddenly, a special unit of liquidators kills all the members of this branch — why? Because one of them has noted in some obscure novel, and passed over to his superiors, the idea of a secret 'organization-within-an-organization' whose existence should be unknown and which controls the legal organization; however, such an organization *already exists* within the CIA. In other words, he proposed a fiction without knowing that he had touched the truth. We can now see, what Lacan is aiming at when he says that 'the Truth has the structure of a fiction'. This is clear from the Lacanian matrix of the four discourses: 'Truth' is an empty *place*, and the 'effect of Truth' is produced when, quite by chance, some piece of 'fiction' (of symbolically structured knowledge) finds itself occupying this place, as in Pollack's movie when some unfortunate lower clerk unwittingly produced an explosive 'effect of Truth'.

The fear of error which conceals its opposite, the fear of Truth: this Hegelian formula encapsulates prefectly the subjective position of the obsessional neurotic: the incessant procrastination, the endless precautions, which characterize his approach. At the same time this reference to obsessional neurosis (not as a clinical entity, of course, but as a subjective position, as what Hegel would call 'the position of thought towards objectivity') enables us to locate properly the Lacanian observation that Hegel is 'the most sublime of all hysterics'. By determining the passage from Kant to Hegel as the hystericization of the obsessional's position, we are already in the midst of the properly Hegelian relation between genus and its species: hysteria and obsessional neurosis are not two species of neurosis as a neutral-universal genus; their relation is a dialectical one — it was Freud himself who noted that obsessional neurosis is a kind of 'dialect of hysteria': hysteria as a fundamental determination of a neurotic position contains two species, obsessional neurosis *and itself as its own species.*

There is, of course, a whole set of differential features enabling us to construct the relation of hysteria to obsessional neurosis as a symmetrical opposition:

- The hysterical symptom articulates, stages, a repressed *desire*, whereas the obsessional symptom stages the *punishment* for realizing this desire;

- A hysterical neurotic cannot bear waiting, he *hastens through*, he 'over-takes himself' and misses the object of desire precisely because of this impatience — because he wants to get at it too quickly — whereas the obsessional neurotic builds up a whole system enabling him to post-pone the encounter of the object *ad infinitum*: the moment is never right.

- To a hysterical neurotic, the object procures *too little* enjoyment: apro-pos of every object, his experience is how 'this is not that', which is why he hastens to reach, finally, the right object; whereas the obsessional neurotic's problem is that the object offers him *too much* enjoyment; the immediate encounter with the object would be unbearable because of its excessive fullness, which is why he post-pones the encounter;

- When the hysterical neurotic feels that he 'doesn't know what he really wants', he addresses the question concerning his desire *to the other* — to the one who embodies for him the 'subject presumed to know' — whereas the obsessional neurotic is tortured by doubt; he cannot decide — that is to say, he addresses his question *to himself*; and so on.

However, a closer look quickly reveals how this impression of a sym-metrical opposition is false: one of the opposite poles (hysterical) is always 'unmarked' — that is, it functions at the same time as a neutral, universal medium of the opposition; while the other (obsessional) is 'marked' and introduces a specific difference. It is thus not difficult to demonstrate how the obsessional staging of the punishment for the real-ization of a desire is nothing but an inverse, 'mediated' way of staging the realization of desire; how the obsessional question the subject addresses to himself (the famous 'obsessional doubt') is nothing but a masked form of the demand addressed to the other; how the obsessional postponement of the encounter with the object out of fear that we would not be able to bear such excessive enjoyment is nothing but a refined way of avoiding disappointment with the object — that is, how it conceals a foreboding that the object itself 'is not that'.

And, to return to the passage from Kant to Hegel, the same goes for the Kantian postponement of the encounter with the Thing — for the Kantian gap dividing for ever the Thing from the world of phenomena: it conceals a foreboding that perhaps this Thing is itself nothing but a lack, an empty place; that beyond the phenomenal appearance there is only a certain negative self-relationship because of which the positively given phenomenal world is perceived as 'mere appearance' — in other words, that

'The supersensible is therefore appearance *qua* appearance'

In the chapter in *Phenomenology* on 'Force and Understanding' — the chapter which accomplishes the passage from consciousness to self-consciousness — Hegel proposes this formula, which blows up the whole Kantian obsessional economy: 'The supersensible is the sensuous and the perceived posited as it is *in truth*; but the *truth* of the sensuous and the perceived is to be *appearance. The supersensible is therefore appearance* qua *appearance*' (Hegel, 1977, p. 89). The appearance implies that there is something behind it which appears through it; it conceals a truth and by the same gesture gives a foreboding thereof; it simultaneously hides and reveals the essence behind its curtain. But what is hidden behind the phenomenal appearance? Precisely the fact that there is nothing to hide. What is concealed is that the very act of concealing conceals nothing.

But is the supersensible therefore a pure illusion of the consciousness, a simple *trompe l'œil*? Is it 'we' who can see that there is nothing behind the curtain, while the 'naïve' consciousness is caught in the web of deception? With Hegel, we should *never* immediately oppose the state of things as 'we' see it 'correctly' and the viewpoint of the erroneous consciousness: if there is deception we cannot subtract it from the Thing; it constitutes its very heart. If, behind the phenomenal veil, there is nothing, it is through the mediation of this 'nothing' that the subject constitutes himself in the very act of his misrecognition. The illusion that there is something hidden behind the curtain is thus a reflexive one: what is hidden behind the appearance is the possibility of this very illusion — behind the curtain is the fact that the subject thinks something must be behind it. The illusion, albeit 'false', is effectively located in the empty place behind the curtain — the illusion has opened a place where it is possible, an empty space that it fills out — where the 'illusory reality', reduplicating the external, factual reality, could find its proper place:

... in order that there may yet be something the void — which, though it first came about as devoid of *objective* Things must, however, as *empty in itself*, be taken as also void of all spiritual relationships and distinctions of consciousness *qua* consciousness — in order, then, that in this *complete void*, which is even called the *holy of holies*, there may yet be something, we must fill it up with reveries, *appearances*, produced by consciousness itself. It would have to be content with being treated so badly for it would not deserve anything better, since even reveries are better than its own emptiness. (Hegel, 1977, pp. 88-9)

The supersensible Holy is thus first an empty place, a space devoid of all positive content, and only subsequently is this emptiness filled out with some content (taken, of course, from the very sensuous world that the supersensible is supposed to negate, to have left behind). The respective contents of the supersensible and of the sensuous world are the same; an object becomes 'holy' simply by changing places — by occupying, filling out, the empty place of the Holy.

This is also the fundamental feature of the logic of the Lacanian object: *the place logically precedes objects which occupy it*: what the objects, in their given positivity, are masking is not some other, more substantial order of objects but simply the emptiness, the void they are filling out. We must remember that there is nothing intrinsically sublime in a sublime object — according to Lacan, a sublime object is an ordinary, everyday object which, quite by chance, finds itself occupying the place of what he calls *das Ding*, the impossible-real object of desire. The sublime object is 'an object elevated to the level of *das Ding*'. It is its structural place — the fact that it occupies the sacred/forbidden place of *jouissance* — and not its intrinsic qualities that confers on it its sublimity.

This point is best illustrated by a whole series of Buñuel's films which are built around the same central motif of the — to use Buñuel's own words — 'non-explainable impossibility of the fulfilment of a simple desire'. In *L'Age d'or* the couple want to consummate their love, but they are again and again prevented by some stupid accident; in *The Criminal Life of Archibaldo de la Cruz* the hero wants to accomplish a simple murder, but all his attempts fail; in *The Exterminating Angel*, after a party, a group of rich people cannot cross the threshold and leave the house; in *The Discreet Charm of the Bourgeoisie* two couples want to dine together, but unexpected complications always prevent the accomplishment of this simple wish; and finally, in *That Obscure Object of Desire*, we have the paradox of woman who, through a series of tricks, postpones again and again the final moment of reunion with her old lover.

What is the common feature of these films? An ordinary, everyday act becomes impossible to accomplish as soon as it finds itself occupying the impossible place of *das Ding* and begins to embody the sublime object of desire. This object or act may be in itself extremely banal (a common dinner, passing the threshold after a party). It has only to occupy the sacred/forbidden, empty place in the Other, and a whole series of impassable obstacles will build up around it; the object or act, in its very vulgarity, cannot be reached or accomplished.

What the object is masking, dissimulating, by its massive, fascinating presence, is not some other positivity but *its own place*, the void, the lack that it is filling in by its presence — the lack in the Other. And what Lacan calls 'going-through the fantasy' consists precisely in the experience of such an inversion apropos of the fantasy-object: the subject must undergo the experience of how the ever-lacking object-cause of desire is in itself nothing but an objectivication, an embodiment of a certain lack; of how its fascinating presence is here just to mask the emptiness of the place it occupies, the emptiness which is exactly the lack in the Other — which makes the big Other (the symbolic order) perforated, inconsistent.

So 'we' (who have already 'gone through the fantasy') can see that there is nothing where the consciousness thought that it saw something, but our knowledge is already mediated by this 'illusion' in so far as it aims at the empty space which makes the illusion possible. In other words, if we subtract from the illusion the illusion itself (its positive content) what remains is not simply nothing but a determinate nothing, the void in the structure which opened the space for the 'illusion'. To 'unmask the illusion' does not mean that 'there is nothing to see behind it': what we must be able to see is precisely this *nothing as such* — beyond the phenomena, there is nothing *but this nothing itself, 'nothing' which is the subject*. To conceive the appearance as 'mere appearance' the subject effectively has to go beyond it, to 'pass over' it, but what he finds there is his own act of passage.

Usually, these Hegelian propositions are reduced to a simple onto-logical elevation of the subject to the status of the substantial Essence of the totality of being: first, the consciousness thinks there is hidden, behind the phenomenal veil, another transcendent Essence; then, with the passage from consciousness to self-consciousness, it experiences how this Essence behind the phenomena, this force which animates them, is the subject himself. However, such a reading, which immediately iden-tifies the subject with the Essence hidden behind the curtain, misses the crucial fact that the Hegelian passage from consciousness to self-consciousness implies the experience of a certain radical *failure*: the subject (consciousness) wants to penetrate the secret behind the curtain; his effort fails because there is nothing behind the curtain, *nothing which 'is' the subject*. It is in this precise sense that, with Lacan too, the subject (of the signifier) and the (fantasy-) object are correlative or even identical: the subject is the void, the hole in the Other, and the object the inert content filling up this void; the subject's entire 'being' thus consists in the fantasy-object filling out his void. This is why these Hegelian formulas recall, point by point, the tale evoked by Lacan in his *Seminar XI*:

> In the classical tale of Zeuxis and Parrahasios, Zeuxis has the advantage of having made grapes that attracted the birds. The stress is placed not on the fact that these grapes were in any way perfect grapes, but on the fact that even the eye of the bird was taken in by them. This is proved by the fact that his friend Parrahasios triumphs over him by having painted on the wall a veil, a veil so lifelike that Zeuxis, turning towards him, said, *Well, and now show us what you have painted behind it.* By this he showed that what was at issue was certainly deceiving the eye [*tromper l'œil*]. A triumph of the gaze over the eye. (Lacan, 1979, p. 103)

We can deceive animals by an appearance imitating a reality for which it can be substitute, but the properly human way to deceive a man is to imitate the dissimulation of reality — the act of concealing deceives us precisely by pretending to conceal something. In other words, there is nothing behind the curtain except the subject who has already gone beyond it:

> It is manifest that behind the so-called curtain which is supposed to conceal the inner world, there is nothing to be seen unless *we* go behind it ourselves as much in order that we may see, as that there may be something behind there which can be seen. (Hegel, 1977, p. 103)

This is how we should read the fundamental Hegelian distinction between substance and subject: the substance is the positive, transcendent Essence supposed to be hidden behind the curtain of phenomena; to 'experience the substance as subject' means to grasp that the curtain of phenomena conceals above all the fact that there is nothing to conceal, and this 'nothing' behind the curtain is the subject. In other words, at the level of the substance the appearance is simply deceiving, it offers us a false image of the Essence; whereas at the level of the subject the appearance deceives precisely by pretending to deceive — by feigning that there is something to be concealed. It conceals the fact that there is nothing to conceal: it does not feign to tell the truth when it is lying, it feigns to lie when it is actually telling the truth — that is, it deceives by pretending to deceive.

A phenomenon can thus tell the truth precisely by presenting itself as a lie, like the Jew in the Freudian joke often quoted by Lacan, who reproaches his friend: 'Why are you telling me that you are going to Cracow and not to Lemberg, when you're really going to Cracow?' (telling the truth represented a breach of the implicit code of deception which ruled their relationship: when one of them was going to Cracow, he was supposed to tell the lie that his destination was Lemberg, and vice versa). In his commentary on the tale of Zeuxis and Parrhasios, Lacan refers to Plato's protest against the illusion of painting:

> It is here that this little story becomes useful in showing us why Plato protests against the illusion of painting. The point is not that painting gives an illusory equivalance to the object, even if Plato seems to be saying this. The point is that the *trompe l'œil* of painting pretends to be something other than what it is. . . . The picture does not compete with appearance, it competes with what Plato designates for us beyond appearance as being the Idea. It is because the picture is the appearance that says it is that which gives the appearance that Plato attacks painting, as if it were an activity competing with his own. (Lacan, 1979, p. 112).

The real danger, for Plato, is this appearance which purports to be an appearance and for this reason is nothing but the Idea itself, as Hegel knows very well ('the supersensible [Idea] is the appearance *qua* appearance'). This is the secret philosophy has to conceal to retain its consistency — the secret that Hegel, at the culminating point of the metaphysical tradition, makes us see. This is why the fundamental Hegelian motif that 'appearance as such is essential' could not be grasped without the hypothesis of the big Other — of the autonomous symbolic order rendering possible the deception in its properly human dimension.

To exemplify this connection let us refer to Stalinism — more specifically, to its obsessive insistence that whatever the cost we must *maintain the appearance*: we all know that behind the scenes there are wild factional struggles going on; nevertheless we must keep at any price the appearance of Party unity; nobody really believes in the ruling ideology, every individual preserves a cynical distance from it and everybody knows that nobody believes in it; but still, the appearance is to be maintained at any price that people are enthusiastically building socialism, supporting the Party, and so on.

This appearance is *essential*: if it were to be destroyed — if somebody were *publicly* to pronounce the obvious truth that 'the emperor is naked' (that nobody takes the ruling ideology seriously . . .) — in a sense the whole system would fall apart: why? In other words: if everybody knows that 'the emperor is naked' and if everybody knows that all the others know it, what is the agency for the sake of which the appearance is to be kept at any price? There is, of course, only one consistent answer: *the big Other* — it is the big Other which should be maintained in ignorance. This also opens up a new approach to the status of deception in ideology: those who should be deceived by the ideological 'illusion' are not primarily concrete individuals but, rather, the big Other; we could thus say that Stalinism has a value as the ontological proof of the existence of the big Other.

On the other hand, not until the emergence of Yugoslav self-management did Stalinism effectively reach the level of deception in its strictly human dimension. In Stalinism, the deception is basically still a simple one: the power (Party-and-State bureaucracy) feigns to rule in the name of the people while everybody knows that it rules in its own interest — in the interest of reproducing its own power; in Yugoslav self-management, however, the same party-and-State bureaucracy reigns, but it reigns in the name of an ideology whose basic thesis is that the greatest obstacle to the full development of self-management consists in the 'alienated' Party-and-State bureaucracy.

The elementary semantic axis which legitimizes Party rule is the opposition between self-managing socialism and 'bureaucratic' State-and-Party socialism — in other words, the Party-and-State bureaucracy legitimizes its rule by an ideology which designates *itself* as the principal enemy, so that an ordinary Yugoslav subject could address to the ruling bureaucracy the same question as was addressed by one Jew to another in the joke recounted earlier: 'Why are you telling me that the greatest enemy of workers' self-management is the Party-and-State bureaucracy, when the greatest enemy is really the Party-and-State bureaucracy?'

We can see now why the thesis by which, in contrast to habitual 'real socialism', Yugoslav self-management represents 'socialism with a human face', is not a mere propaganda ploy but is to be taken quite liter-ally: in Yugoslavia people are, of course, deceived, just as in all 'real socialism', but they are at least deceived on a specifically human level. After what we have said about the Hegelian distinction between substance and subject, we should not be surprised to find that the differ-ence between habitual 'real socialism' and Yugoslav self-management coincides with this distinction. There is a well-known Yugoslav political joke expressing the quintessence of this: 'In Stalinism, the representatives of the people drive Mercedes, while in Yugoslavia, the people themselves drive Mercedes by proxy, through their representatives.' That is to say, Yugoslav self-management is the point at which the subject must recognize, in the figure embodying the 'alienated' substantial power (the bureaucrat driving the Mercedes), not only a foreign force opposed to him — that is, his other — but *himself in his otherness*, and thus 'reconcile' himself with it.

'Not Only as *Substance*, but Also as *Subject*'

The Logic of Sublimity

In his essay on 'The Religion of Sublimity' (Yovel, 1982), Yirmiahu Yovel has pointed out a certain inconsistency in Hegel's systematization of religions, an inconsistency which does not result directly from the very principle of Hegel's philosophy but expresses rather a contingent, empirical prejudice of Hegel's as an individual, and can therefore be rectified by consequent use of Hegel's own dialectical procedure. This inconsistency concerns the place occupied respectively by Jewish and by ancient Greek religion: in Hegel's *Lessons on the Philosophy of Religion*, Christianity is immediately preceded by three forms of the 'religion of spiritual individuality': the Jewish religion of Sublimity [*Erhabenheit*], the Greek religion of Beauty, and the Roman religion of Understanding [*Verstand*]. In this succession the first, lowest place is taken by the Jewish religion — that is, Greek religion is conceived as a higher stage in spiritual development than the Jewish religion. According to Yovel, Hegel has here given way to his personal anti-Semitic prejudice, because to be consistent with the logic of the dialectical process it is undoubtedly the Jewish religion which should follow the Greek.

Despite some reservations about the detail of Yovel's arguments, his fundamental point seems to hit the mark: the Greek, Jewish and Christian religions do form a kind of triad which corresponds perfectly to the triad of reflection (positing, external and determinate reflection), to this elementary matrix of the dialectical process. Greek religion embodies the moment of 'positing reflection': in it, the plurality of spiritual individuals (gods) is immediately 'posited' as the given spiritual essence of the world. The Jewish religion introduces the moment of 'external reflection' — all positivity is abolished by reference to the unapproachable, transcendent God, the absolute Master, the One of absolute negativity; while Christianity conceives the individuality of man not as something external to God but as a 'reflective determination' of God himself (in the figure of Christ, God himself 'becomes man').

It is something of a mystery why Yovel does not mention the crucial argument in his favour: the very interconnection of the notions of 'Beauty' and 'Sublimity'. If Greek religion is, according to Hegel, the religion of Beauty and Jewish religion that of Sublimity, it is clear that the very logic of the dialectical process compels us to conclude that Sublimity should *follow* Beauty because it is the point of its breakdown, of its mediation, of its self-referential negativity. In using the couple Beauty/Sublimity Hegel relies, of course, on Kant's *Critique of Judgement*, where Beauty and Sublimity are opposed along the semantic axes quality–quantity, shaped–shapeless, bounded–boundless: Beauty calms and comforts; Sublimity excites and agitates. 'Beauty' is the sentiment provoked when the suprasensible Idea appears in the material, sensuous medium, in its harmonious formation – a sentiment of immediate harmony between Idea and the sensuous material of its expression; while the sentiment of Sublimity is attached to chaotic, terrifying limitless phenomena (rough sea, rocky mountains).

Above all, however, Beauty and Sublimity are opposed along the axis pleasure–displeasure: a view of Beauty offers us pleasure, while 'the object is received as sublime with a pleasure that is only possible through the mediation of displeasure' (Kant, 1964, p. 109). In short, the Sublime is 'beyond the pleasure principle', it is a paradoxical pleasure procured by displeasure itself (the exact definition – one of the Lacanian definitions – of enjoyment [*jouissance*]). This means at the same time that the relation of Beauty to Sublimity coincides with the relation of immediacy to mediation – further proof that the Sublime must *follow* Beauty as a form of mediation of its immediacy. On closer examination, in what does this mediation proper to the Sublime consist? Let us quote the Kantian definition of the Sublime:

> The Sublime may be described in this way: It is an object (of nature) the *representation [Vorstellung] of which determines the mind to regard the elevation of nature beyond our reach as equivalent to a presentation [Darstellung] of ideas.* (Kant, 1964, p. 119)

– a definition which, so to speak, anticipates Lacan's determination of the sublime object in his Seminar on *The Ethic of Psychoanalysis*: 'an object raised to the level of the (impossible–real) Thing'. That is to say, with Kant the Sublime designates the relation of an inner-worldly, empirical, sensuous object to *Ding an sich*, to the transcendent, trans-phenomenal, unattainable Thing-in-itself. The paradox of the Sublime is as follows: in principle, the gap separating phenomenal, empirical objects of experience from the Thing-in-itself is insurmountable — that is, no empirical object, no representation [*Vorstellung*] of it can adequately present [*darstellen*] the Thing (the suprasensible Idea); but the Sublime is an object in which we can experience this very impossibility, this permanent failure of the representation to reach after the Thing. Thus, by means of the very failure of representation, we can have a presentiment of the true dimension of the Thing. This is also why an object evoking in us the feeling of Sublimity gives us simultaneous pleasure and displeasure: it gives us displeasure because of its inadequacy to the Thing-Idea, but precisely through this inadequacy it gives us pleasure by indicating the true, incomparable greatness of the Thing, surpassing every possible phenomenal, empirical experience:

> The feeling of the Sublime is, therefore, at once a feeling of displeasure, arising from the inadequacy of imagination in the aesthetic estimation of magnitude to attain to its estimation by reason, and a simultaneously awakened pleasure, arising from this very judgement of the inadequacy of the greatest faculty of sense being in accord with ideas of reason, so far as the effort to attain to these is for us a law. (Kant, 1964, p. 106)

We can now see why it is precisely nature in its most chaotic, boundless, terrifying dimension which is best qualified to awaken in us the feeling of the Sublime: here, where the aesthetic imagination is strained to its utmost, where all finite determinations dissolve themselves, the failure appears at its purest.

The Sublime is therefore the paradox of an object which, in the very field of representation, provides a view, in a negative way, of the dimension of what is unrepresentable. It is a unique point in Kant's system, a point at which the fissure, the gap between phenomenon and Thing-in-itself, is abolished in a negative way, because in it the phenomenon's very inability to represent the Thing adequately *is inscribed in the phenomenon itself* — or, as Kant puts it, 'even if the Ideas of reason can be in no way adequately represented [in the sensuous-phenomenal world], they can be revived and evoked in the mind by means of this very inadequacy which can be presented in a sensuous way.' It is this mediation of the inability —

this successful presentation by means of failure, of the inadequacy itself — which distinguishes *enthusiasm* evoked by the Sublime from fanciful *fanaticism* [*Schwärmerei*]: fanaticism is an insane visionary delusion that we can immediately see or grasp what lies beyond all bounds of sensibility, while enthusiasm precludes all positive presentation. Enthusiasm is an example of purely negative presentation — that is, the sublime object evokes pleasure in a purely negative way: the place of the Thing is indicated through the very failure of its representation. Kant himself pointed out the connection between such a notion of Sublimity and the Jewish religion:

> We have no reason to fear that the feeling of the Sublime will suffer from an abstract mode of presentation like this, which is altogether negative as to what is sensuous. For though the imagination, no doubt, finds nothing beyond the sensible world to which it can lay hold, still this thrusting aside of the sensible barriers gives it a feeling of being unbounded; and that removal is thus a presentation of the infinite. As such it can never be anything more than a negative presentation — but still it expands the soul. Perhaps there is no more sublime passage in the Jewish Law than the commandment: Thou shalt not make unto thee any graven image, or any likeness of any thing that is in heaven or on earth, or under the earth, and so forth. This commandment can alone explain the enthusiasm which the Jewish people, in their moral period, felt for their religion when comparing themselves with others. . . . (Kant, 1964, p. 127)

In what consists, then, the Hegelian criticism of this Kantian notion of the Sublime? From Kant's point of view, Hegel's dialectics appears, of course, as a repeated fall, as a return to the *Schwärmerei* of traditional metaphysics which fails to take into account the abyss separating phenomena from the Idea and pretends to mediate the Idea with phenomena (as with the Jewish religion, to which Christianity appears as a return to pagan polytheism and the incarnation of God in a multitude of man-like figures).

In Hegel's defence, it is not enough to point out how in his dialectics none of the determinate, particular phenomena represents adequately the suprasensible Idea — that is, how the Idea is the very movement of sublation [*Aufhebung*] — the famous *Flüssigwerden*, 'liquidizing' — of all particular determinations. The Hegelian criticism is much more radical: it does not affirm, in opposition to Kant, the possibility of some kind of 'reconciliation'–mediation between Idea and phenomena, the possibility of surmounting the gap which separates them, of abolishing the radical 'otherness', the radical negative relationship of the Idea–Thing to phenomena. Hegel's reproach of Kant (and at the same time of Jewish religion) is, on the contrary, that *it is Kant himself who still remains a prisoner of the field of representation*. Precisely when we determine the Thing as a transcendent surplus beyond what can be represented, we determine it on the basis of the field of representation, starting from it, within its horizon, as its negative limit: the (Jewish) notion of God as radical Otherness, as unrepresentable, still remains the extreme point of the logic of representation.

But here again, this Hegelian approach can give way to misunderstanding if we read it as an assertion that — in opposition to Kant, who tries to reach the Thing through the very breakdown of the field of phenomena, by driving the logic of representation to its utmost — in dialectical speculation, we must grasp the Thing 'in itself', from itself, as it is in its pure Beyond, without even a negative reference or relationship to the field of representation. This is *not* Hegel's position: the Kantian criticism has here done its job and if this were Hegel's position, Hegelian dialectics would effectively entail a regression into the traditional metaphysics aiming at an immediate approach to the Thing. Hegel's position is in fact 'more Kantian than Kant himself' — it adds nothing to the Kantian notion of the Sublime; it merely takes it more *literally* than Kant himself.

Hegel, of course, retains the basic dialectical moment of the Sublime, the notion that the Idea is reached through purely negative presentation — that the very inadequacy of the phenomenality to the Thing is the only appropriate way to present it. The real problem lies elsewhere: Kant still presupposes that the Thing-in-itself exists as something positively given beyond the field of representation, of phenomenality; the breakdown of phenomenality, the experience of phenomena, is for him only an 'external reflection', only a way of indicating, within the domain of phenomenality, this transcendent dimension of the Thing which persists in itself beyond phenomenality.

Hegel's position is, in contrast, that there is *nothing* beyond phenomenality, beyond the field of representation. The experience of radical negativity, of the radical inadequacy of all phenomena to the Idea, the experience of the radical fissure between the two — this experience is already *Idea itself as 'pure', radical negativity*. Where Kant thinks that he is still dealing only with a negative presentation of the Thing, we are already in the midst of the Thing-in-itself — *for this Thing-in-itself is nothing but this radical negativity*. In other words — in a somewhat overused Hegelian speculative twist — the negative experience of the Thing must change into the experience of the Thing-in-itself as radical negativity. The experience of the Sublime thus remains the same: all we have to do is to subtract its transcendent presupposition — the presupposition that this experience indicates, in a negative way, some transcendent Thing-in-itself persisting in its positivity beyond it. In short, we must limit ourselves to what is strictly immanent to this experience, to pure negativity, to the negative self-relationship of the representation.

Homologous to Hegel's determination of the difference between the death of the pagan god and the death of Christ (the first being merely the death of the terrestrial embodiment, of the terrestrial representation, figure, of God, while with the death of Christ it is God of beyond, God as a positive, transcendent, unattainable entity, which dies) we could say that what Kant fails to take into account is the way the experience of the nullity, of the inadequacy of the phenomenal world of representation, which befalls us in the sentiment of the Sublime, means at the same time the nullity, the nonexistence of the transcendent Thing-in-itself as a positive entity.

That is to say, the limit of the logic of representation is not to 'reduce all contents to representations', to what can be represented, but, on the contrary, in the very presupposition of some positive entity (Thing-in-itself) *beyond phenomenal representation*. We overcome phenomenality not by reaching beyond it, but by the experience of how there is nothing beyond it — how its beyond is precisely this Nothing of absolute negativity, of the utmost inadequacy of the appearance to its notion. The suprasensible essence is the 'appearance *qua* appearance' — that is, it is not enough to say that the appearance is never adequate to its essence, we must also add that *this 'essence' itself is nothing but the inadequacy of the appearance to itself*, to its notion (inadequacy which makes it '[just] an appearance').

Thus the status of the sublime object is displaced almost imperceptibly, but none the less decisively: the Sublime is no longer an (empirical) object indicating through its very inadequacy the dimension of a transcendent Thing-in-itself (Idea) but an object which occupies the place, replaces, fills out the empty place of the Thing as the void, as the pure Nothing of absolute negativity — the Sublime is an object whose positive body is just an embodiment of Nothing. This logic of an object which, by its very inadequacy, 'gives body' to the absolute negativity of the Idea, is articulated in Hegel in the form of the so-called 'infinite judgement', a judgement in which subject and predicate are radically incompatible, incomparable: 'the Spirit is a *bone*', *Wealth* is the Self', 'the State is *Monarch*', 'God is *Christ*'.

In Kant, the feeling of the Sublime is evoked by some boundless, terrifying imposing phenomenon (raging nature, and so on), while in Hegel we are dealing with a miserable 'little piece of the Real' — the Spirit *is* the inert, dead skull; the subject's Self *is* this small piece of metal that I am holding in my hand; the State as the rational organization of social life *is* the idiotic body of the Monarch; God who created the world *is* Jesus, this miserable individual crucified together with two robbers. . . . Herein lies the 'last secret' of dialectical speculation: not in the dialectical mediation–sublimation of all contingent, empirical reality, not in the deduction of all reality from the mediating movement of absolute negativity, but in the fact that this very negativity, to attain its 'being-for-itself', must embody itself again in some miserable, radically contingent corporeal leftover.

'The Spirit is a Bone'

At the immediate level, that of 'understanding', of 'representation [*Vorstellung*]', this proposition appears, of course, as an extreme variation of vulgar materialism; reducing the spirit, the subject, pure negativity, the most mobile and subtle element, an ever-escaping 'fox', to a rigid, fixed, dead object, to total inertia, to an absolutely non-dialectial presence. Consequently, we react to it like the shocked Soviet bureaucrat in the Rabinovitch joke: we are startled, it is absurd and nonsensical; the proposition 'the Spirit is a bone' provokes in us a sentiment of radical, unbearable contradiction; it offers an image of grotesque discord, of an extremely negative relationship.

However, as in the case of Rabinovitch, it is precisely thus that we produce its speculative truth, because *this negativity, this unbearable discord, coincides with subjectivity itself*, it is the only way to make present and 'palpable' the utmost — that is, self-referential — negativity which characterizes the spiritual subjectivity. We *succeed* in transmitting the dimension of subjectivity *by means of the failure itself*, through the radical insufficiency, through the absolute maladjustment of the predicate in relation to the subject. This is why 'the Spirit is a bone' is a perfect example of what Hegel calls the 'speculative proposition', a proposition whose terms are incompatible, without common measure. As Hegel points out in the

Preface to the *Phenomenology of Spirit*, to grasp the true meaning of such a proposition we must go back and read it over again, because this true meaning arises from the very failure of the first, 'immediate' reading.

Does not the proposition 'the Spirit is a bone' — this equation of two absolutely incompatible terms, pure negative movement of the subject and the total inertia of a rigid object — offer us something like a Hegelian version of the Lacanian formula of fantasy: $\$ \lozenge a$? To convince ourselves that it does, it is enough to place this proposition in its proper context: the passage from physiognomy to phrenology in the *Phenomenology of Spirit*.

Physiognomy — the language of the body, the expression of the subject's interior in his spontaneous gestures and grimaces — still belongs to the level of language, of signifying representation: a certain corporeal element (a gesture, a grimace) represents, signifies, the non-corporeal interior of the subject. The final result of physiognomy is its utter *failure*: every signifying representation 'betrays' the subject; it perverts, deforms what it is supposed to reveal; there is no 'proper' signifier of the subject. And the passage from physiognomy to phrenology functions as the change of level from *representation* to *presence*: in opposition to gestures and grimaces, the skull is not a sign expressing an interior; it represents nothing; it is — in its very inertia — the immediate presence of the Spirit:

> In physiognomy, Spirit is supposed to be known in its *own* outer aspect, as in a being which is the *utterance* of Spirit — the visible invisibility of its essence. . . . In the determination yet to be considered, however, the outer aspect is lastly a wholly *immobile* reality which is not in its own self a speaking sign but, separated from self-conscious movement, presents itself on its own account and is a mere Thing. (Hegel, 1977, p. 195)

The bone, the skull, is thus an object which, by means of its *presence*, fills out the void, the impossibility of the signifying *representation* of the subject. In Lacanian terms it is the objectification of a certain lack: a Thing occupies the place where the signifier is lacking; the fantasy-object fills out the lack in the Other (the signifier's order). The inert object of phrenology (the skullbone) is nothing but a positive form of certain failure: it embodies, literally 'gives body' to, the ultimate failure of the signifying representation of the subject. It is therefore correlative to the subject in so far as — in Lacanian theory — the subject is *nothing but* the impossibility of its own signifying representation — the empty place opened up in the big Other by the failure of this representation. We can now see how meaningless is the usual reproach according to which Hegelian dialectics 'sublates' all the inert objective leftover, including it in the circle of the dialectical mediation: the very movement of dialectics implies, on the contrary, that there is always a certain remnant, a certain leftover escaping the circle of subjectivation, of subjective appropriation-mediation, and *the subject is precisely correlative to this leftover*: $\$ \Diamond a$. The leftover which resists 'subjectivation' embodies the impossibility which 'is' the subject: in other words, the subject is strictly correlative to its own impossibility; its limit is its positive condition.

The Hegelian 'idealist wager' consists, rather, in the conversion of this lack of the signifier into the signifier of the lack; from Lacanian theory we know that the signifier of this conversion, by means of which lack as such is symbolized, is the phallus. And — here we encounter the last surprise in the Hegelian text — at the end of the section on phrenology, Hegel himself evokes the phallic metaphor to designate the relationship between the two level of reading the proposition 'the Spirit is a bone': the usual reading, that of 'representation'/'understanding', and the speculative one:

> The *depth* which Spirit brings forth from within — but only as far as its picture-thinking consciousness where it lets it remain — and the *ignorance* of this consciousness about what it really is saying, are the same conjunction of the high and the low which, in the living being, Nature naïvely expresses when it combines the organ of its highest fulfilment, the organ of generation, with the organ of urination. The infinite judgement, *qua* infinite, would be the fulfilment of life that comprehends itself; the consciousness of the infinite judgement that remains at the level of picture-thinking behaves as urination. (Hegel, 1977, p. 210)

'Wealth is the Self'

When, in the *Phenomenology of Spirit*, we encounter a certain 'figure of consciousness', the question to ask is always: Where does this figure repeat itself — that is, where do we find a later, richer, more 'concrete' figure which, by repeating the original one, offers us, perhaps, the key to its true meaning? Concerning the passage from physiognomy to phrenology, we do not have to look far: it is resumed in the chapter on the 'Self-alienated Spirit', in the form of a passage from 'language of flattery' to Wealth.

The 'language of flattery' is a middle term in the triad *Noble-minded consciousness-The language of flattery-Wealth*. Noble-minded consciousness occupies the position of extreme alienation: it posits all its contents in the common Good embodied in the State — noble-minded consciousness serves the State with total and sincere devotion, attested by its acts. It does not speak: its language is limited to 'counsels' concerning the common Good. This Good functions here as an entirely substantial entity, whereas with the passage to the next stage of dialectical development it assumes the form of subjectivity: instead of the substantial State, we obtain the Monarch who is able to say 'l'État, c'est moi'. This subjectivation of the State entails a radical change in the mode of serving it: 'The *heroism of silent service* becomes the *heroism of flattery*' (Hegel, 1977, p. 310). The medium of activity of the consciousness is no longer deeds, it is now language, flattery addressed to the person of the Monarch, who embodies the State.

It is not difficult to detect the historical background of this passage: the transformation of medieval feudalism, with its notions of honourable service, and so on, into absolute Monarchy. But here we are far from a simple corruption or degeneration of silent and devoted service into hypocritical flattery. The paradoxical syntagm 'heroism of flattery' is not to be taken as an ironic conjunction of two otherwise opposed notions; here we are concerned with heroism in the full sense of the word. The 'heroism of flattery' is a notion that deserves to be interpreted on the same level as that of 'voluntary servitude'; it announces the same theoretical deadlock: how can 'flattery', usually perceived as a non-ethical activity *par excellence*, as a renunciation of the ethical stance in pursuit of 'pathological' interests of gain and pleasure, obtain a properly ethical status, the status of an obligation whose fulfilment draws us 'beyond the pleasure principle'?

According to Hegel, the key to this enigma is the role played in it by language. Language is, of course, the very medium of the 'journey of consciousness' in *Phenomenology*, to such a point that it would be possible to define every stage of this journey, every 'figure of consciousness', by a specific modality of language; even in its very beginning, in the 'sense-certainty', the dialectical movement is activated by the discord between what the consciousness 'means to say' and what it effectively says. In this series, the 'language of flattery' none the less presents an exception: only here is language not reduced to a medium of the dialectical process but becomes as such, in its very form, what is at stake in the struggle; it 'has for its content the form itself, the form which language itself is, and is authoritative as *language*. It is the power of speech, as that which performs what has to be performed' (Hegel, 1977, p. 308).

This is why 'flattery' is not to be conceived at the psychological level, in the sense of hypocritical and avaricious adulation: what announces itself here is rather the dimension of an *alienation proper to language as such* — it is the very form of language which introduces a radical alienation; noble-minded consciousness betrays the sincerity of its internal conviction *as soon as it starts talking*. That is to say, as soon as we start talking, truth is on the side of the Universal, of what we are 'effectively saying', and the 'sincerity' of our innermost feelings becomes something 'pathological' in the Kantian sense of the word: something of a radically non-ethical nature, something which belongs to the domain of the pleasure principle.

The subject can pretend that his flattery is nothing but a simple feigning, accommodation to an external ritual which has nothing whatsoever to do with his innermost and sincere convictions. The problem is that as soon as he pretends to feign, he is already the victim of his own feigning: his true place is out there, in the empty external ritual, and what he takes for his innermost conviction is nothing but the narcissistic vanity of his null subjectivity — or, in modern parlance, the 'truth' of what we are saying depends on the way our speech constitutes a social bond, on its performative function, not on the psychological 'sincerity' of our intention. The 'heroism of flattery' carries this paradox to its extreme. Its message is: 'Although what I'm saying disavows completely my innermost convictions, I know that this form emptied of all sincerity is truer than my convictions, and in this sense I'm sincere in my eagerness to renounce my convictions'.

This is how 'flattering the Monarch against one's convictions' can become an ethical act: by pronouncing empty phrases which disavow our innermost convictions, we submit ourselves to a compulsive disrupting of our narcissistic homeostasis, we 'externalize' ourselves completely — we heroically renounce what is most precious in us, our 'sense of honour', our moral consistency, our self-respect. The flattery achieves a radical voidance of our 'personality'; what remains is the empty form of the subject — the subject as this empty form.

We encounter a somewhat homologous logic into the passage of the revolutionary Leninist consciousness to the post-revolutionary Stalinist one: here as well, after the revolution, faithful service and devotion to the revolutionary Cause turns necessarily into a 'heroism of flattery' addressed to the Leader, to the subject presumed to embody and personify the revolutionary power. Here too, the properly heroic dimension of this flattery consists in the fact that in the name of our fidelity to the Cause we are ready to sacrifice our elementary sincerity, honesty and human decency – with the supplementary 'turn of the screw' that we are prepared *to confess this very insincerity* and to declare ourselves 'traitors'.

Ernesto Laclau was quite right to remark that *it is language which is, in an unheard-of sense, a 'Stalinist phenomenon'.* The Stalinist ritual, the empty flattery which 'holds together' the community, the neutral voice, totally freed of all 'psychological' remnants, which pronounces the 'confessions' in the staged political processes – they realize, in the purest form to date, a dimension which is probably essential to language as such. There is no need to revert to the pre-Socratic foundation if we want to 'penetrate the origins of language'; the *History of the Communist Party (Bolsheviks)* is more than sufficient.

Where can the subject who is thus 'emptied' find his objective correlative? The Hegelian answer is: in Wealth, in money obtained in exchange for flattery. The proposition 'Wealth is the Self' repeats at this level the proposition 'The Spirit is a bone': in both cases we are dealing with a proposition which is at first sight absurd, nonsensical, with an equation the terms of which are incompatible; in both cases we encounter the same logical structure of passage: the subject, totally lost in the medium of language (language of gestures and grimaces; language of flattery), finds his objective counterpart in the inertia of a non-language object (skull, money).

The paradox, the patent nonsense of money – this inert, external, passive object that we can hold in our hands and manipulate – serving as the immediate embodiment of Self, is no more difficult to accept than the proposition that the skull embodies the immediate effectivity of the Spirit. The difference between the two propositions is determined solely by the difference in the starting point of the respective dialectical movement: if we start from language reduced to 'gestures and grimaces of the body', the objective counterpart to the subject is what at this level presents the total inertia – the skullbone; but if we conceive language as the medium of the social relations of domination, its objective counterpart is of course wealth as the embodiment, as the materialization of social power.

Positing, External, Determinate Reflection

This paradox of the 'infinite judgement' is what escapes Kant — why? To put it in Hegelian terms, because Kant's philosophy is one of 'external reflection' — because Kant is not yet able to accomplish the passage from 'external' to 'determinate' reflection. In Kant's view, the whole move-ment which brings forth the feeling of the Sublime concerns only our subjective reflection external to the Thing, not the Thing-in-itself — that is, it represents only the way we, as finite subjects caught in the limits of our phenomenal experience, can mark in a negative mode the dimension of the trans-phenomenal Thing. In Hegel, however, this movement is an immanent reflexive determination of the Thing-in-itself — that is, the Thing is *nothing but* this reflexive movement.

To exemplify this movement of reflection — namely the triad of positing, external and determinate reflection (Hegel, 1966), let us take the eternal hermeneutical question of how to read a text. 'Positing reflec-tion' corresponds to a naïve reading claiming immediate access to the true meaning of the text: we know, we pretend to grasp immediately what a text says. The problem arises, of course, when there are a number of mutually exclusive readings claiming access to the true meaning: how do we choose between them, how do we judge their claims? 'External reflection' provides a way out of this impasse: it transposes the 'essence', the 'true meaning' of a text into the unattainable beyond, making of it a transcendent 'Thing-in-itself'. All that is accessible to us, finite subjects, are distorted reflections, partial aspects deformed by our subjective perspective; the Truth-in-itself, the true meaning of the text, is lost for ever.

All we have to do to pass from 'external' to 'determinate' reflection is to become aware how *this very externality of the external reflexive determin-ations of the 'essence'* (the series of distorted, partial reflections of the true meaning of the text) *is already internal to this 'essence' itself,* how the internal 'essence' is already in itself 'decentred', how the 'essence' of this essence itself consists in this series of external determinations.

To make this somewhat speculative formulation clearer, let us take the case of conflicting interpretations of some great classical text — *Anti-gone*, for example. 'Positing reflection' claims a direct approach to its true meaning: '*Antigone* is in fact a drama about . . .'; 'external reflection' offers us a gamut of historical interpretations conditioned by different social and other contexts: 'We don't know what Sophocles really meant, the immediate truth about *Antigone* is unattainable because of the filter of

historical distance, all that is within our grasp is the succession of
historical influence of the text: what *Antigone* meant in the Renaissance,
to Hölderlin and Goethe, in the nineteenth century, to Heidegger, to
Lacan. . . .' And to accomplish the 'determinate reflection', we have only
to experience how this problem of the 'true', 'original' meaning of *Anti-*
gone — that is, the status of *Antigone*-'in-itself', independent of the
string of its historical efficacy — is ultimately a pseudo-problem: to
resume the fundamental principle of Gadamer's hermeneutics, there is
more truth in the later efficacy of a text, in the series of its subsequent
readings, than in its supposedly 'original' meaning.

The 'true' meaning of *Antigone* is not to be sought in the obscure
origins of what 'Sophocles really wanted to say', it is constituted by this
very series of subsequent readings — that is, it is constituted *afterwards*,
through a certain structurally necessary *delay*. We achieve the 'determinate reflection' when we become aware of the fact that this delay is
immanent, internal to the 'Thing-in-itself': *the Thing-in-itself is found in its*
Truth through the loss of its immediacy. In other words, what appears, to
'external reflection', as an *impediment* is in fact a *positive condition* of our
access to Truth: the Truth of a thing emerges because the thing is not
accessible to us in its immediate self-identity.

Yet what we have just said is insufficient inasmuch as it still leaves
room for a certain misunderstanding: if we grasp the plurality of
phenomenal determinations which at first sight blocked our approach to
the 'essence' as so many self-determinations of this very 'essence' — if we
transpose the fissure separating the appearance from essence into the
internal fissure of the essence itself — it could still be said that in this way
— through 'determinate reflection' — the appearance is ultimately reduced
to the self-determination of the essence, 'sublated' in its self-movement,
internalized, conceived as a subordinate moment of self-mediation of the
essence. We have yet to add the decisive emphasis: it is not only that the
appearance, the fissure between appearance and essence, is a fissure
internal to the essence itself; the crucial point is that, inversely, *'essence'*
itself is nothing but the self-rupture, the self-fissure of the appearance.

In other words, the fissure between appearance and essence is internal
to the appearance itself; it must be reflected in the very domain of
appearance — *this* is what Hegel calls 'determinate reflection'. The basic
feature of Hegelian reflection is thus the structural, conceptual necessity
of its *redoubling*: it is not only that the essence must appear, must articulate its inner truth in a multiplicity of determinations (this being one of
the commonplaces of Hegelian commentary: 'the essence is only as deep

as it is broad'); the point is that it must appear *for the appearance itself* — as essence in its difference to appearance, in the form of a phenomenon which, paradoxically, gives body to the nullity of phenomena as such. This redoubling characterizes the movement of reflection; we run into it at all levels of the Spirit, from the State to religion. The world, the universe, is of course the manifestation of divinity, the reflection of God's infinite creativity; but for God to become effective he must again reveal himself to his creation, embody himself in a particular person (Christ). The State is, of course, a rational totality; but its establishes itself as an effective sublation-mediation 'of all particular contents only by embodying itself again in the contingent individuality of the Monarch. This redoubling movement is what defines 'determinate reflection', and the element which embodies again, which gives positive form to the very movement of sublation of all positivity, is what Hegel calls 'reflexive determination'.

What we must grasp is the intimate connection, even identity, between this logic of reflection (positing, external, determinate reflection) and the Hegelian notion of the 'absolute' subject — of the subject which is no longer attached to some presupposed substantial contents but posits its own substantial presuppositions. Roughly speaking, our thesis is that what is constitutive for the Hegelian subject is precisely this redoubling of the reflection, the gesture by means of which the subject posits the substantial 'essence' presupposed in the external reflection.

Positing the Presuppositions

To exemplify this logic of 'positing the presuppositions', let us take one of the most famous 'figures of consciousness' from Hegel's *Phenomenology of Spirit*: the 'beautiful soul'. How does Hegel undermine the position of the 'beautiful soul', of this gentle, fragile, sensitive form of subjectivity which, from its safe position as innocent observer, deplores the wicked ways of the world? The falsity of the 'beautiful soul' lies not in its inactivity, in the fact that it only complains of a depravity without doing something to remedy it; it consists, on the contrary, in the very mode of activity implied by this position of inactivity — in the way the 'beautiful soul' structures the 'objective' social world in advance so that it is able to assume, to play in it the role of the fragile, innocent and passive victim. This, then, is Hegel's fundamental lesson: when we are active, when we intervene in the world through a particular act, the real act is not this particular, empirical, factual intervention (or non-intervention); the real act is of a strictly symbolic nature, it consists in the very mode in which we structure the world, our perception of it, in advance, in order to make our intervention possible, in order to open in it the space for our activity (or inactivity). The real act thus *precedes* the (particular-factual) activity; it consists in the previous restructuring of our symbolic universe into which our (factual, particular) act will be inscribed.

To make this clear, let us take the care of the suffering mother as the 'pillar of the family': all other members of the family — her husband, her children — exploit her mercilessly; she does all the domestic work and she is of course continually groaning, complaining of how her life is nothing but mute suffering, sacrifice without reward. The point, however, is that this 'silent sacrifice' is her imaginary identification: it gives consistency to her self-identity — if we take this incessant sacrificing from her, nothing remains; she literally 'loses ground'.

This is a perfect case of Lacanian communication (by which the speaker gets back from the recipient his own message in its inverted — that is, true — meaning). The meaning of the mother's incessant groaning is a demand. 'Keep on exploiting me! My sacrifice is all that gives meaning to my life!', so that by exploiting her mercilessly, other members of the family return to her the true meaning of her own message. In other words, the true meaning of the mother's complaint is: 'I'm ready to give up, to sacrifice everything ... *everything but the sacrifice itself!*' What the poor mother must do, if she wants to liberate herself effectively from this domestic enslavement, is to *sacrifice the sacrifice itself* — to stop accepting or even actively sustaining the social network (of the family) which confers on her the role of exploited victim.

The mother's fault is therefore not simply in her 'inactivity' in silently enduring the role of exploited victim, but in actively sustaining the social-symbolic network in which she is reduced to playing such a role. Here, we could also refer to the distinction between 'constituting' and 'constituted' identification — between the ideal ego and the ego-ideal. On the level of the ideal-imaginary ego, the 'beautiful soul' sees herself as a fragile, passive victim; she identifies with this role; in it she 'likes herself', she appears to herself likeable; this role gives her a narcissistic pleasure; but her real identification is with the formal structure of the intersubjective field which enables her to assume this role. In other words, this structuring of the intersubjective space (the family network) is the point of her symbolic identification, the point from which she observes herself so that she appears to herself likeable in her imaginary role.

We could also formulate all this in terms of the Hegelian dialectics of form and content, in which the Truth is of course in the form: by means of a purely formal act, the 'beautiful soul' structures its social reality in advance in such a way that it can assume the role of passive victim; blinded by the fascinating content (the beauty of the role of 'suffering victim'), the subject overlooks his or her *formal responsibility* for the given state of things. To explain this notion of form, let us take a historical example: the debate between Sartre and the French Communists immediately after the Second World War (the so-called 'existentialism debate'). The Communists' main reproach to Sartre was as follows: by conceiving the subject as pure negativity, void, emptied of all positive substantial contents, of all determination by some pre-given 'essence', Sartre rejected all bourgeois *content*. What remained, however, was the pure *form* of bourgeois subjectivity, so Sartre had still to accomplish the last and most difficult task: to reject this very form of bourgeois individualistic subjectivity and give himself up to the working class. . . . Despite its simplicity, there is a grain of truth in this argument: is not the blind-spot of so-called 'bourgeois libertarian radicalism' precisely in the way its pathetic sacrificing of all bourgeois content affirms the form of bourgeois subjectivity? In overlooking the fact that the real 'source of evil' is not the positive content but this form itself? This dialectic of form and content is the background for our understanding of the following enigmatic passage from Hegel's *Phenomenology*:

> Action *qua* actualization is thus the pure form of will — the simple conversion of a reality that merely *is* into a reality that results from *action*, the conversion of the bare mode of objective knowledge into that of knowing *reality* as something produced by consciousness. (Hegel, 1977, p. 385)

Before we intervene in reality by means of a *particular* act, we must accomplish the *purely formal* act of converting reality as something which is objectively given into reality as 'effectivity', as something produced, 'posited' by the subject. Here the interest of the 'beautiful soul' is to make us see this gap between the two acts (or two aspects of the same act): on the level of positive content she is an inactive victim, but her inactivity is already located in a field of effectivity, of social reality 'that results from *action*' — in the field constituted by the 'conversion' of the 'objective' reality into effectivity. For the reality to appear to us as the field of our own activity (or inactivity), we must conceive it in advance as 'converted' — *we must conceive ourselves as formally responsible-guilty for it.*

Here we finally encounter the problem of posited presuppositions: in his particular-empirical activity, the subject of course presupposes the 'world', the objectivity on which he performs his activity, as something given in advance, as a positive condition of his activity; but his positive-empirical activity is possible only if he structures his perception of the world in advance in a way that opens the space for his intervention — in other words, only if he retroactively posits the very presuppositions of his activity, of his 'positing'. This 'act before act' by means of which the subject posits the very presuppositions of his activity is of a strictly formal nature; it is a purely formal 'conversion' transforming reality into something perceived, assumed as a result of our activity.

The crucial moment is this previousness of the act of formal conversion in relation to positive-factual interventions, whereby Hegel differs radically from Marxian dialectics: in Marx, the (collective) subject first transforms the given objectivity by means of the effective-material process of production; he first gives it 'human form', and thereupon, reflecting the results of his activity, he formally perceives himself as the 'author of its world', while in Hegel the order is reversed — before the subject 'actually' intervenes in the world, he must formally grasp himself as responsible for it.

In ordinary language, the subject 'doesn't really do anything', he only assumes the guilt-responsibility for the given state of things — that is, he accepts it as 'his own work' by a purely formal act: what was a moment ago perceived as substantial positivity ('reality that merely *is*') is suddenly perceived as resulting from his own activity ('*reality* as something produced by consciousness'). 'In the beginning' is thus not an active intervention but a paradoxical act of 'imitation', of 'pretending': the subject *pretends* that the reality which is given to him in its positivity — which he encounters in its factual substantiality — is his own work. The first 'act' of this kind, the act defining the very emergence of man, is the funeral ritual; Hegel develops this in a formal, explicit way apropos of Polynices' burial in *Antigone*:

> This universality which the individual *as such* attains is *pure being, death*; it is a state which has been reached *immediately*, in the *course of Nature*, not the result of an action *consciously done*. The duty of the member of a Family is on that account to add this aspect, in order that the individual's ultimate being, too, shall not belong solely to Nature and remain something irrational, but shall be something *done*, and the right of consciousness be asserted in it. . . . Blood-relationship supplements, then, the abstract natural process by

adding to it the movement of consciousness, interrupting the work of Nature and rescuing the blood-relation from destruction; or better, because destruction is necessary, the passage of the blood-relation into mere being, it takes on itself the act of destruction. (Hegel, 1977, pp. 270–71)

The crucial dimension of the funeral rite is indicated in the last phrase quoted: the passage into pure being, death, natural disintegration, is something that happens anyway, with inevitable natural necessity; by means of the funeral rite the subject takes upon himself this process of natural disintegration, he symbolically repeats it, he pretends that this process resulted from his own free decision.

Of course, from a Heideggerian perspective we can here reproach Hegel with bringing subjectivism to its extreme: the subject wants to dispose freely even with death, this limiting condition of human existence; he wants to transform it into his own act. However, the Lacanian approach opens up the possibility of another, opposite reading: the funeral rite presents an act of symbolization *par excellence*; by means of a forced choice, the subject assumes, repeats as his own act, what happened anyway. In the funeral rite, the subject confers the *form* of a free act on an 'irrational', contingent natural process.

Hegel articulates the same line of thought in a more general way in his *Lectures on the Philosophy of Religion*, when he discusses the status of the Fall of man in Christianity — more specifically, the relationship between Evil and human nature. His starting point is of course that human nature is in itself innocent, in a state 'before the Fall' — that guilt and Evil exist only when we have freedom, free choice, the subject. But — and this is the crucial point — it would be quite erroneous to conclude, from this original innocence of human nature, that we can simply distinguish in man the part of nature — which was given to him, for which he is consequently not responsible — from the part of free spirit — a result of his free choice, the product of his activity. Human nature 'in itself' — in its abstraction from culture — is indeed 'innocent', but as soon as the form of spirit begins to reign, as soon as we enter culture, man becomes, so to speak, retroactively responsible for his own nature, for his most 'natural' passions and instincts. 'Culture' consists not only in transforming nature, in conferring on it spiritual form: human nature itself, as soon as it is put in relation to culture, *changes into its own opposite* — what was a moment ago spontaneous innocence becomes retroactively pure Evil. In other words, as soon as the universal form of the Spirit comprises natural contents, the subject is formally *responsible* for it even if it is materially something which he simply *found*: the subject is treated as if, by means of an eternally past, primordial act, he freely chose his own natural-substantial base. It is this formal responsibility, this fissure between the spiritual form and the given content, which drives the subject to incessant activity (Hegel, 1969).

It is thus not difficult to realize the connection between this gesture of 'choosing what is given', this act of formal conversion by means of which the subject assumes — determines as his own work — the given objectivity and the passage from external to determinate reflection accomplished when the positing-producing subject posits the very presuppositions of his activity, of his 'positing': what is 'positing of presuppositions' if not that very gesture of formal conversion by means of which we 'posit' as our own work what is given to us?

It is likewise not difficult to recognize the connection between all this and the fundamental Hegelian thesis that the substance is to be conceived as subject. If we do not want to miss the crucial point of this Hegelian conception of substance as subject, we have to take into account the break that separates the Hegelian 'absolute' subject from the Kantian-Fichtean, still 'finite' subject: the latter is the subject of practical activity, the 'positing' subject, the subject which actively intervenes in the world, transforming-mediating the given objective reality; he is consequently *bound* to this presupposed reality. In other words, the Kantian-Fichtean subject is the subject of the work-process, the subject of the productive relationship to reality. Precisely for this reason he can never entirely 'mediate' the given objectivity, he is always bound to some transcendent presupposition (Thing-in-itself) upon which he performs activity, even if this presupposition is reduced to the mere 'instigation [*Anstoß*]' of our practical activity.

The Hegelian subject is, however, 'absolute': he is no longer a 'finite' subject bound to, limited, conditioned by some given presuppositions; he himself posits these very presuppositions — how? Precisely through the act of 'choosing what is already given' — that is, through the symbolic act, mentioned above, of a purely formal conversion; by pretending that the given reality is already his work; by assuming responsibility for it.

The current notion according to which the Hegelian subject is 'even more active' than the Fichtean subject in so far as he succeeds where the Fichtean subject still fails — that is, in 'devouring'-mediating-internalizing the whole effectivity without any leftover — is entirely wrong: what we must add to the Fichtean 'finite' subject to arrive at the Hegelian 'absolute' subject is just some purely formal, empty gesture —

in common parlance: an act of pure feigning by means of which the subject pretends to be liable for what is happening anyway, without taking part in it. *This is the way 'substance becomes subject'*: when, by means of an empty gesture, the subject takes upon himself the leftover which eludes his active intervention. This 'empty gesture' receives from Lacan its proper name: the signifier; in it resides the elementary, constitutive act of symbolization.

In this way, it is also clear how we connect the Hegelian concept of 'substance as subject' with the fundamental feature of the dialectical process: in this process, we can say that in a sense *everything has already happened*; all that is actually going on is a pure change of form through which we take note of the fact that what we arrived at *has always already been*. For example, in the dialectial process the fissure is not 'sublated' by being actively overcome: all we have to do is to state formally that *it never existed*. This happens in the Rabinovitch joke, where the bureaucrat's counter-argument is not actively refuted by Rabinovitch's more accurate arguments; all Rabinovitch has to do is to accomplish a purely formal act of conversion by simply stating that the bureaucrat's very counter-argument is effectively an argument in his favour.

There is no contradiction between this 'fatalistic' aspect of Hegelian dialectics — the idea that we are simply taking note of what has already happened — and his claim to conceive substance as subject. Both really aim at the same conjunction, because the 'subject' is precisely a name for this 'empty gesture' which changes nothing at the level of positive content (at this level, everything has already happened) but must nevertheless be added for the 'content' itself to achieve its full effectively.

This paradox is the same as that of the last grain of sand to be added before we have a heap: we can never be sure which grain is the last one; the only possible definition of the heap is that *even if we take away one grain, it will still be a heap*. So this 'last grain of sand' is by definition superfluous, but none the less necessary — it constitutes a 'heap' by its very superfluity. This paradoxical grain materializes the agency of the signifier — paraphrasing the Lacanian definition of the signifier (that which 'represents the subject for another signifier'), we are even tempted to say that this last, superfluous grain represents the subject for all the other grains in the heap. It is the Hegelian Monarch which embodies this paradoxical function at its purest. The State without the Monarch would still be a *substantial* order — the Monarch represents the point of its subjectivation — but what precisely is his function? Only 'dotting the i's' (Hegel, 1969b, par. 280) in a formal gesture of taking upon himself (by putting his signature on them) the decrees proposed to him by his ministers and councillors — of making them an expression of his personal will, of adding the pure form of subjectivity, of 'It is our will . . .', to the objective content of decrees and laws. The Monarch is thus a subject *par excellence*, but only in so far as he limits himself to the purely formal act of subjective decision: as soon as he aims at something more, as soon as he concerns himself with questions of positive content, he crosses the line separating him from his councillors, and the State regresses to the level of Substantiality.

We can now return to the paradox of the phallic signifier: in so far as, according to Lacan, the phallus is a 'pure signifier', it is precisely a signifier of this act of formal conversion by means of which the subject assumes the given, substantial reality as his own work. This is why we could determine the basic 'phallic experience' as a certain 'everything depends on me, but for all that I can do nothing'. Let us exemplify it by reference to two cases which should be read together: the theory of the phallus found in St Augustine, and a certain well-known vulgar joke.

St Augustine developed his theory of sexuality in one of his minor but none the less crucial texts, *De Nuptiis et Concupiscentia*. His reasoning is extremely interesting because at its very outset it differs from what is commonly regarded as the basic premises of the Christian notion of sexuality: far from being the sin which caused man's Fall, sexuality is on the contrary, the *punishment*, *penitence* for the sin. Original sin lies in man's arrogance and pride; it was committed when Adam ate from the Tree of Knowledge, wanting to elevate himself to the divine heights and to become himself master of all creation. God subsequently punished man — Adam — by implanting in him a certain drive — the sexual drive — which strikes out, which cannot be compared with other drives (hunger, thirst, and so on); a drive which radically exceeds its organic function (reproduction of human species) and which, precisely because of this non-functional character, cannot be mastered, tamed. In other words, if Adam and Eve had stayed in the Garden of Eden they would have had sexual intercourse, but they would have accomplished the sexual act in the same way as they accomplished all other instrumental acts (ploughing, sowing . . .). This excessive, non-functional, constitutively perverse character of human sexuality represents God's punishment for man's pride and his want of power.

How can we detect, where can we locate this uncontrollable character of sexuality? It is at this point that St Augustine proposes his theory of the phallus: if man has a strong will and self-control, he can master the movement of all parts of his body (here Augustine evokes a series of extreme cases: an Indian fakir who is able to stop the beating of his heart for a moment, and so on); all parts of the body are thus in principle submitted to man's will, their uncontrollabilities subsisting only in the *factual* degree of weakness or power of man's will — all parts except *one*: the erection of the phallus escapes *in principle* man's free will. This is therefore according to St Augustine, the 'meaning of the phallus': the part of man's body which escapes his control, the point at which man's own body takes revenge on him for his false pride. Someone with a strong enough will can starve to death in the middle of a room full of delicious food, but if a naked virgin passes his way, the erection of his phallus is in no way dependent on the strength of his will. . . .

This, however, is only one side of the phallus paradox; its reverse is indicated by a well-known riddle/joke: 'What is the lightest object on earth? — The phallus, because it is the only one that can be elevated by mere thought.' And to obtain the true 'meaning of phallus', we have to read both examples together: 'phallus' designates the juncture at which the radical externality of the body as independent of our will, as resisting our will, joins the pure interiority of our thought. 'Phallus' is the signifier of the short circuit whereby the uncontrollable externality of the body passes immediately into something bound to pure interiority of 'thought' and, in contrast, the point at which the innermost 'thought' assumes features of some strange entity, escaping our 'free will'. To use the traditional Hegelian terms, 'phallus' is the point of the 'unity of opposites': not a 'dialectical synthesis' (in the sense of a kind of mutual completion) but the *immediate passage* of one extreme into its opposite, as in Hegel's example where the lowest, most vulgar function of urination passes into the most sublime function of procreation.

It is this very 'contradiction' that constitutes the 'phallus experience': EVERYTHING *depends on me* — the point of the riddle — *but for all that I can do* NOTHING — the point of St Augustine's theory. And from here — from this notion of the phallus as pulsation between 'all' and 'nothing' — we can conceive the 'phallic' dimension of the act of formal conversion of reality *as given* into reality *as posited*. This act is 'phallic' in so far as it marks the point of coincidence between omnipotence ('everything depends on me': the subject posits all reality as his work) and total impotence ('but for all that I can do nothing': the subject can formally assume only what is given to him). It is in this sense that the phallus is a 'transcendental signifier': if, following Adorno, we define as 'transcendental' the inversion by means of which the subject experiences his radical limitation (the fact that he is confined to the limits of his world) as his constitutive power (the a priori network of categories structuring his perception of reality).

Presupposing the Positing

There is, however, one crucial weakness in what we have just articulated: our presentation of the process of reflections was oversimplified at a decisive point which concerns the passage from positing to external reflection. The usual interpretation of this passage, which we have accepted automatically, is as follows: positing reflection is the activity of the essence (pure movement of mediation) which posits the appearance — it is the negative movement sublating every given immediacy and positing it as 'mere appearance'; — but this reflexive sublation of the immediate, this positing of it as 'mere appearance', is in itself bound to the world of appearance; it *needs* appearance as something already given, as the basis upon which to perform its negative mediation activity. In short, reflection *presupposes* the positive world of appearance as the starting point of its activity of mediating it, of positing it as 'mere appearance'.

To exemplify this presupposing, let us take the classical procedure of the 'criticism of ideology': this procedure 'unmasks' a certain theoretical, religious, or other edifice by enabling us to 'see through it', by making us see in it 'just an [ideological] appearance', an expression-effect of some concealed mechanisms; this procedure consists thus in a purely negative movement which *presupposes* a 'spontaneous', 'non-reflected' ideological experience in its given-immediate positivity. To accomplish the passage from positing to external reflection, the movement of reflection has only to take note of how it is always bound to some given, external presuppositions which are subsequently mediated-sublated through its negative activity. In short, the activity of positing has to take note of its presuppositions — *external* to the movement of reflection are precisely its *presuppositions*.

In contrast to this current view, Dieter Heinrich, in his excellent study on Hegel's logic of reflection (Heinrich, 1971), demonstrated how *the whole dialectic of positing and presupposing still falls within the category of 'positing reflection'*. Let us refer to Fichte as a philosopher of positing reflection *par excellence*: by means of his productive activity, the subject 'posits', sublates-mediates, transforms the given positivity of objects; he transforms it into a manifestation of his own creativity; but this positing remains for ever bound to its presuppositions — to the positively given objectivity upon which it performs its negative activity. In other words, the dialectic of positing-presupposing implies the subject of the working process, the subject which by means of its negative activity, mediates the presupposed objectivity, transforming it into an objectivation of itself; in short, it implies the 'finite', not the 'absolute' subject.

In this case — if the whole dialectic of positing and presupposing falls within the field of positing reflection — in what consists the passage from positing to external reflection? Now we arrive at the crucial distinction elaborated by Heinrich: it is not enough to determine external reflection by the fact that the essence presupposes the objective world as its basis, as the starting point of its negative movement of mediation, external to this movement; the decisive feature of external reflection is that the essence *presupposes itself as its own other, in the form of externality, of something objectively given in advance* — that is to say, in the form of immediacy. We find ourselves in external reflection when the essence — the movement of absolute mediation, pure, self-referential negativity — presupposes ITSELF in the form of an Entity existing in itself, excluded from the movement of meditation. To use exact Hegelian terms, we are in external reflection when the essence not only presupposes its other (objective-phenomenal immediacy), but presupposes ITSELF in the form of otherness, in the form of some alien substance.

To exemplify this decisive twist, let us refer to a case which is misleading in so far as it is too 'concrete' in the Hegelian sense; in so far, that is, as it implies that we have already accomplished the passage from pure logical categories to concrete historical spiritual content: the analysis of religious alienation as developed by Feuerbach. This 'alienation', whose formal structure is clearly that of external reflection, does not consist simply in the fact that man — a creative being, externalizing his potentials in the world of objects — 'deifies' objectivity, conceiving the objective natural and social forces out of his control as manifestations of some supernatural Being. 'Alienation' means something more precise: it means that man presupposes, perceives *himself*, his own creative power, in the form of an external substantial Entity; it means that he 'projects', transposes his innermost essence into an alien Being ('God'). 'God' is thus man himself, the essence of man, the creative movement of mediation, the transforming power of negativity, but perceived in the form of externality, as belonging to some strange Entity existing in itself, independently of man.

This is the decisive but usually overlooked lesson of Hegel's theory of reflection: we can speak of the difference, the fissure separating the essence from appearance, only in so far as the essence is itself split in the way described above — only, that is, in so far as the essence presupposes itself as something alien, as its own Other. If the essence is not in itself split; if — in the movement of extreme alienation — it does not perceive itself as an alien Entity, then the very duality essence/appearance cannot establish itself. *This self-fissure of the essence means that the essence is 'subject' and not only 'substance'*: to express this in a simplified way, 'substance' is the essence in so far as it reflects itself in the world of appearance, in phenomenal objectivity; it is the movement of mediation–sublation–positing of this objectivity, and the 'subject' is substance in so far as it is itself split and experiences itself as some alien, positively given Entity.

We could say, paradoxically, that the subject is *substance precisely in so far as it experiences itself as substance* (as some alien, given, external, positive Entity, existing in itself): 'subject' is nothing but the name for this inner distance of 'substance' towards itself, the name for this empty place from which the substance can perceive itself as something 'alien'. Without this self-fissure of the essence, there can be no place distinguished from essence in which essence can *appear* as distinct from itself — that is, as 'mere appearance': essence can appear only in so far as it is already external to itself.

What, then, is the nature of the passage from external to *determinate* reflection? If we remain on the level of the common interpretation of the logic of reflection, in which the passage of positing into external reflection coincides with that of positing into presupposing, things are, of course, clear. To accomplish the passage in question, we simply have to take note of the fact that the very presuppositions are already posited — thus we find ourselves already in determinate reflection; in the reflexive movement which retroactively posits its own presuppositions. To refer again to the active-producing subject which mediates–negates–forms the presupposed objectivity: all he has to do is to experience how the ontological status of this presupposed objectivity is *nothing but* the presupposition of his activity, how it exists, how it is here only for him to use, to perform on it his mediating activity: how, then, it is itself retroactively 'posited' through his activity. 'Nature', the presupposed object of activity, is so to speak already 'by its own nature', in itself, the object, the material for the subject's activity; its ontological status is determined by the horizon of the process of production. In short, it is in advance *posited* as such — that is, as a presupposition of subjective positing.

If, however, external reflection cannot be sufficiently defined by the fact that positing is always bound to some presuppositions; if, to reach external reflection, essence must presuppose *itself* as its other, things become a little complicated. At first sight, they are still clear enough; let us refer again to the Feuerbachian analysis of religious alienation. Does not the passage from external to determinate reflection consist simply in the fact that man has to recognize in 'God', in this external, superior, alien Entity, the inverse reflection of his own essence — its own essence in the form of otherness; in other words, the 'reflexive determination' of its own essence? And thus to affirm himself as 'absolute subject'? What is amiss with this conception?

To explain it, we have to return to the very notion of reflection. The key for the proper understanding of the passage from external to determinate reflection is given by the double meaning of the notion of 'reflection' in Hegel — by the fact that in Hegel's logic of reflection, reflection is always on two levels:

(1) in the first place, 'reflection' designates the simple relation between essence and appearance, where the appearance 'reflects' the essence — that is to say, where the essence is the negative movement of mediation which sublates and at the same time posits the world of appearing. Here we are still dwelling within the circle of positing and presupposing; the essence posits the objectivity as 'mere appearance' and at the same time presupposes it as the starting point of its negative movement;

(2) as soon as we pass from positing to external reflection, however, we encounter quite another kind of reflection. Here the term 'reflection' designates the relationship between the essence as self-referential negativity, as the movement of absolute mediation, and the essence in so far as it presupposes itself in the inverse-alienated form of some substantial immediacy, as some transcendent entity *excluded* from the movement of reflection (which is why reflection is here 'external': external reflecting which does not concern the essence itself).

At this level, we pass from external to determinate reflection simply by experiencing the relationship between these two moments — essence as movement of self-mediation, self-referential negativity; essence as substantial-positive entity excluded from the tremor of reflection — *as that of reflection*: by experiencing how this image of the substantial-immediate, positively given essence is *nothing but* the inverse-alienated reflection of the essence as pure movement of self-referential negativity.

Strictly speaking, it is only this second reflection which is 'reflection-into-itself' of the essence, reflection in which the essence redoubles itself and thus reflects itself in itself, not only in appearance. This is why this second reflection is reflection *redoubled*: on the level of 'elementary' reflection, reflection in sense (1), essence is simply opposed to appearance as the power of absolute negativity which, by mediating–sublating–positing every positive immediacy, makes it 'mere appearance'; while on the level of the redoubled reflection, reflection in sense (2), essence reflects *itself* in the form of its own presupposition, of a given–immediate substance. Reflection of the essence into itself is an immediacy which is not 'mere appearance' but an inverse–alienated image of the very essence, essence itself in the form of its otherness, in other words, a presupposition which is not simply posited by the essence: in it, *essence presupposes itself as positing*.

As we have already indicated, the relationship between these two reflections is not that of a simple succession; the first, elementary reflection (1) is not simply followed by the second, redoubled reflection (2). The second reflection is, strictly speaking, the *condition* of the first — it is only the redoubling of the essence, the reflection of the essence into itself, which opens the space for the appearance in which the hidden essence can reflect itself. By taking into consideration this necessity of the redoubled reflection, we can also demonstrate what is amiss with the Feuerbachian model of surpassing the external reflection.

This model, in which the subject overcomes alienation by recognizing, in the alienated substantial Entity, the inverse image of his own essential potential, implies a notion of religion that corresponds to the Enlightenment's portrait of the Jewish religion (almighty God as an inverse image of man's powerlessness, and so on); what escapes such an understanding is the logic behind the fundamental motif of Christianity: God's incarnation. The Feuerbachian gesture of recognizing that God as an alien essence is nothing but the alienated image of man's creative potential does not take into account the necessity for this reflexive relationship between God and man to reflect itself *into God himself*; in other words, it does not suffice to ascertain that 'man is the truth of God', that the subject is the truth of the alienated substantial Entity. It is not enough for the subject to recognize–reflect himself in this Entity as in his inverse image; the crucial point is that this substantial Entity must itself split and 'engender' the subject (that is, 'God himself must become man').

As regards the dialectics of positing and presupposing, this necessity means that it is not enough to affirm that the subject posits its own presuppositions. This positing of presuppositions is already contained in the logic of positing reflection; what defines determinate reflection is, rather, that the subject must *presuppose himself as positing*. More precisely: the subject effectively 'posits his presuppositions' by presupposing, by reflecting himself in them as positing. To exemplify this crucial twist, let us take the two usual examples: the Monarch and Christ. In the immediacy of their lives, subjects as citizens are, of course, opposed to the substantial State which determines the concrete network of their social relations. How do they overcome this alienated character, this irreducible otherness of the State as the substantial presupposition of the subjects' activity-'positing'?

The classical Marxist answer would be, of course, that the State as an alienated force must 'wither away', that its otherness must be dissolved in the transparency of non-alienated social relations. The Hegelian answer is, on the contrary, that in the last resort, subjects can recognize the State as 'their own work' only by reflecting free subjectivity into the very State at the point of the Monarch; that is to say, by presupposing in the State itself — as its 'quilting point', as a point which confers its effectivity — the point of free subjectivity, the point of the Monarch's empty-formal gesture 'This is my will . . .'.

From this dialectic, we can very neatly deduce the necessity behind the double meaning of the word 'subject' — (1) a person subject to political rule; (2) a free agent, instigator of its activity — subjects can realize themselves as free agents only by means of redoubling themselves, only in so far as they 'project', transpose, the pure form of their freedom into the very heart of the substance opposed to them; into the person of the subject–Monarch as 'head of the State'. In other words, subjects are subjects only in so far as they presuppose that the social substance, opposed to them in the form of the State, is already in itself a subject (Monarch) to whom they are subjected.

Here we should rectify — or, more precisely, supplement — our previous analysis: the empty gesture, the act of formal conversion by means of which 'substance becomes subject', is not simply dispersed among the multitude of subjects and as such proper to each of them in the same manner; it is always centred at some point of exception, in the One, the individual who takes upon himself the idiotic mandate of performing the empty gesture of subjectivation — of supplementing the given, substantial content by the form of 'This is my will'. This is homologous with Christ: the subjects overcome the Otherness, the strangeness, of the

Jewish God not by immediately proclaiming him their own creature but by presupposing in God himself the point of 'incarnation', the point at which God becomes man. This is the significance of Christ's arrival, of his 'It is fulfilled!': for freedom to take place (as our positing), *it must already have taken place* in God as his incarnation — without it, subjects would remain for ever bound to the alien substance, caught in the web of their presuppositions.

The necessity of this redoubling explains perfectly why the strongest instigation to free activity was procured by Protestantism — by religion putting so much emphasis on predestination, on the fact that 'everything is already decided in advance'. And now, finally, we can also give a precise formulation to the passage from external to determinate reflection: the condition of our subjective freedom, of our 'positing', is that it must be reflected in advance into the substance itself, as its own 'reflexive determination'. For that reason, Greek religion, Jewish religion and Christianity form a triad of reflection: in Greek religion, divinity is simply posited in the multitude of beautiful appearance (which is why, for Hegel, Greek religion was religion of the work of art); in Jewish religion, the subject perceives its own essence in the form of a transcendent, external, unattainable power; while in Christianity, human freedom is finally conceived as a 'reflexive determination' of this strange substance (God) itself.

The significance of these at first sight purely speculative ruminations for the psychoanalytic theory of ideology cannot be overestimated. What is the 'empty gesture' by means of which the brute, senseless reality is *assumed*, accepted as our own work, if not the most elementary ideological operation, the symbolization of the Real, its transformation into a meaningful totality, its inscription into the big Other? We can literally say that this 'empty gesture' *posits the big Other, makes it exist*: the purely formal conversion which constitutes this gesture is simply the conversion of the pre-symbolic Real into the symbolized reality — into the Real caught in the web of the signifier's network. In other words, through this 'empty gesture' the subject *presupposes the existence of the big Other*.

Now, perhaps we are able to locate that radical change which, according to Lacan, defines the final stage of the psychoanalytic process: 'subjective destitution'. What is at stake in this 'destitution' is precisely the fact that *the subject no longer presupposes himself as subject*; by accomplishing this he annuls, so to speak, the effects of the act of formal conversion. In other words, he assumes not the existence but the *nonexistence* of the big Other; he accepts the Real in its utter, meaningless idiocy; he keeps open the gap between the Real and its symbolization. The price to be paid for this is that by the same act he also *annuls himself as subject*, because — and this would be Hegel's last lesson — the subject is subject only in so far as he presupposes himself as absolute through the movement of double reflection.

Bibliography

Adorno, Theodor W. (1970), 'Society', *Salmagundi* 10–11.

Althusser, Louis (1965), *Pour Marx*, Paris (translated as *For Marx*, London 1977).

—— (1976), 'Idéologie et appareils idéologiques d'État', *Positions*, Paris (translated as 'Ideology and Ideological State Apparatuses' in *Essays in Ideology*, London 1984).

Baas, Bernard (1987), 'Le désir pur', *Ornicar?* 43, Paris.

Benjamin, Walter (1955), *Gesammelte Schriften* I, Frankfurt.

—— (1969), *Illuminations*, New York.

Bodenheimer, Aron (1984), *Warum? Von der Obszönität des Fragens*, Stuttgart.

Božovič, Miran (1988), 'Immer Ärger mit dem Körper', *Wo es war* 5–6, Ljubljana-Vienna.

Derrida, Jacques (1987), *The Post Card*, Chicago.

Descartes, René (1976), *Discourse on Method*, Harmondsworth.

Dolar, Mladen (1986), 'Hitchcock's Objekt', *Wo es war* 2, Ljubljana-Vienna.

—— (1987), 'Die Einführung in das Serail', *Wo es war* 3–4, Ljubljana-Vienna.

Elster, Jon (1982), *Sour Grapes*, Cambridge.

Eysenck, Hans-Jürgen (1966), *Sense and Nonsense in Psychology*, Harmondsworth.

Fenichel, Otto (1928), 'Die "lange Nase"', *Imago* 14, Vienna.

Foucault, Michel (1984), *Power/Knowledge*, Brighton.

Freud, Sigmund (1977), *The Interpretation of Dreams*, Harmondsworth.

Habermas, Jürgen (1985), *Der philosophische Diskurs der Moderne*, Frankfurt (translated as *The Philosophical Discourse of Modernity*, Cambridge 1988).

Hegel, G.W.F. (1966), *Wissenschaft der Logik* I/II, Hamburg.

—— (1969), *Philosophie der Religion* I/II, Frankfurt.

—— (1969a), *Vorlesungen uber die Philosophie der Geschichte*, Frankfurt.

—— (1969b), *Grundlinien der Philosophie des Rechts*, Frankfurt.

—— (1977) *Phenomenology of Spirit*, Oxford.

Heinlein, Robert (1986), *The Door Into Summer*, New York.

Heinrich, Dieter (1971), *Hegel im Kontext*, Frankfurt.

Kafka, Franz (1978), *Wedding Preparations in the Country and Other Stories*, Harmondsworth.

—— (1985), *The Trial*, Harmondsworth.

Kant, Immanuel (1964), *Critique of Judgement*, Oxford.

Kantorowicz, Ernst (1959), *The King's Two Bodies*, Princeton.

Kovel, Joel (1988), *White Racism*, London.

Kripke, Saul (1980), *Naming and Necessity*, Cambridge MA.

Lacan, Jacques (1966), *Écrits*, Paris.

—— (1975), *le Séminaire XX - Encore*, Paris.

—— (1975a), 'R.S.I.', *Ornicar?* 4, Paris.

—— (1977), 'Subversion of the subject and dialectic of desire', *Écrits: A Selection*, New York/London.

—— (1979), *The Four Fundamental Concepts of Psycho-Analysis*, Harmondsworth.

—— (1981), *le Séminaire III - Les psychoses*, Paris.

—— (1986), *le Séminaire VII - L'éthique de la psychanalyse*, Paris.

—— (1988), *The Seminar of Jacques Lacan, Book I: Freud's Papers on Technique*, Cambridge.

—— (1988a), 'Joyce le symptôme', in *Joyce avec Lacan*, Paris.

Laclau, Ernesto (1977), *Politics and Ideology in Marxist Theory*, London.

Laclau, Ernesto and Mouffe, Chantal (1985), *Hegemony and Socialist Strategy*, London.

Lefort, Claude (1981), *L'invention démocratique*, Paris.

Lord, Walter (1983), *A Night to Remember*, New York.

Marcuse, Herbert (1955), *Eros and Civilization*, Boston MA.

Marx, Karl (1974), *Capital* I, London.

—— (1977), *Les 'sentirs escarpés' de Karl Marx* I, Paris.

Miller, Jacques-Alain (1987), 'Les reponses du réel', in *Aspects du malaise dans la civilisation*, Paris.

Močnik, Rastko (1986), 'Ueber die Bedeutung der Chimären fur die *conditio humana*', *Wo es war* 1, Ljubljana–Vienna.

Nancy, Jean-Luc and Lacoue-Labarthe, Philippe (1973), *Le titre de la lettre*, Paris.

Pascal, Blaise (1966), *Pensées*, Harmondsworth.

Pêcheux, Michel (1975), *Les vérités de la Palice*, Paris (translated as *Language, Semantics and Ideology*, London 1979).

Riha, Rado (1986), 'Das Dinghafte der Geldware', *Wo es war* 1, Ljubljana–Vienna.

Schelling, F.W.J. (1978), *Ueber das Wesen der menschlichen Freiheit*, Frankfurt.

Searle, John (1984), *Intentionality*, Cambridge.

Silvestre, Michel (1986), *Demain la psychanalyse*, Paris.

Sloterdijk, Peter (1983), *Kritik der zynischen Vernunft*, Frankfurt (translated as *Critique of Cynical Reason*, London 1988).

Sohn-Rethel, Alfred (1978), *Intellectual and Manual Labor*, London.

Yovel, Yirmiahu (1982), 'La religion de la sublimité, in *Hegel et la religion*, Paris.

Žižek, Slavoj (1988), *Le plus sublime des hystériques*, Paris.

Index